AFRICAN AMERICAN HISTORY AND CULTURE

edited by

GRAHAM RUSSELL HODGES
COLGATE UNIVERSITY

A GARLAND SERIES

AFRICAN AMERICAN WOMEN DURING THE CIVIL WAR

ELLA FORBES

GARLAND PUBLISHING, Inc.
A MEMBER OF THE TAYLOR & FRANCIS GROUP
NEW YORK & LONDON / 1998

Library of Congress Cataloging-in-Publication Data

Forbes, Ella, 1948–
    African American women during the Civil War / Ella Forbes.
       p.   cm. — (Studies in African American history and
culture)
    Includes bibliographical references and index.
    ISBN 0-8153-3115-0 (alk. paper)
    1. United States—History—Civil War, 1861–1865—Afro-
Americans. 2. United States—History—Civil War, 1861–1865—
Women. 3. Afro-American women—History—19th century.
I. Title. II. Series.
E540.N3F67 1998
973.7'089'96073—dc21

                                        97-52754

Printed on acid-free, 250-year-life paper
Manufactured in the United States of America

Contents

Preface

One of the major drawbacks for the researcher seeking to resurrect the African American woman during the Civil War is the depersonalized objectification of the black female presence in most historical treatments of this period. And resurrected she must be because the part the African American woman played in this epoch of immense importance and transition to the nation, and most especially to African Americans, has faded into obscurity—she is all but invisible. Rarely is she the subject under study, in any case; if mentioned at all, she is often a nameless, faceless, and voiceless appendage, an exotic afterthought or a superwoman like Harriet Tubman or Sojourner Truth. It is usually the perspective of the white male participant which prevails when the Civil War is under discussion. When African American Civil War participation is the focus, the African American male is highlighted. If women are the focus, the perspective belongs to white women. Implicit in the historiography is the value placed on gender: heroes tend to be white males, white women play a supporting role to white male heroes and the experience of African American men represents the experience of all African Americans.

Given this reality, then, it is most often through the prism of the experience and actions of African American men that the African American female presence is detected, if seen at all. The women being reconstructed in this volume, however, would not have found this insulting. Rather, they achieved a certain nobility by playing a supporting role to their husbands, fathers, sons and brothers and they knew that African American history cannot be divided by gender. The history of black males and females in this country is inextricably intertwined and informed by a common racial experience. This is not to say that gender, or sexism, was not an issue, however minor, in the African American community, just as it was in the larger society. However, the role that black women defined, for themselves, as women, was a position which recognized that racial solidarity was paramount to gender.

Therefore, this text is not about proving that the contributions of African American women during the Civil War were *just as* important as what African American men did and it is not about "in spite of" as in "in spite of being a woman," or about the nature of gender roles. It doesn't mean that African American men were less brave than African American women or that their contributions are somehow diminished by acknowledging the contributions of African American women. It also doesn't mean that a value can be placed on the type of contribution women made during this period for, in fact, any action in support of black liberation was important. Rather, this volume seeks, in a practical way, to bring some of the African American female participants in the Civil War, in Susie King Taylor's words, *"in history before the people"* by reconstructing, reclaiming and resurrecting the lives and deeds of ordinary African American women forced to perform extraordinary feats in a world and situation not of their making.

In seeking to reclaim the presence of African American women during this era we must depend upon the narratives of some of the women themselves, passing references in the letters and diaries of male and white female Civil War participants, African American newspapers and journals and marginal notes in documents about something other than African American women to get a glimpse of what the war was like for African American women. This text, then, relies quite heavily on primary sources because they allow us to discern, at most every stage and level of the Civil War, the presence of African American women either in the forefront as actors or obliquely in the shadows being acted upon or reacting to events.

However, the best sources for information are the communications of the women themselves because conjectures can be made about a collective African American female experience by focusing on specific women. Rebecca Primus, for example, recorded her experience as a teacher of freedpeople in letters to her family, friends and sponsoring organizations. Her words place her in history by showing what the experience was like for her personally and African American female teachers, generally. Her family, proud of its history, preserved her letters as a part of their family record, leaving a valuable historical legacy to their heirs as well as the entire field of African American studies.

Some of the finest locations for the reports and feelings of women are African American newspapers and journals because the women let their community know what they were doing and who was doing it through the African American press, especially organs such as the *Christian Recorder* and the *Weekly Anglo-African*. It is also in these documents that we find out particulars about African American women during the Civil War—such information, for example, as names and places which are often missing from other sources. We also see how they wanted to be seen—as deserving of the traditional respect "ladies" were given. This is reflected in their writings and speeches which carry a strong moral overtone because they concentrated their attention on the uplift and elevation of their people through their own conduct and behavior.

Yet, even many African American sources neglect to provide information about particular women. The ladies are often not identified by name in the minutes, reports and accounts of African American male organizations and church records. Rather there are references to female organizations, auxiliaries and subsidiaries but, too often, none which give the individual ladies' names. For example, the men at the February 1865 State Equal Rights Convention of the Colored People of Pennsylvania, while praising African American women for their relief work in a long, controversial resolution, did not see fit to distinguish the women by name. Even Susie King Taylor doesn't say much about other African American women in her autobiography. William Wells Brown lumps the heroic women determined to defend themselves during the New York City Draft Riot under the sobriquet, "amazons," without giving other data which might identify specific women. It would be wonderful to point to these women as examples of African American female resistance, if we only knew something more about them.

One thing which African American sources often supply, however, is written descriptions of the women. In an age when photography was just blossoming, not many of the women, unless they were famous or well-to-do, routinely had pictures taken so writers presented a mental picture for readers. This text adopts the technique of furnishing physical descriptions, wherever possible, of the women under discussion to make them more human and real, especially when photographs are lacking. Most of the pictures that are included are of lesser-known African American women as a way of resurrecting and reclaiming a larger black female presence.

One possible explanation for the fact that sources, in a great many instances, do not identify African American women by name might be that the narrator was usually providing an anecdote, using an African American woman or women, as an illustration of a particular point and the issue was considered more important than the specific participants. This holds true for black as well as white sources. Also, understandably, the raconteur is usually telling his or her own story so that the focus is on the narrator and not other individuals.

George Clary, a white army officer, for instance, recorded his own Civil War experience in his letters to his family and friends. However, such sources are valuable because even though they most often give a jaundiced view of African American women, they exhibit better than any scholarly treatise the insidious, ubiquitous effect of racism on the African American community. Racist comments, spoken in an offhand manner which objectifies the black presence, explain why racism continues to pervade American society. Of course, objectification allows a certain distance from the problem; it is someone else's fault or solution. Nevertheless, such comments allow us to see just what the African American community, and black women, in particular, were up against—a white public clearly and openly hostile to their presence. White diarists and letter writers routinely referred to African Americans as "niggers" and "darkies."[1] African American women were lumped under these pejoratives, even when the writers are referring only to women. Almost without exception, the letters, diaries and journals of whites confirm that African American women were not afforded any special consideration or courtesy because they were members of a "fragile" gender.

White objectification allowed black women to make a major contribution to black liberation because it forced them to directly confront and challenge negative stereotypes of black womanhood. They understood that how they conducted themselves as women, and as African Americans, reflected on the black community as a whole. To be sure, we are familiar with mythical one-dimensional black women—Sapphire, Mammy and the harlot—which are traditionally presented as representations of African American women during enslavement. These are the "disfigured images"[2] that the African American revolutionary Angela Davis, said "must be consciously repudiated as myth and the black woman in her true historical contours must be resurrected. We, the black women of today, must accept the full weight of a legacy wrought in blood by our mothers in chains. Our fight, while identical in spirit, reflects different conditions and thus implies different paths of struggle. But as heirs to a tradition of supreme perseverance and heroic resistance, we must hasten to take our place wherever our people are forging on toward freedom."[3] Davis wrote these words while she, herself, was being held in the Marin County jail in San Rafael, California, facing three capital charges of murder, kidnaping and conspiracy to commit both. She wrote during another epoch of immense struggle for African Americans—the 1960s and 1970s. Many young black women identified with Davis' plight just as African American women during the Civil War saw themselves in common cause with other black women.

Therefore, Sapphire, the emasculating, domineering harpy, is missing from this study. Mammy, the fat, happy neutered darkey who was more concerned with her "white folks" than her own family, and indeed, her own life, is also absent. Eliminated, too, is the wanton African woman who seduces the hapless, helpless white man or slaveowner. Making no attempt to reappropriate or reinterpret these images, I contend that a true picture of African American womanhood shows that through assertiveness, negotiation, self-empowerment, resistance, activism, and even just surviving, African American women during the Civil War demolished such stereotypes by assuming a kind of nobility as ladies who were determined to elevate and uplift the image of the African American community. They resolutely accepted the charge of doing whatever they could to make a life for their people in a nation which was inimical to their presence. The dictates of the time demanded a new commitment to black liberation and African American women were up to the challenge.

This book is also, inescapably, about what African American women endured during this period because it is impossible to recount any portion of African American history without talking about what has been done to black people in this country. Black women during the Civil War era were routinely subjected to racial and gender indignities because they existed in a racist, patriarchal society which did not value them either as African Americans or as women. Too often, however, attention to what has happened to African Americans is labeled "oppression studies" so that documentation of atrocities and disfranchisement seems like whining about things best forgotten and forgiven and the raconteur is branded and dismissed as assuming the role of victim. Nevertheless, this is not an exercise in "oppression studies" because the women empowered themselves by exercising an agency they felt was their birthright and although they knew they were being victimized, they knew no one had the right to oppress them.

This text necessarily generalizes some points because it is understood that not all whites were racist and that not every black woman reacted or acted in the same way. Nonetheless, in assessing what the Civil War experience of African American women was like, it would be remiss not to deal with the major defining issue for the black community—race. After all, by its very nature, the Civil War was ultimately about race. Besides, there would have been no reason to write this book if the racism which created the need to reclaim and reconstruct African American women to history did not exist.

Moreover, the text is African-centered. For example, to reinforce the volume's African-centeredness, when no racial designation is given, it is to be assumed that the persons under discussion are African American. African-centeredness also means that close attention has been paid to semantics because what is said or written gives an indication of perspective and perspective often indicates the value placed on what is being discussed. For instance, while the term "freedpeople" indicates that the persons are no longer enslaved, "refugees" or "displaced persons" frequently give a better picture of their situation. Additionally, wherever possible, the terms "enslaved" or "enslavement" have been used rather than "slave" or "slavery" because they show the imposition of a condition rather than a birthright. And, as C. Tsehloane Keto says, expressions such as "slave and slave trade may appear neutral but from an African-centered perspective, the terms harbor an implicit element of submission to enslavement by Africans and an acceptance of the condition by African Americans."[4] The women in this book were anything but accepting of the conditions imposed upon them.

Most of the misspellings, grammar and punctuation errors in quotations from narratives, letters, diaries, and journals have been revised so as not to distract the reader. The meanings and tones of the writers and speakers have not been changed, however. This is also done because often the use of so-called "black dialect" is a means of marginalization and is a technique whose intent is to show perceived inferiority. Since recorders did not transcribe the long vowels of whites from the northeast or the peculiarities of their speech or southern white speech patterns (which were nearly identical to southern African American speech), then it is improper to retain the vernacular presumed to represent African Americans. The same courtesy of revision has been given in this volume to white speakers and writers also.

Admittedly, this document's treatment of the women is celebratory. The first reason is that very little work, of a practical nature, has been done on African American women during the Civil War. Secondly, their endeavors deserve celebration and acknowledgment because they were performed in the interest of the larger African American community. Ergo, the names of as many of the women as possible have been included, leading sometimes to an almost encyclopedic recitation. The retrieval of their names, however, is one of the main reasons for the text: addressing the problem of the invisibility and omission of African American history from "traditional" history and the invisibility and omission of black women from African American history. Still, much work remains to be done before the contributions of African American women during the Civil War are truly "*in history before the people.*"

NOTES

1. An interesting comparison between the letters, diaries and journals of African Americans with similar white writings shows that African Americans rarely recorded racially disparaging remarks about whites, even when recounting racial incidents. Most often they ascribed such behavior to ignorance rather than some innate racial deficiency.

2. Patricia Morton, *Disfigured Images: the Historical Assault on Afro-American Women* (New York: Praeger Publishers, 1991).

3. Angela Davis, "Reflections on the Black Woman's Role in the Community of Slaves," *Black Scholar* (December, 1971): 15.

4. C. Tsehloane Keto, *The Africa Centered Perspective of History* (Blackwood, New Jersey: K.A. Publications, 1991), 40.

Abbreviations

AMA	American Missionary Association
A.M.E.	African Methodist Episcopal
CRA	Contraband Relief Association
FAP	Friends' Association of Philadelphia, and Its Vicinity, for the Relief of Colored Freedmen
ICY	Institute for Colored Youth [later Cheyney University]
LSASTC	Ladies' Sanitary Association of St. Thomas's African Episcopal Church
LUA	Ladies' Union Association
NFRA	National Freedmen's Relief Association
NFRADC	National Freedmen's Relief Association of the District of Columbia
OR	United States. War Department. *The War of the Rebellion: a Compilation of the Official Records of the Union and Confederate Armies*
USCI	United States Colored Infantry
USCT	United States Colored Troops
WFAC	Western Freedmen's Aid Commission

African American Women
during the Civil War

CHAPTER 1

In History Before the People: Introduction

"There are many people who do not know what some of the colored women did during the war . . . These things should be kept in history before the people. There has never been a greater war in the United States than the one of 1861, where so many lives were lost,—not men alone but noble women as well."[1] Susie King Taylor wrote these words in her 1902 narrative, *Reminiscences of My Life in Camp,* to show "that there were 'loyal women,' as well as men, in those days, who did not fear shell or shot, who cared for the sick and dying; women who camped and fared as the boys did . . . "[2] She could speak authoritatively because she experienced "the terrors of that war" as an active participant.[3] One of the few firsthand African American female accounts, King's memoir documented her own ordeal during the Civil War but her experience represents the determined, noble spirit that innumerable black women displayed during a period of great importance to the African American community. And it is still true that many people do not know that African American women played an important role in the Civil War—they have been largely lost to history.

186,000 African American men served the Union as soldiers and an additional 30,000 as sailors. They represented approximately 10% of all Union troops. African Americans, though, suffered disproportionate casualties when compared to white soldiers. About 37,000 of them died during the Civil War: 2,870 died in combat; 4,000 from unknown causes;

and 29,756 from illness due to inferior food, clothing, equipment and medical care.[4] Many of the nearly one quarter million African Americans who performed other service as laborers, cooks, laundresses, and servants were women. A far greater number of black women simply subsisted, resisted and survived this terrible conflict.

Most African Americans saw the Civil War as an opportunity to end the enslavement of Africans in the United States and to make real the ultimate truism: that the liberation of African Americans was only going to come about through the efforts of African Americans. Although the war itself was relatively short, it was a pivotal and defining period in African American history because it was the culmination of many years of one type of struggle and its end signaled a new and different battle. African American history is still referred to in terms of antebellum and post-bellum activities, in terms of what African Americans were doing before the Civil War and what has happened to us since the war.

Therefore, black women had as much a stake in the outcome of the conflict as African American men. To show their commitment to the cause, they participated in a variety of ways, offering whatever skills they possessed: directly as spies, scouts, camp workers, nurses, cooks, seamstresses, recruiting agents, teachers, activists, fundraisers, organizers, and relief workers; less directly and more covertly by engaging in resistance activities such as work slowdowns, strikes, sabotage, insubordination and fleeing if they were enslaved; and indirectly, by entrepreneurial activities and by keeping families and homes together for returning soldiers and sailors. In the process they elaborated on and further developed an existing paradigm of black female charity, activism and resistance.

Coming from all backgrounds and walks of life, the women's service was fueled by incalculable and varied experiences. Nevertheless, they all tapped into the existing tradition of black female benevolence. Categorization of the women's contributions, consequently, is a bit difficult because they did not confine themselves to one sphere or activity. Sallie Daffin may have been an educator but she was also a relief worker and a journalist. Harriet Tubman was a spy, scout and soldier as well as a nurse. Mary Ann Shadd Cary was a recruiter, journalist and a paid agent for a relief organization. Most women who did aid work among refugees were involved in other benevolent activities such as succoring African American soldiers.

A large number of free women were already activists in a multiplicity of causes, usually racial, before the Civil War and they were well-known in their own right. Some were participants in numerous organizations and they used their networking skills to further their Civil War activities. Often the women came from families which had long histories of anti-slavery activism. Some women, on the other hand, were forced to act because they or loved ones may have been enslaved and they needed to relieve aspects of that particular burden. Occasionally, women, such as Harriet Tubman and Sojourner Truth, are memorable because they are considered nontypical, larger-than-life figures. However, most of the women were ordinary people who seized the opportunity to work for African American liberation by striving for their own freedom.

Like any other community, ideological, religious, social and class differences existed within African American society. But despite these differences, any debate about race always centered on how best to relieve the racist oppression everyone suffered. Black women were involved in the debate, not as women, but as African Americans and they were well aware that they were not oppressed because they were women, but because they were African women, African being the operative word.

Class differences were often imposed on, and sometimes assimilated by, the African American community. One area of class determination was seen in the treatment of "free" African Americans versus the treatment of newly-freed people, or refugees. Generally, free African Americans were seen, by whites, as more civilized and deserving of some rights, however limited, while the formerly enslaved were seen as so degraded by the experience of enslavement that they were incapable of exercising citizenship. Some middle and upper class African Americans held opinions about freedpeople which were similar. However, free blacks, most often, felt that the formerly enslaved could be elevated to citizenship with a little education and training. After all, most of them had come out of the enslavement experience in one way or another and class distinctions within the African American community did not blur the racial discrimination that all African Americans experienced.

Therefore, they were thoroughly familiar with racism because they experienced discrimination in most social and civil areas. The same racism that prevented their fathers, husbands, brothers and sons from exercising the rights of citizenship affected African American women in very concrete and material ways. It was a constant—always there to be dealt with, regardless of gender, status or class. Consequently, whatever happened to African American men, impacted upon African American women. The Delaware, Ohio Ladies' Anti-Slavery Society issued a written address to the Convention of Disfranchised Citizens of Ohio in 1856 which spoke to this point. The discourse urged the black men of the state to continue fighting for the rights the state legislature had deprived them of, saying, "we offer this testimonial of our sympathy and interest in the cause in which you are engaged . . . " The deposition, written by Sara G. Stanley, later to be an important and dedicated teacher of freedpeople, went on to assert, "press on! Manhood's prerogatives are yours by Almighty fiat." In a collective crusade with the black men of Ohio, the "Christian wives, mothers and daughters" of the Ladies' Anti-Slavery Society "pledge ourselves to exert our influence unceasingly in the cause of Liberty and Humanity."[5] This sentiment was translated into action during the Civil War when liberation became the black community's common cause, no matter what gender, rank, class or ideology.

The infamous Dred Scott Decision, rendered in 1857, had left no doubt about the status of Africans in this country: they were not considered citizens. Roger B. Taney, the Chief Supreme Court Justice, said about African Americans in the course of stating the Court's decision: "They had more than a century before [the signing of the Declaration of Independence] been regarded as beings of an inferior order, and altogether unfit to be associated with the white race, either in social or political relations; and so far inferior, that they had no rights which the white man was bound to respect; and the Negro might justly and lawfully be reduced to slavery for his benefit. He was bought and sold, and treated as an ordinary article of merchandise and traffic, whenever a profit could be made by it. This opinion was at that time fixed and universal in the civilized portion of the white race. It was regarded as an axiom in morals as well as in politics."

White public opinion, therefore, determined public policy and public policy mandated the disfranchisement of African Americans. In most northern states African American men did not have the right to vote. African Americans were denied passports because they were not considered citizens. Discrimination in public accommodations was rampant. The judicial system was racially unfair. Whites engaged in physical intimidation and violent actions against African Americans. Nonetheless, African Americans expected that black participation in the Civil War would finally establish their place as viable citizens in American society once and for all by reversing white public opinion. Women were to play a major, if sometimes supporting, role in that process.

In that context, Anne Demby asked the question,

> What should the colored race do in the present crisis? is a question that forces itself upon the mind of every thinking man and woman. Should we meekly submit to the threats, insults, and bruises that have been heaped upon our ancestors, and upon ourselves for so long a period, or should we go forth and cry our wrongs from the hill-sides or from the mountain tops? No. Then what should we do?

She began with "we" because white supremacy was not gender-biased; African American men and women both suffered the same racism. However, she placed the role of African American women in the traditional realm of nurturer and educator:

> Mothers should inculcate it into the minds of their children that, although many of them may have been born slaves, and held in that brutal condition and forced to drink to the dregs that most bitter cup of human degradation—and although they have, for many years been subjected to the most demoralizing influences that slavery, in its hideous form, and subtle nature could impart—while the design of this creation was not that they should stand with folded hands and cry for help, but that they should, with uplifted hands, and willing hearts, rush forward to conquer and to the conquest, never fearing while they have truth and justice on their side . . .

According to Demby, men had a more direct and active part to play in the conflict,

> The fathers should also teach their sons that although the colored man is denied the right of political franchise, the right is not denied

him of shouldering his musket, and marching to the field of battle
shouting, for their watch-word, 'Liberty or Death.' . . . names that
are borne by sable sons, shall shine with a lustre that the darkness
and shame of slavery can never extinguish . . .

Apparently no believer in passive resistance, Demby, like several of her
contemporary African American male activists, recognized the necessity
of armed action.

It is to be considered a menial act for any one of the colored race
to shrink from the duties that are now devolved upon them, but
they should aspire, and, by having God on the one hand, and the
sword in the other, they should, by the might of God, and by their
own might and patriotism, slay the grim monster slavery, and
trample his mangled corpse beneath their feet, crying Truth and
Justice, Liberty or Death . . . [6]

While placing her words in the context of the Civil War, she echoed
activists like David Walker, Henry Highland Garnet and Frederick
Douglass who had previously loudly proclaimed the right of African
Americans to violently resist enslavement and oppression.

Demby and other African American women, free or freed, consciously
resolved not to shrink from the new duties that the Civil War visited upon
them. They operated on whatever level they could to make a contribution
to their community during the Civil War. Acting with an agency they had
always possessed, they went forward, "crying Truth and Justice, Liberty
or Death." Their actions secure their place in history.

NOTES

1. Susie King Taylor, *Reminiscences of My Life in Camp With the 33rd
United States Colored Troops* (New York: Arno Press, 1968, 1902), 67-68.
    2. Ibid., preface.
    3. Ibid., 51.
    4. Otto Friedrich, "We Will Not Do Duty Any Longer For Seven Dollars Per
Month," *American Heritage* (February 1988): 68.
    5. Herbert Aptheker, ed., *A Documentary History of the Negro People in the
United States: From the Colonial Times Through the Civil War* (New York:
Citadel Press, 1979, 1951), 381, 383.
    6. *Christian Recorder*, 8 October 1864.

CHAPTER 2

Full of the Spirit of Freedom: Freedwomen and the System

The experience and contributions of newly-freedwomen were understandably different from the "civilized" contributions made by free African American women. That was mainly because of the imposition of an inferior status which determined, right from the beginning of their freedom, that they would have to contend with more obstacles than just gender. A major hindrance was the assumption on the part of whites that freedpeople required control disguised as guardianship. Greed, racism and classism were also added to the mix.

Most of the fugitives who fled to Union lines were considered "contraband" or confiscated property. The term was used, initially, to indicate that as spoils of war, the Africans who escaped to Union lines would not be returned to Confederate slaveholders, inflicting a serious blow to the South's labor force and, hence, to their ability to function during the war. According to Edward L. Pierce, white Treasury agent in charge of abandoned plantations, "Thenceforward the term 'contraband' bore a new signification, with which it will pass into history, designating the negroes who had been held as slaves, now adopted under the protection of the Government."[1]

The connotation of the term, however, came to be quite negative. The Western Freedmen's Aid Commission noted in 1865 that "the term 'Freedmen,' . . . we are pleased to notice is passing into general use instead of the word 'contraband.'"[2] African American groups, speakers and writers tended to dislike the term and used "freedmen" or "freedpeople" instead, to emphasize the liberation of the formerly enslaved.

Pierce remarked in 1863 that the refugees "were first called contrabands at Fortress Monroe; but at Port Royal, where they were next introduced to us in any considerable number, they were generally referred to as freedmen. These terms are milestones in our progress; and they are yet to be lost in the better and more comprehensive designation of citizens, or, when discrimination is convenient, citizens of African descent." He acknowledged the change when he wrote an article for *Atlantic Monthly* in 1863 entitled, "The Freedmen at Port Royal," after he had written an essay for the same journal in 1861 with the title, "The Contrabands at Fortress Monroe."

His words capture the point—the use of the term, contraband, in an official capacity by the government allowed the denial of basic civil rights to the African Americans who had liberated themselves by fleeing enslavement or who had been freed by the Union army. It also placed the former bondspeople at the mercy of a generally racist bureaucracy which exploited their labor and humanity. These terms—contraband, freedmen and ex-slaves—which were used to describe refugees served to label them for years as undeserving of United States' citizenship.

George Clary, white Union army surgeon, wrote jokingly to his brother, Timothy, from New Orleans in 1862: "Our building is filling with contrabands of all sorts, shades, and sizes. If you want a domestic black enough to pay the fare home, I could easily supply you with one, who would be glad to go and very likely might prove constant and faithful. They are a drug here. We know not what to do with them. Every day brings new ones to us . . . They are a nuisance."[3] Clary's comments were commonplace. Clearly, many whites felt that the refugees constituted a problem, analogous to the twentieth-century "Negro Problem," and the terms denoted the nature of the problem: these were a people who were supposedly so debilitated by their former enslavement that they were unused to "civilization" and independent thinking. On the one hand, they should have been able to take care of themselves. On the other hand, they were seen as so crippled by enslavement that they had been stripped of the ability to be self-sufficient, that they were unready for freedom, citizenship and the means for sustaining either.

Comments by the American Freedmen's Inquiry Commission to Edwin Stanton, Secretary of War, in their final report of May 15, 1864, reinforce this point. "The Anglo-Saxon race, with great force of character, much mental activity, an unflagging spirit of enterprise, has a certain hardness, a stubborn will, only moderate geniality, a lack of habitual cheerfulness . . . It is a race more calculated to call forth respect than love; better fitted to do than enjoy. The African race is, in many respects, the reverse of this. Genial, lively, docile, emotional, the affections rule; the social instincts maintain the ascendant. Except under cruel repression, its cheerfulness and love of mirth overflow with the exuberance of childhood . . . It is a knowing rather than a thinking race . . . It is not a race that will ever take a lead in the material improvement of the world . . . " Although the Commission held such an opinion, they went on to assert, "Let us beware the temptation to treat the colored people with less than even justice, because they have been, and still are, lowly and feeble."[4] But, that is exactly what happened to a people thought to have no material contributions to make to the world.

This negative opinion prevailed among whites and some African Americans, so that decisions were made for the refugees, and by extension the African American community, with no regard for the wishes and desires of the people affected. The white speculator and agent, Edward Philbrick from Boston, articulated this stripping of black autonomy in paternalistic terms: "Such a course, by keeping the control of the work, in the hands of white men, who have a larger share of forethought and energy than the negroes, besides acquired knowledge would conduce to the misprovement [improvement] of their methods of culture . . . "[5] Such a system, however, benefited Philbrick much more than it did freedpeople.

It is probable, also, that whites dreaded the specter of thousands of African Americans being unleashed into the white population with the still raw memories of being brutally enslaved by white people; physical, social and economic controls were ways to address their fear. One of the government's solutions was to put newly liberated or self-liberated African men, women and children to work as menial laborers, by force when necessary, under the supervision of government agents. Freedpeople built battlements and other military fortifications, worked as servants for officers or raised cotton and other crops, often without pay. The government sold the yields produced by the freedpeople to factories and sources in the north and paid wages, rations and supplies from the proceeds.

In other words, the federal government took over where slaveholders left off, depriving African Americans of the right to decide how to dispose of their own labor and denying them the profits of that labor. In an attempt to address one aspect of "the problem," William D. Whipple, the Adjutant General issued the following October 14, 1861 directive:

> All colored persons called 'contrabands,' employed as servants by officers . . . will be furnished with their subsistence, and at least eight dollars per month for males, and four dollars per month for females, by the officers or others employing them. So much of the above-named sums as may be necessary to furnish clothing, to be decided by the commanding officers . . . will be applied for that purpose, and the remainder will be paid into the hands of the chief quartermaster, to create a fund for the support of those 'contrabands' who are unable to work for their own support.[6]

Even though this was meant for the servants of officers, the same treatment held true for most of the workers. It was to be a particularly sore point with formerly enslaved African American soldiers because the government designated them as contraband laborers and paid them much less than regular soldiers. As this order showed, no special consideration was given to the women, although they performed the same type of backbreaking labor as the men and in a typical display of wage discrimination coupled with racism, they received half as much pay as the underpaid men.

The notion that the formerly enslaved were unready to take care of themselves can also be seen in the fact that Africans were denied the right to plant what they wanted—specifically corn and sweet potatoes—on their own plots of land in locations like Port Royal. Instead they were forced to plant, cultivate and gin cotton for the government and other white speculators. The freedpeople, on the other hand, wanted to use cash crops to amass capital.

Pierce noted that the newly-freed people, before he came along "to guide and care for them," were "beginning to plant corn in their patches, but were disinclined to plant cotton, regarding it as a badge of servitude." It *was* a badge of servitude, and the formerly enslaved knew that quite well—there were very few white people working out in the cotton fields.

African Americans wished to relinquish all remnants of their enslavement—the distinctive clothes and shoes, particular foods, inferior housing and, most definitely, dependence on whites; they wanted nothing to remind them of their former bondage.

Pierce used coercion to force the people to plant cotton. "The culture of the cotton is voluntary, the only penalty for not engaging in it being the imposition of a rent for the tenement and land adjacent thereto occupied by the negro, not exceeding two dollars per month. Both the Government and private individuals, who have become owners of one-fourth of the land by recent tax-sales, pay twenty-five cents for a standard day's-work." He noted that "the work both upon the cotton and the corn is done only by the women, children and disabled men" because the men had been drafted as laborers into the Union army.[7]

Most of the black farmers were renting their land because, of course, having just come out of enslavement they did not possess the capital, on the whole, to purchase properties outright. Twenty-five cents a day was not a living wage and two dollars a month was a stiff penalty for a poor worker to pay. Cotton was profitable for the government and speculators; corn and other truck crops were not. In fact, Pierce's job required the dependence of the African workers; there would have been no need for agents like him if the land had been redistributed and freedpeople allowed to sink or swim on their own.

Paradoxically, Pierce equated land ownership with manhood and thought it was a good thing for African Americans to own their own land. African Americans also equated property ownership with manhood; they wanted to be able to support their families, as men. "The instinct for land—to have one spot on earth where a man may stand, and whence no human being can of right drive him—is one of the most conservative elements of our nature; and a people who have it in any fair degree will never be nomads or vagabonds."[8] Pierce conceded that African Americans were going to great lengths to get land so they would be self-sufficient.

Major Martin Delany of the 104th USCT was detailed for duty at Hilton Head, South Carolina to work with freedpeople in August 1865. He decided that in order for them to be self-sufficient they needed land. "Let, then, such lands as belong to the government, by sale from direct taxation, be let or sold to these freedmen, and other poor loyal men of the South, in small tracts of from twenty to forty acres to each head of a family." He included poor whites in his plan because he felt they, too, were oppressed. What he really wanted was for freedpeople to be extended the rights of citizenship. "Place no impediment in the way of the freedman; let his right be equally protected and his chances be equally regarded, and . . . he will stand and thrive . . . "[9] By 1867, however, he was documenting the obstacles placed in the way of freedpeople due to speculators such as Pierce and the lack of black landownership. "It was apparent from observation and experience that the custom of renting lands to speculators, who sub-let them to freedmen, or employed them to work at disadvantageous rates—that these poor people, at the end of the planting year, habitually came out with nothing."[10]

A delegation of mostly formerly enslaved men was interviewed by Secretary of War Edwin M. Stanton, Union General William T. Sherman and the Assistant Adjutant-General of the Army, E.D. Townsend, in January 1865 in Savannah, Georgia. The deputation, recognizing that black women were the primary laborers, at the time, on abandoned plantations because most able-bodied men had been conscripted, insisted, "The way we can best take care of ourselves is to have land, and turn in and till it by our labor—that is, by the labor of the women, and children, and old men—and we can soon maintain ourselves and have something to spare . . . We want to be placed on land until we are able to buy it, and make it our own."[11]

The soldiers of the 33rd USCI went so far as to create a building association in 1863 through which they hoped to obtain land by cooperative means. The leader of the association, Sergeant Prince Rivers, declared, "Every colored man will be a slave, and feel himself a slave until he can *raise his own bale of cotton* and *put his own mark upon it* and say *This is mine!*"[12]

It is obvious that freedpeople were not ever going to be self-sufficient under a system which prevented them from benefiting fully from their own labor. They were not going to be equal in a competitive, capitalistic economy without having that which drives such an economy—property, specifically, land. Ideally, according to African Americans, the government should have given the necessary initial aid and then left the freedpeople alone. As William Wells Brown said, "All I demand for the black man is, that the white people shall take their heels off his neck, and let him have a chance to rise by his own efforts."[13]

African American leaders, and some whites, clearly saw the need for land and called for the redistribution of the properties abandoned by rebels. Sojourner Truth was one leader who recognized the necessity of property as she sought to have land in the west set aside for freedpeople. Frances Ellen Watkins Harper asserted, "While I am in favor of Universal suffrage, yet I know that the colored man needs something more than a vote in his hand . . . A man landless, ignorant and poor may use the vote against his interests; but with intelligence and land he holds in his hand the basis of power and elements of strength."[14] She urged in a speech to freedpeople, "Get land, every one that can, and as fast as you can. A landless people must be dependent upon the landed people. A few acres to till for food and a roof, however humble, over your head, are the castle of your independence, and when you have it you are fortified to act and vote independently whenever your interests are at stake."[15]

Evidently freedpeople understood the nature of the property-conscious culture they were being forced to operate in and they vigorously challenged attempts to thwart their independence. Often the only real laborers on abandoned plantations and the ones responsible for the physical survival of their families, black women came to represent the ability of the African American community to be self-reliant. Certain of their own capabilities, the freedwomen, themselves, through their labor and resourcefulness, attempted to be independent. In one instance, the women, led by the elderly Grace, on a plantation at Port Royal protested, in a body, to Edward S. Philbrick about their pay, exploitation by white storekeepers and not being able to make their own decisions about what to plant.[16]

The February 8, 1862 *Weekly Anglo-African* denounced the government's attempts to place freedpeople into a position closely resembling enslavement. "The 'contraband' system is but another name for Government slavery . . . the Government had already made at least fifteen thousand dollars out of these Government slaves [at Fortress Monroe.] General [Thomas John] Wood says there is now a fund of $7,000 on hand from the avails of their labor. And yet the Government had laid out no expense on the women and children that do not work for Government, or have none to work for them, they are suffering for want of comfortable quarters and clothing. Nor will the authorities allow charity to come in and make up the deficiency of Government about the fort, in supplying clothing, lest it take away an incentive to labor for Government. *No money is promised to women who work for Government* [emphasis added], and the only stimulus offered is clothing . . . the women would prefer to work for officers and soldiers, and get a little pay for it."

For African American women, as this article shows, being designated "spoils of war" severely hampered their ability to provide for themselves and their families since their men were impressed into government service. The women were relegated to the same menial tasks that had generally been their lot in enslavement but now, instead of working for slaveholders, they were working for the government, seemingly for their own keep.

Many of the men who were conscripted as laborers were later absorbed into regular USCT regiments, leaving their women to fend for themselves while they were away at the front. In the absence of the men, African women labored on farms set up by the federal government to provide food, cotton and supplies to the Union army, themselves and other freedpeople. Francis W. Bird, a white abolitionist on a tour of the South, in his testimony before a War Department commission in 1863, acknowledged the self-sufficiency of African American women. "It is . . . to be borne in mind that very few able-bodied men are now employed upon these farms, nearly all of that class having been drawn either into the army or employed in other labor for the Government. Notwithstanding these drawbacks I think it is safe to say, that on all these farms the laborers have raised crops abundantly sufficient to support themselves and their families until the next harvest."[17]

Bird's testimony also highlighted another successful farm in Virginia being run primarily by the women after the former owner, Confederate General Henry Wise, abandoned it. "The whole number of able bodied men is five stout boys and men over 15, four. Boys under fifteen, five. Able bodied women, fifteen. Girls under fifteen who work occasionally, seven . . . Two hundred and fifty acres of land were cultivated. The amount of produce sent off or on hand was, potatoes 100 Barrells, corn 2100 bushels. It should be observed to the credit of the experiment, how small the proportion of able-bodied men is to the non-producers on these farms, to the infirm and the women and children, whom they have had to support. With the exception of Herrings place one half of the crops on these farms belongs to the Government; and in all cases so far as I could understand this half more than pays for all the materials furnished by the

Government."[18] Nevertheless, in spite of his acknowledgment of the women, Bird failed to give proper credit to them, assuming that the "able-bodied men" were primarily responsible for the success of the farms. Surely, the women were putting as much, if not more, sweat equity in the endeavor. It is to be assumed that he was attempting to define the African American family by the parameters of the "traditional" family structure and attempting to show that African Americans were capable of fulfilling such a social norm.

The policy of forced labor was very lucrative for the government as evidenced by a local camp supervisor in 1863: "I am well satisfied, from careful calculations, that the freedmen of this Camp [Corinth, Mississippi] and District have netted the Government, over and above all their expenses, including rations, tents, &c., at least $3000 per month, *independent of what the women do*, [emphasis added] & all the property brought through our lines from the rebels."[19]

The June 30, 1863 *Preliminary Report* of the American Freedmen's Inquiry Commission gives further evidence of how profitable the pseudo-enslavement of African Americans was. The Commission reported to Secretary of War Edwin Stanton, "Even under the present faulty or imperfect system of management, the refugee Negroes furnish to the government in various localities, in the shape of military labor, the full equivalent of the rations and the wages they and their wives and children receive . . . in all the localities visited by the commission, the demand for able-bodied Negroes as laborers in the military service has greatly exceeded the supply."[20]

More than a year later, the *Pennsylvania Freedmen's Bulletin* furnished additional proof. The paper carried the text of a November 21, 1864 speech by William F. Mitchell, who had toured the South to assess the condition of the former bondspeople. "Last spring I visited the Contraband Camp at Huntsville, Ala. It contained about 300 persons, one-half of whom were ill. It was entirely dependent on the government and charity of the North. It was the scene of squalor and misery beyond description. Mark the change. But a few weeks since I visited it again—population about the same; on the sick-list *two*—camp nearly self-supporting, and had it not been for the raid upon the plantation they would have returned to the Government all with which they were supplied last year. *And these were women and children, and a few men unfit for the army* . . . [emphasis added]" Mitchell had reported earlier that a refugee camp in the Department of the Cumberland [Nashville, Tennessee] had raised $300,000 worth of cotton.[21] The African Americans who worked for the army and federal government under a system too reminiscent of enslavement, did not materially benefit from their labor.

In a scathing attack on the government and the National Freedmen's Relief Association (NFRA,) Thomas Knox, a white assistant surgeon in the Military Department of South Carolina, charged northern speculators with fraud in the management of abandoned plantations. He said they made "mere serfs" of the freedpeople and that the white "Northern oppressors" were a "horde of plunderers" who did not pay the people a fair living wage. He noted that African American women got $4 a month as opposed to $8 for black men while white laborers on Beaufort's wharf received $30 to $50 per month.

Knox also accused agents of the NFRA of "deceiving and defrauding these poor colored people, who had escaped from bondage only to fall into the hands of God-forsaken Northern sharks." He said the agents made the refugees pay exorbitant prices for clothes which were sent to them via the Freedmen's Bureau by northerners. Many of these clothes were sent by African American female relief groups. Knox was subsequently relieved of his duties, imprisoned and charged with attempting to incite an insurrection among the refugees.[22]

Although dismissed by most relief leaders as a troublemaker, fraud and crackpot, Knox's contentions were somewhat supported in the NFRA's own records. Their minutes of March 15, 1862 show that Rev. Mansfield French, their representative at Port Royal, suggested that " . . . all *new* and second rate clothing shall be sold to the working hands and paid for in labor . . . The children, the sick, the aged will be furnished without charge. All cases of destitution among those coming from the 'main,' i.e. the rebels, and all cases where no employment is afforded by either class of agents, will be promptly attended to by the ladies and with no charge for any article. So far as I can learn, all the friends of the colored people oppose this plan of operation. It is proposed in giving the clothes to those receiving wages, to note carefully the name of the person receiving the goods, the kind and prices and pass the bills over to the cotton or plantation agents. There is no money here to pay the laborers and even if the government had the money, it is very questionable whether it would be best to pay it to the people. They have no idea of its value . . . If the above plan shall meet the approval of the Association, it will soon bring a large sum from the government . . . " The NFRA approved French's plan.[23] Such a policy, of course, placed the newly free Africans in a subservient, dependent position and kept them there, at the mercy of white agents, planters, and the government. By denying African Americans the right to handle their own financial affairs, the NFRA crushed the autonomy required to be self-reliant. It is obvious why charges of fraud could be made because donors supplied money and clothes to be given, not sold, to the destitute refugees.

African American relief workers were, consequently, often at odds with the federal government and some white charitable organizations over whether the formerly enslaved were, or should be, able to take care of themselves. Of course, some few black relief workers held the view that the freedpeople were, as yet, too uncivilized to be self-sufficient but most felt it was necessary for them to have full access to citizenship rights. They had too long themselves, as ostensibly "free" people, lived lives proscribed by racism. Most African Americans, including the newly-freed people, wanted what other Americans had—the right to make their own decisions and live their lives without the impediment of white intervention and racism. They called for help for, not control of, the former bondspeople.

Freedmen's Village in Arlington, Virginia housed more than a thousand refugees who were raising food for the Union army and purchasing homes in the community. For Elizabeth Keckley, president of Contraband Relief Association, this was evidence that African Americans were capable of taking care of themselves:

> . . . emancipated blacks . . . went to work with commendable energy, and planned with remarkable forethought. They built themselves cabins, and each family cultivated for itself a small patch of ground. The colored people are fond of domestic life, and with them domestication means happy children, a fat pig, a dozen or more chickens, and a garden. Whoever visits the Freedmen's Village now in the vicinity of Washington will discover all of these evidences of prosperity and happiness.[24]

Although the lineage and facts are somewhat murky, it ironically appears that the community was built on seventeen acres which had been deeded to Mary Syphax[25] by her white father, George Washington Parke Custis. Syphax's mother had been enslaved by Custis who was Martha [wife of George] Washington's grandson.[26]

Robert E. Lee, the Confederate general, was Custis' son-in-law and the executor of his will which manumitted about two hundred enslaved Africans, possibly including Mary Syphax.[27] According to Luther Porter Jackson, John B. Syphax, a member of Virginia's House of Delegates from 1874 to 1875, was the son of Charles and Maria Custis Syphax and was born on the Parke Custis estate. Jackson says, John's "parents, once slaves, had been freed by the will of Parke Custis."[28] John remained a major landowner in Alexandria County in the location of Custis' Arlington estate.

The December 9, 1864 *Liberator* carried a report that Lee kept some of these freedpeople enslaved, however. "It will be remembered that several slaves on the Arlington estate, who were left free by the will of Mr. Curtis [Custis], but kept in slavery by Gen. R.E. Lee, ran away, were recaptured, whipped severely by the general, and afterwards taken to Richmond. A gentleman who has lately visited Arlington informs us that these have been released by Gen. Lee's son, and have returned to Arlington, free. The young woman who was so badly treated by Lee, and whose case was the subject of some controversy in the papers about the time of the rebellion, is among them, and is living near her aged and worthy parents."

The article was referring to two letters in the June 24, 1859 *New York Tribune* which alleged that Lee had the two men and one woman stripped and given thirty-nine lashes each after they were recaptured. When the whipper refused to flog the woman, the letters claimed that Lee whipped her himself. One of the letters, from "A Citizen," said that the writer lived only a mile from the Arlington estate and that he had confirmed the incident with "near relatives of the men whipped." He also asserted that "Custis had fifteen children by his slave women. I see his grandchildren every day; they are of a dark yellow." Such reports simply confirmed the North's vision of a decadent southern white ruling class.

In a vein similar to Elizabeth Keckley's, Harriet Jacobs, a leading relief worker, declared to the white abolitionist, Lydia Maria Child, that though destitute, many of the freedpeople had jobs and were "supporting themselves and their families." According to Jacobs, who is defending her "abused and suffering people" from the derision and contempt heaped on them by white philanthropists, they "are quick, intelligent, and full of the spirit of freedom."[29]

William Evans, Jr. and J. Wistar Evans, white members of the Friends' Association of Philadelphia for the Relief of Colored Freemen, concurred with Jacobs' assessment. They reported on their visit to Freedmen's Village in Alexandria, Virginia in June 1864. "This city contains a very large number of freedmen, who appear to be the most self-supporting of any locality which came under our observation. It is known that they have spent at least thirty thousand dollars of their earnings in the erection of dwelling houses, and have besides put up a school-house at a cost of $500, which is held by trustees selected from among themselves. They have been much assisted and stimulated in their efforts by a colored woman, Harriet Jacobs, who has established herself here, and relieves destitution by the distribution of clothing, furnished by Northern societies, and in other ways."[30] Harriet and her daughter, Louisa, later went to Savannah, Georgia in 1866 to give medical and educational aid to freedpeople.

Laura M. Towne, a white abolitionist sent by the Port Royal Relief Association of Philadelphia to the Sea Islands, on the other hand, considered the freedpeople she worked among childlike and in need of control and civilizing. She remarked appreciatively that the women on Pope's Plantation, St. Helena Island, South Carolina, were "obliged to work. All who can are kept busy with the cotton, but there are some women and young girls unfit for the field, and these are made to do their share of housework and washing, so that they may draw pay like the others—or rations—for Government must support them all whether they work or not . . . So far as I have seen, they are eager to get a chance to do housework or washing . . . "[31] Evidently the belief that free Africans had to be compelled to work and that they had no right to their own time, labor and wages (the very things that denoted "freedom") was prevalent among even the whites like Towne who devoted their energies to aiding freedpeople. She, no doubt, missed the irony in the fact that her efforts on behalf of the former bondspeople were partially funded by the government which seized, as contraband, cotton and other crops grown by Africans on plantations. The labor of Africans during the Port Royal Experiment supported her own "philanthropic" work among them.

Edward L. Pierce concurred with Towne's position, stating, "It has been suggested that field-work does not become women in the new condition [freedom]; and so it may seem to some persons of just sympathies who have not yet learned that no honest work is dishonorable in man or woman . . . Field-work, as an occupation, may not be consistent with the finest feminine culture or the most complete womanliness; but it

in no way conflicts with virtue, self-respect, and social development . . .
Better a woman with a hoe than without it, when she is not yet fitted for
the needle or the book."[32]

Pierce's comments illuminate the warped view of the freedpeople that
far too many of their "friends" held. White southerners, including those
who had fled the plantations, saw no value in physical labor. If they had,
they would not have needed the forced labor of Africans. Certainly,
sweaty, laborious fieldwork was not seen as "consistent with the finest
feminine culture" or "complete womanliness." White female refugees were
not being forced into the fields; they were being allowed to retain their
position on the pedestal of "true womanhood." In any case, the decision
about whether or not to engage in fieldwork was not the freedwomen's to
make because Pierce, as the overseer of the plantations, had the authority,
and exercised it, to force the women back into the fields, regardless of
their wishes.

It was this lack of choice which freedpeople objected to. When they
were working for themselves, the women were more than willing to do
such difficult work. This process and Pierce's bias also show how an
inferior status was imposed on the freedwomen from the beginning of their
freedom. Someone else—Pierce in this instance—was to determine a
definition of them and their status and that definition determined that they
would not measure up to "true womanhood," precisely because fieldwork
was not for "real ladies." This definition was to plague African American
women for decades.

A broadside distributed in Robertson and Sumner Counties in
Tennessee in January 1867 illustrates this point further. The leaflet,
obviously by a racist organization similar to the Ku Klux Klan, sets forth
the conditions of black life with special reference to African American
women.

> 1st. No man shall squat negroes on his place unless they are all
> under his employ male and female. 2d. Negro women shall be
> employed by white persons. 3d. All children shall be hired out for
> something. 4th. Negroes found in cabins to themselves shall suffer
> the penalty. 5th. Negroes shall not be allowed to hire negroes. 6th.
> Idle men, women or children, shall suffer the penalty.[33]

African American women were clearly to be denied the status of "true
womanhood" and it is significant that most sharecropping contracts after
the Civil War stipulated or mandated the labor of wives and children,
thereby ensuring this fact.

Most white philanthropic organizations and government officials relied on the opinions of whites such as Pierce, whose word, as a government official, carried a lot of weight. Another white whose opinion was thought highly of was Frederick Law Olmsted who wrote to his friend, Charles E. Norton, a white refugee relief supporter, in 1863: "The Negro is not a gentleman and a Christian . . . He is little better than a cunning idiot and a cowed savage. He does not on this account need an owner, but he does need a guardian, and he knows that he does. He would rather have an owner than no guardianship."[34] Olmsted was (and sometimes is still) mistakenly thought of as an abolitionist because he contended that "free" or wage labor was more efficient than the forced labor of enslaved Africans. Olmsted was being considered for a position heading the NFRA's work with refugees. However, as his letter shows, he may have found fault with the economic institution of enslavement but his opinion of African Americans made him no friend of the black community.

Norton was little better. An article in the July 1865 *North American Review*, under his editorial direction, propounded the view that newly freed African Americans were "stunted, misshapen children" who were good imitators but were "deficient in the more ideal operations, which require reflection and reasoning." According to Norton, friend of the freedpeople, African Americans suffered from a "mental degradation" which can be seen in "the confusion of ideas that blurs their common statements. It even accounts for much of their apparent dishonesty, and most curiously distorts the structure of their language." Ironically, while the article was an attempt to solicit support for the freedpeople, it explicated the racist attitudes which motivated much of the white charity extended to refugees. A race of imbecilic children such as the one Norton described required white control and guardianship and that is exactly what white philanthropists and the government set out to provide.

An order issued by General Lorenzo Thomas on March 11, 1864 concerning plantations in Mississippi confirmed this. A cynic might, however, see such an attitude as self-serving rationalization on the part of those who benefited from black labor. The following excerpt is lengthy but instructive because it shows just how the dependence of the recently-freed people was officially codified. Later sharecropping contracts followed the same format.

The first thing that Thomas did was to divide the area into "police districts" under the direction of provost-marshals. Then, he allowed the establishment of schools for "the instruction of colored children under twelve years of age." A child over twelve, one could surmise, was considered an adult.

Provision IV stated: "Soldiers will not be allowed to visit plantations without the written consent of the commanding officer of the regiment or post to which they are attached, and never with arms, except when on duty, accompanied by an officer." Read, African American soldiers, in much the same way as the black and slave codes which prohibited African American men from carrying arms, were treated as criminals. This was reinforced in Provision XI, "The possession of arms or concealed or dangerous weapons, without authority will be punished by fine and imprisonment."

This police state was further strengthened by Provision V: "Plantation hands will not be allowed to pass from one place to another, except under such regulations as may be established by the provost-marshal of the police district." Under such a police state, African Americans were denied some very basic rights.

Provision VI eliminated one of the remnants of enslavement when it outlawed the use of "flogging and other cruel or unusual punishment" but it reinstituted other aspects as Provision XII showed:

> Laborers shall render to their employer, between daylight and dark, ten hours in summer and nine hours in winter, of respectful, honest, faithful labor, and receive therefore, in addition to just treatment, healthy rations, comfortable clothing, quarters, fuel, medical attendance, and instruction for children, wages per month as follows, payment of one-half of which, at least, shall be reserved until the end of the year, and lessees will discourage all payment of monthly wages as far as it can be done without discontent, and reserve the same as above stated: The minimum wages for males over fourteen years of age, and competent to do a well man's work, $10 per month; for females over fourteen years of age, and competent to do a well woman's work, $7 per month; children from twelve to fourteen years of age, inclusive, and of those too feeble to earn full wages, half the above amounts will be paid . . . Wages will be deducted in case of sickness, and rations also when sickness is feigned. Indolence, insolence, disobedience of orders, and crime will be suppressed by forfeiture of pay—such forfeitures to go to the fund for the support of the helpless freed people—and such punishments as are provided for similar offenses by Army Regulations.[35]

Provision XIII continued the descent into quasi-enslavement: "In cases of attempted imposition, by feigning sickness or stubborn refusal of duty, they will be turned over to the provost-marshal of the police districts for labor upon the public works without pay." There was no way out for African Americans caught in such a system.

Provision XIV illustrated the hypocrisy of this scheme: "Laborers will be permitted to cultivate land on private account, as shall be agreed between them and the employers, subject to the approval of the provost-marshal of the district. *The encouragement of independent industry will strengthen all the advantages which capital derives from labor, and enable the laborer to take care of himself and to prepare for the time when he can render so much labor for so much money, which is the great end to be attained* [emphasis added.]" African Americans were ready to be paid a living wage for their labor; they were ready to work for themselves on their own land. However, this system, as proposed, was not going to provide them with access to capital. Certainly, no one knew better than they the value of their labor—it had been taken from them by force for nearly two hundred and fifty years.

More hypocrisy was evident in Provision XX: "These regulations are based on the assumption that labor is a public duty and idleness and vagrancy is a crime." Labor was not a public duty for whites since the provision went on to explain, "That portion of the people identified with the cultivation of the soil, however changed in condition by the revolution through which we are passing, is not relieved from the necessity of toil, which is the condition of existence with all the children of God. The revolution has altered its tenure, but not its law . . . Indolence, disorder, and crime will be suppressed." Of course, African Americans were identified with the soil so this pseudo-enslavement was meant only for them and not the ignorant, shiftless, lazy poor whites that white northerners continually wrote about in their diaries, journals and newspapers.

The rest of the order extends clemency to rebels. The irony of this is inescapable—African Americans who were not in rebellion and who did not take up arms against the United States, did not have their situation made materially better while rebel whites simply had to swear an oath of allegiance to the United States in order to resume their privileged position with their feet still firmly on the necks of the people they had formerly enslaved.

When compared to many of the "rules for governing Negroes" that slaveowners gave to overseers and agents, these conditions must have seemed, to the formerly enslaved, uncomfortably similar to the enslavement from which these supposedly "freed" people had just been "liberated." In addition to making provisions for military punishments for infractions such as "indolence, insolence, disobedience of orders," this order demanded that the laborers give "respectful, honest, faithful labor" to their employers who did not have to afford them the same treatment. Of course, whites were to decide what constituted "proper" behavior as well as infractions.

The restrictions reflected the old slaveholding mentality, as noted by W.E.B. Du Bois, "If they fought for freedom, they were beasts; if they did not fight, they were born slaves. If they cowered on the plantations, they loved slavery; if they ran away, they were lazy loafers. If they sang, they were silly; if they scowled, they were impudent."[36] What they weren't, according to the new outlook, was truly free. Attitudes such as those held by General Benjamin Butler made this abundantly clear. Butler, like General Thomas, believed that "political freedom rightly defined is liberty to work" and that African Americans had "rights so long as they fulfill their duties"[37]—duties, that is, to the existing plantation labor system which was still in place despite the war. Emancipation did not a citizen make.

African American women were not exempted from these strictures, interpositions, interdictions and impositions. General Butler again serves as an example. He placated slaveholders in Louisiana when, as commander of the Department of the Gulf in 1862, he set about maintaining the plantation economy by returning fugitives to slaveholders and by instituting a labor contract system which was virtually identical to enslavement because people who had been freed by the Emancipation Proclamation were physically forced to labor for plantation owners. When he was replaced by General Nathaniel Banks in 1863, his successor carried on his policies and, in fact, strengthened them. By way of illustration: a female plantation worker in Ascension Parish, Louisiana had a conflict with the plantation's white mistress over rations. "The planter and his overseer later entered the woman's cabin, disarmed her of a knife, and while restraining her husband at gunpoint, administered, by the planter's own account, about forty or fifty blows with a stick. 'This woman,' the planter charged before the provost marshal, 'cursed us all the time, using very insolent language.'" Using Banks' restrictive labor regulations which were very similar to Thomas', a Union officer sentenced the woman to one month in jail for "insolence and disobedience of orders."[38]

Major-General William T. Sherman, however, took issue with General Thomas' plan because it did not take into consideration the entrenched racism of the rebels. He wrote to Thomas in April 1864, "I heard a young lady in Canton [Mississippi], educated at Philadelphia, who was a communicant of a Christian church, thank her God that her negroes, who had attempted to escape into our lines at Big Black, had been overtaken by [General L.S.] Ross' Texas brigade and killed. She thanked God, and did so in religious sincerity. Now a stranger to the sentiment of the South would consider this unnatural, but it is not only natural but universal. All the people of the South, old and young, rich and poor, educated and ignorant, unite in this, that they will kill as vipers the whites who attempt to free their slaves, and also the 'ungrateful slaves' who attempt to change their character from slave to free. Therefore, in making this change, which I regard as a decree of nature, we have to combat not only with organized resistance of the Confederate forces, but the entire people of the South." His words were prophetic because it is this unreconstructed mentality with which African Americans had to contend after the War.

Sherman proposed a more equitable solution, "I would prefer much to colonize the negroes on lands clearly forfeited to us by treason." He pointed out several areas along the Mississippi River, a "rich alluvial region . . . as the very country in which we might collect the negroes, and where they will find more good land already cleared . . . [It] would enable the negro at once to be useful." If the government went along with Thomas' plan, and it did, then Sherman wanted to at least have "the occupation of a black brigade of Harrisonburg [Louisiana]."[39] Sherman, presumably, thought that African American soldiers would have the interests of the freedpeople at heart.

Colonel William Birney also had a plan of action, proposed at the same time as Sherman's: "As my plan involves bringing off large numbers of women and children, as well as men (because you cannot get the latter without bringing off the former), the first step is to make proper and adequate provision for their support. If placed on land, sheltered, and provided with houses, the women and children can support themselves after the first crop, with the aid of the father's pay . . . What I ask, therefore, is that the Government shall give the enlisting soldier forty acres of land as a bounty and furnish his family commissary stores at cost . . . It is implied that the soldiers are to be paid as much as white soldiers. How legislators can imagine we can raise troops, as a permanent thing, at $7 a month I cannot see. The man must have $2 for himself, and he cannot support his family on the other $5."[40] Birney's plan addresses several issues: the strength of the black family—he assumed that freedpeople formed legitimate and traditional family units; the need for land in a capitalistic economy; and the inequitable pay structure and its impact on the families.

The quasi-enslavement of the sharecropping system which grew out of the government's actions toward freedpeople during the Civil War was noted by the *Pennsylvania Freedmen's Bulletin* in 1867: "The rate of wages given to the freedmen in [Person County, North Carolina] is very low, and being paid in orders upon stores kept by the planters themselves, they do not receive a just equivalent for their wages."[41] Another example of this pseudo-enslavement, with its overlay of "legality," can be seen in the following contract issued shortly after the war ended:

> This article of agreement, witnesseth that I the undersigned S.C. Montgomery the employer and the freedmen whose names appear below the labourers have made this contract, whereby the freedmen agree to live upon and labour for the said Montgomery on Belmont Plantation in the county of Claiborne, State of [Mississippi]; for the year (1867) eighteen hundred & sixty seven for the wages as specified below.
>
> For No. 1 male field hands $15.00 per month
>   "   2 "   "   "   12.00 " "
>   "   3 "   "   "   10.00 " "
>   "   1 female "   "   12.00 " "
>   "   2 "   "   "   10.00 " "
>   "   3 "   "   "   8.00 " "
>
> The said Montgomery will give 4 lbs of mess pork, 1 peck of meal weekly, to each labourer; charging cost price delivered for all extra rations furnished idle members of families. Obey all rules & regulations made by the said Montgomery, or, his agent. Done this the 19th day of Jan 1867[42]

The laborers, thirteen men and eight women, all made marks rather than signatures as they apparently could not read or write. Note that the women were paid less than the men and none were paid a living wage. The inequities of the sharecropping system can be seen in this contract which clearly benefits the plantation owner at the expense of the workers. Elements of the former condition of enslavement can be seen also, i.e., "Obey all rule & regulations, made by . . . Montgomery, or his agent." No provisions were made to assure that white employers rendered fair and equitable treatment to their employees.

George Clary, a white surgeon who attempted to participate in the lucrative business of speculating by leasing an abandoned plantation and using captive black labor to run it—remarked, "The question of labor and the cultivation of cotton crops is the one of interest to those who have any faith in the free negro."[43] That faith resided, however, in white exploitation of black labor, not in African American self-reliance.

He knew just how lucrative such a venture would be for the speculators: "It is to be a great business for some years to come, and the Southerners can't manage the darks now as the Yankees can."[44] As a Northerner, he felt particularly suited to "take the plantations and run them upon shares."[45] He assumed he had some measure of Yankee thrift and ability which Southerners presumably lacked. Clary and three other white officers in his regiment had "been agitating the subject of taking a plantation on the St. John River in Florida and planting 1000 acres of cotton. We estimated that, with a moderate yield and allowing a large margin for adverse circumstances, we could easily clear $20,000 a year each. There is no doubt that cotton is to be a very profitable crop to raise, and it takes the Yankees to make the negroes work."[46]

The only way for this to be successful, however, would be by having a captive black labor force, which was tied to the land. In such a system the laborers were not going to reap the benefits of their labor but the "free-market," "free-labor" capitalists, like Clary, were. Clary understood this quite distinctly.

He considered poor whites shiftless and lazy but did not think them worthy of being enslaved and "compelled to labor." He noted that the sugar mills in New Orleans in October 1863 "are at work and will make from ½ to 1/4 of a crop of sugar. There is a lack of help on account of the ablest of the negroes having either volunteered or having been conscripted in the army. The old men and women and children are principally left to do the work. *The white men are too lazy to work generally and are not accustomed to it* [emphasis added.]"[47] The white men were not expected, or required, to do the work even though they were captured rebels. On the other hand, African American elderly men, women and children were compelled to perform necessary labor in the absence of their men. They were being made to toil again in a system which required the same type of brutality and force to keep them captive and dependent.

However, Clary's conscience required a rationalization for instituting the quasi-enslavement of African Americans: "I have a sympathy for the race, though it is modified by a familiarity with their exceedingly indolent and vicious habits. They as a race need for years to come the protection and the care of the Gen'l Government, with regulations compelling them to labor and to fulfill their contracts, and the same in regard to the whites. They must be made to fulfill *their* contracts with the negro, or the negro will suffer more than in a state of slavery. When the negro was property, his master took care of him as carefully as he would his horse and more in proportion to the value, but now that the negro is free, he is an object of hatred and neglect."[48] He goes on to say that African Americans have "a propensity to steal." Nevertheless, this tendency, according to Clary, "is a natural result of their having been deprived of the just remuneration for their labor. They have in their ignorance an innate sense of a right to share in the produce of their toil, and they strive blindly to obtain it."[49] He made no mention of the fact that he recognized that he was attempting to do exactly that - deprive the African Americans who would have been sharecroppers on his own plantation of just remuneration for their labor. He justified his exploitation by assuming the basic criminality of those on whose labor he hoped to capitalize. This man, who had "sympathy for the race," would have reduced the African Americans once again to a type of enslavement, for his own profit. To call a people who had been forced to labor under the lash, the whip, chains and coercion, "indolent" and "vicious," while simultaneously depriving them of land in a property-based capitalistic economy was the height of insensitive self-serving racism. To attempt to benefit from their continued oppression compounded his hypocrisy. Apparently Clary did not participate in the speculation scheme, not because of his moral principles but because he and his partners could not get the project off the ground.

Edward Pierce also considered poor whites less than desirable. "In natural tact and the faculty of getting a livelihood the contrabands are inferior to the Yankees, but quite equal to the mass of the Southern population. It is not easy to see why they would be less industrious, if free, than the whites, particularly as they would have the encouragement of wages . . . Of the [white] Virginians who took the oath of allegiance at Hampton, not more than one in fifteen could write his name, and the rolls captured at Hatteras disclose an equally deplorable ignorance."[50] Many northern Civil War participants noted the illiteracy and ignorance of white Southerners but they might have been swayed by the fact that, at one point, as rebels, they were considered the enemy.

Poor white northerners, especially the Irish, also came into their fair share of disdain from middle and upper-class whites. Colonel Robert Gould Shaw, white commander of the Massachusetts 54th USCT, said of the black soldiers he led, "They learn all the details of guard duty and camp service infinitely more readily than most of the Irish I have had under may command."[51] Orrin Cook, a white Union soldier from Massachusetts, said to his diary, " . . . the nigger is a gentleman and a saint compared to the Irishman. There is little difference in the intelligence of the two, but the Irishman smells and behaves the worst. If the North could exchange its Irish population for the same no. of negroes, person and property would be far safer there than they now are."[52] In any case, poor whites were generally exempted from the mistreatment that blacks endured at the hands of Union soldiers and, later, at the hands of government agents and speculators.

While many of the whites involved in refugee relief efforts were surely motivated by philanthropic impulses, the overwhelming conclusion that can be drawn from the results of their work is that in many cases the advancement and independence of the African American community were retarded by their paternalistic and maternalistic benevolence. The established antebellum order of white dominance and black subordination did not substantially change because African Americans gained very little political, social or economic advantages from the intervention of white northern philanthropists.

A white representative of NFRA of New York, Mrs. Harlan, flatly rejected the idea that freedpeople were unwilling or incapable of taking care of themselves. She reported to the organization on March 31, 1862, "All with whom I conversed, or observed, male and female, manifested a strong desire to be put to work, either for wages, or, on the gardens and lands, on their own account. None seemed to hesitate. All seem anxious to provide for their own necessities, and implored us to give them seeds and let them begin at once. They are confident of their own ability to work and even manage the estates on which they were left. When doubts were expressed they would promptly reply, 'Didn't we work and raise enough for master and ourselves to eat, and a heap more, when he was here?'"[53] Since the able-bodied men were most likely absent due to conscription, Harlan is undoubtedly referring to women.

What is clear from the records, however, is that the women had a strong desire to be self-sufficient and independent. They wanted employment, not charity. Jacob Willets, a white agent of the Indiana Freedmen's Aid Commission and Refugee Relief Association, wrote to L. Abbott, the General Secretary of the American Freedmen's and Union Commission, "With few exceptions, I have found the whites as ignorant of letters as the blacks, and far more helpless in providing for their support. The black women were far ahead of the whites in the knowledge of housekeeping and domestic economy, and required much less assistance in procuring a living, and those in health soon ceased to be a burden, while the whites required continual assistance, as long as they remained. They were anxious to return as soon as the way opened for it, and by government aid and otherwise, they have mostly returned to their former homes, and taken their places again as citizens of their respective States, and are ready to exercise the rights and privileges of citizens."[54] African American women had to be self-sufficient; they did not have former homes worthy of going back to and they had never been citizens.

The Western Freedmen's Aid Commission reported, "Degraded as they have been by slavery, they still manifest a purpose to support themselves in preference to depending solely upon the Government and private charities. Hence the inmates of the camps are chiefly women with children, orphan children, and the sick, the infirm, and the aged. Some of the camps are composed mostly of the families of colored soldiers."[55]

The same *Report* carried a message from Chaplain George Stokes, Superintendent of Freedmen at Huntsville, Alabama: "Have a large field of labor, where eleven months' experience has given sufficient assurance that we can put to silence all who have pleaded the incapacity of the negro or freedman for self-management, education, or advancement, self-protection, or self-support. Though opposed in our work by rebel sympathizers, or those of pro-slavery proclivities, the year of trial has been a prosperous one till military strategy caused us to evacuate our camp at Huntsville where we had raised four thousand bushels of corn, about seven or eight bales of cotton, and sorghum for thirty barrels of syrup. This was raised principally by women and children."[56] Unfortunately, however, the camp had been broken up by a retreat of Union forces.

Samuel Shipley, the president of the Executive Board of the Friends' Association of Philadelphia, reported on his visit to refugee camps on the Mississippi River. "You are aware that all able-bodied men have been taken into Government employ. The women, children, and infirm men who remain are represented as very willing to work, when they can find the occupations to which they are accustomed. They show a commendable spirit of independence, and desire to provide for themselves. The Superintendent at Columbus said, he regarded them as more industrious than the whites . . . In the Vicksburg Department, they have cut 10,000 cords of wood during the past three months. For this, they have received from fifty cents to one dollar and fifty cents per cord. They have built 220 houses in the same time. Where the camps of white regiments are accessible, the women earn a considerable amount by washing for them."[57]

Despite such glowing testimonials, the view that African Americans were too debased to operate as full citizens was too ingrained in the white psyche to be dislodged easily. The opinion which mandated black dependency continued to hold sway and the negative stereotypes of African Americans, male and female, proliferated. Nevertheless, as the examples of freedwomen have shown, African American women were in the vanguard of seeking true independence and self-reliance for themselves and their community.

NOTES

1. Edward L. Pierce, "The Contrabands at Fortress Monroe," *Atlantic Monthly*, 8 (November 1861): 627.

2. Western Freedmen's Aid Commission, *Second Annual Report* (Cincinnati: Methodist Book Concern, 1865), 6.

3. George Clary Papers, May 25, 1862, Connecticut Historical Society, Hartford.

4. OR, Series III, volume 4, 378, 380.

5. Ira Berlin, et al., eds., *Free At Last: a Documentary History of Slavery, Freedom, and the Civil War* (New York: New Press, 1992), 263.

6. Bernard C. Nalty and Morris J. MacGregor, eds., *Blacks in the Military: Essential Documents* (Wilmington, Delaware: Scholarly Resources, 1981), p. 22.

7. Edward L. Pierce, "The Freedmen at Port Royal," *Atlantic Monthly*, 12 (September 1863): 308-309.

8. Ibid., 310.

9. Frank [Frances] A. Rollin, *Life and Public Services of Martin R. Delany* (New York: Arno Press, 1969, 1883), 239, 241.

10. Ibid., 272.

11. *Liberator*, 24 February 1865.

12. Joseph T. Glatthaar, *Forged in Battle: the Civil War Alliance of Black Soldiers and White Officers* (New York: Free Press, 1990), 246.

13. *Liberator*, 16 May 1862.

14. William Still, *The Underground Railroad* (New York: Arno Press, 1968, 1872), 770.

15. Ibid., 775-776.

16. Elizabeth Ware Pearson, *Letters from Port Royal, 1862- 1868* (New York: Arno Press, 1969, 1906), 303-304.

17. Berlin, *Free*, 280.

18. Ibid., 283-284.

19. Ibid., 196.

20. Nalty, 30.

21. *Pennsylvania Freedmen's Bulletin* 1(February 1865): 15- 16.

22. Thomas P. Knox, *Startling Revelations from the Department of South Carolina, and An Expose of the So Called National Freedmen's Relief Association* (Boston: William M. Kindall, 1864), 5-7.

23. National Freedman's Relief Association (NFRA), New York, *By-Laws and Minutes* [Rare Books and Manuscripts Department, Boston Public Library].

24. Elizabeth Keckley, *Behind the Scenes: Thirty Years a Slave and Four Years in the White House* (New York: Arno Press, 1968, 1868), 142-143.

25. Variously Mary or Marie Syphas

26. Dorothy Sterling, ed., *We Are Your Sisters: Black Women in the Nineteenth Century* (New York: W.W. Norton, 1984), 247; William Loren Katz, *History of Schools for the Colored Population* (New York: Arno Press, 1969, 1871), 256.

27. Ervin Jordan, Jr., *Black Confederates and Afro-Yankees in Civil War Virginia* (Charlottesville: University of Virginia, 1995), 138, 258, 324-325.

28. Luther Porter Jackson, *Negro Office-Holders in Virginia, 1865-1895* (Norfolk, Virginia: Guide Quality Press, 1945), 41.

29. C. Peter Ripley, ed., *The Black Abolitionist Papers, Volume V: the United States, 1859-1965* (Chapel Hill: University of North Carolina Press, 1992), 193.

30. *Freedman's Friend* 1 (June 1864): 4.

31. Laura M. Towne, *Letters and Diary* (New York: Negro Universities Press, 1969, 1912), 13.

32. Pierce, "Freedmen," 309.

33. Ira Berlin and Leslie Rowland, eds., *Families and Freedom: a Documentary History of African-American Kinship in the Civil War Era* (New York: New Press, 1997), 189.

34. NFRA, *By-Laws.*

35. United States. War Department, *The War of the Rebellion: a Compilation of the Official Records of the Union and Confederate Armies*, Series III, Volume IV (Washington, D.C.: Government Printing Office, 1900), 167.

36. W.E.B. Du Bois, *Black Reconstruction in America 1860-1880* (Cleveland: World Publishing Company, 1962), 125.

37. OR, Series III, Volume 3, 1139-44.

38. Louis Gerteis, *From Contraband to Freedman: Federal Policy Toward Southern Blacks 1861-1865* (Westport, Connecticut: Greenwood Press, 1973), 105.

39. OR, Series III, vol. 4, 225.

40. Ibid., 226-227.

41. *Pennsylvania Freedmen's Bulletin* (October 1867): 6.

42. Manuscript, ms.E.94, Rare Books and Manuscripts Department, Boston Public Library.

43. George Clary Papers, October 23, 1865, Connecticut Historical Society, Hartford.

44. Ibid., October 24, 1865.

45. Ibid., October 23, 1865.

46. Ibid., November 7, 1865.

47. Ibid., November 6, 1863.
48. Ibid., December 11, 1865.
49. Ibid.
50. Pierce, "Contrabands," 639.
51. Luis F. Emilio, *A Brave Black Regiment: History of the Fifty-fourth Regiment of Massachusetts Volunteer Infantry 1863-1865* (New York: Bantam Books, 1992, 1894), 23.
52. Guy McLain, et al., eds., *Springfield Fights the Civil War* (Springfield, Massachusetts: Connecticut Valley Historical Museum, 1990), 76.
53. NFRA, *By-Laws*.
54. *American Freedmen*,1 (April 1866): 7.
55. WFAC, *Second*, 7.
56. Ibid., 29.
57. Friends' Association of Philadelphia (FAP), and Its Vicinity, for the Relief of Colored Freedmen, *Statistics of the Operations of the Executive Board* (Philadelphia: Inquirer Printing Office, 1864), 20.

Fearing Shell Nor Shot: Soldiers, Spies, Recruiters & Other Heroes

Some African American women were directly involved in military activities during the Civil War. They performed daring deeds, fearing neither, as Susie King Taylor said, "shell nor shot." Their heroism covered a wide range of actions; they donned uniforms, took up guns, actively solicited African American male participation, and died for principle.

Harriet Tubman is one of the most famous African American women directly involved in the Civil War. For three years, she was a nurse, scout and spy whose intelligence information allowed Colonel James Montgomery, Commander of the 2nd South Carolina Volunteers (African American), to lead several successful raids on Confederate strongholds including ammunition depots and supply warehouses. Her official contributions to the Union were finally recognized when she received a funeral with full military honors at her death in 1913.

Short and slight at five feet tall, Tubman's appearance belied the strong physique and endurance she had gained doing "man's work" while enslaved. William Still, an abolitionist from Philadelphia who sometimes aided Tubman when she helped enslaved Africans to escape, said, "Harriet was a woman of no pretensions, indeed, a more ordinary specimen of humanity could hardly be found among the most unfortunate-looking farm hands of the South. Yet, in point of courage, shrewdness and disinterested exertions to rescue her fellow-men . . . she was without her equal."[1] Her ability to assume the guise of an old cowering enslaved woman greatly aided her in her spying activities.

In June 1863, 756 enslaved Africans on the Combahee River fled, at Tubman's urging, to Union lines in South Carolina in one of her most successful missions. Thousands of dollars worth of Confederate supplies and equipment were destroyed. Tubman wrote to a friend about the foray: "You have, without doubt, seen a full account of the expedition I refer to. Don't you think we colored people are entitled to some credit for that exploit, under the lead of the brave Colonel Montgomery? We weakened the rebels somewhat on the Combahee river by taking and bringing away seven hundred and fifty-six head of their most valuable livestock, known up in your region as 'contrabands,' and this, too, without the loss of a single life on our part, though we have good reason to believe that a number of rebels bit the dust."[2] Of course, Tubman was well-experienced in spiriting Africans out of enslavement, having been responsible for liberating in excess of three hundred Africans.

Most of the able-bodied men among this Combahee group, about 400, enlisted in the United States Colored Troops (USCT).[3] The women aided their men by attempting to keep their families together. They, too, worked for the government and themselves as farm workers, menial laborers, laundresses, cooks and nurses, and they belong to the group of heroic and resourceful Sea Island women so often mentioned in the letters, diaries and journals of soldiers, teachers, missionaries and relief workers.

Luis Emilio gave an account of this raid in his history of the Massachusetts 54th but he does not credit Harriet Tubman at all.[4] The *Boston Commonwealth*, July 10, 1863 also reported on the military maneuver. "Col. Montgomery and his gallant band of 300 black soldiers, under the guidance of a black woman, dashed into the enemy's country, struck a bold and effective blow, destroying millions of dollars worth of commissary stores, cotton and lordly dwellings, and striking terror into the heart of rebeldom, brought off near 800 slaves and thousands of dollars worth of property, without losing a man or receiving a scratch. It was a glorious consummation . . . The Colonel was followed by a speech from the black woman who led the raid and under whose inspiration it was originated and conducted. For sound sense and real native eloquence her address would do honor to any man, and it created a great sensation."[5] Although the newspaper's coverage is laudatory, not enough is thought of Tubman by the white reporter to give her name! Like so many other African Americans, particularly women, she is objectified as simply "the black woman."

In the African American community and white abolitionist circles, however, she was renowned as her people's "Moses." John Brown, who led the famous 1859 raid on Harper's Ferry, called Tubman "the most of a man naturally that I ever met with. There is abundant material here and of the right quality."⁶ Charlotte Forten, a well-to-do poet and educator from Philadelphia, related the honor she felt in meeting Harriet Tubman in Beaufort, South Carolina in 1863 as she worked with refugees in the Sea Islands: "She is a wonderful woman—a real heroine . . . My own eyes were full as I listened to her—the heroic woman!"⁷

She was present at Fort Wagner in South Carolina with the Massachusetts 54th USCT, the first regiment of African American soldiers raised in the north which was primarily composed of free northern African Americans. Her description of the battle, in which more than three hundred black soldiers were killed, is poignant: "Then we saw the lightening, and that was the guns; and then we heard the thunder, and that was the big guns; and then we heard the rain falling, and that was the drops of blood falling; and when we came to get in the crops, it was dead men that we reaped." Tubman may have served Colonel Robert Gould Shaw's last meal before he was killed along with his African American troops in that famous battle.⁸

She was also the commander of eight or nine male scouts who acted as lookouts and guides for the Union army. This activity alone should have justified an army for her military service but it did not. Instead, it was her marriage, in 1869, to Civil War veteran, Nelson Davis, which allowed her to receive his pension of $20 per month after his death in 1888. Ironically, she was not awarded a government pension for her own service during the Civil War for more than thirty years and only then after a protracted struggle. Indeed, Tubman serves as an example of the depreciation and objectification of African American women. Her own experience of being marginalized and not properly compensated for her service, because she was a black woman, throws the treatment of other African American women into relief.

In 1898, thirty-three years after the end of the Civil War, Tubman wrote a petition making a claim for $1800 for her services during the war. Until she received the pension of $20 per month (shaved from $25 due to the opposition of southern congressmen), she was reduced to selling reprints of her autobiography to support herself and a home she had established for aged freedpeople in Auburn, New York.⁹

William H. Seward, an abolitionist and Secretary of State during the Civil War, wrote a letter of support for Tubman to Major General David Hunter in July of 1868: "Harriet Tubman, a colored woman, has been nursing our soldiers during nearly all the war. She believes she has a claim for faithful services to the command in South Carolina with which you are connected, and she thinks that you would be disposed to see her claim justly settled. I have known her long, and a nobler, high spirit, or a truer, seldom dwells in the human form. I commend her, therefore, to your kind and best attentions."[10] Seward only made mention of Tubman's service as a nurse, not the other valuable services she rendered. Tubman had known Seward a long time, having purchased land from him while he was the governor of New York to build a house in Auburn, New York for her aged parents. This house became a home for indigent freedpeople.

General Rufus Saxton stated the other activities in another letter of support in 1868. "I can bear witness to the value of her services rendered in the Union Army during the late war in South Carolina & Florida. She was employed in the Hospitals and as a spy. She made many a raid inside the enemy's lines displaying remarkable courage, zeal and fidelity. She was employed by Genl Hunter and I think both Generals [Isaac I.] Stevens and Sherman—and is as deserving of a pension from the Government for her services as any other of its faithful servants."[11] In spite of such support, Tubman's claim was given short shrift by government officials.

After the Civil War, she was active in the interracial women's suffrage movement which sought to achieve the vote for women. Tubman also helped to organize the National Federation of Afro-American Women, a confederation of several organizations devoted to the special concerns of African American women. In a display of unparalleled unity, this new organization combined with the National League of Colored Women to form the National Association of Colored Women which addressed such issues as lynching, suffrage for African Americans, support for African American domestics and impoverished women and the negative image of African American women among whites.

Another woman whose service was not officially recognized by a pension was Susie King Taylor. Like Tubman, she received the pension of her spouse, Edward King. Traveling with her husband's regiment, the 1st South Carolina Volunteers (33rd USCI), Taylor was ostensibly hired as a laundress and nurse in South Carolina, Georgia and Florida. She did whatever was necessary, however. "My services were given at all times for the comfort of [the] men. I was on hand to assist whenever needed. I was enrolled as company laundress, but I did very little of it, because I was always busy doing other things through camp, and was employed all the time doing something for the officers and comrades."[12] She also taught many of the soldiers of her husband's regiment to read and she made sure she learned to use a musket. Taylor said she " . . . could shoot straight and often hit the target. I assisted in cleaning the guns and used to fire them off, to see if the cartridges were dry, before cleaning and reloading, each day"[13]

Another woman, Maria Lewis of Virginia, served as a soldier with the Eighth New York Cavalry. "Lewis was not a camp follower but a full-fledged soldier who accompanied the New Yorkers to Washington to present seventeen captured rebel flags to the War Department."[14] Mary Dyson, "enslaved and suffering in her younger days"[15] was a "unique figure . . . in Philadelphia . . . Her claim to recognition and homage, was for the reason of her having disguised her sex, and taking part in several battles as a man."[16]

Lucy Carter, a fugitive, was given a special "official" status similar to Harriet Tubman's which allowed her access to the front lines. Lieutenant Colonel George S. Hollister issued the following order in 1864 while encamped in Vienna, Virginia: "Guards and Patrols. Will you please pass Lucy Carter, Colored, through the lines of the 16th Regiment New York Cavalry at pleasure until further orders."[17] According to Ervin L. Jordan, Jr., Carter was a spy for the Union[18] so the pass was presumably so she could carry out her duties while disguised as a laborer of some sort.

As an employee at the Gosport Navy Yard in Norfolk, Mary Louveste was able to provide valuable information to Gideon Welles, Secretary of the Union Navy, about the Confederate plans and ships. Welles remarked on her service in his reminiscences, "Mrs. Louveste encountered no small risk in bringing this information . . . and other facts. I am aware of none more meritorious than this poor colored woman whose zeal and fidelity I remember and acknowledge with gratitude."[19] Louveste was enslaved by an engineer working to convert the captured USS Merrimac into a Confederate ironclad vessel. She stole some of his plans which she gave to Welles.[20]

Another spy was Mary Elizabeth Bowser, a free woman, who went undercover as Ellen Bond, an illiterate enslaved woman, in the Richmond home of Jefferson Davis, the Confederate president. By pretending to be mentally impaired, she was able to overhear important military information being discussed by Davis and his visitors which she passed on to Union soldiers. The social more which believed that servants were invisible probably operated in her favor as much as her charade. When she came under suspicion, Bowser fled to Union lines after attempting to burn the Confederate White House in January 1864.[21]

Elizabeth Draper Mitchell worked for the famous white Union spy, Elizabeth Van Lew, as an assistant cook in Richmond, and among other activities, helped Union soldiers being held prisoner escape. "'Lizzie' they called her, and of her Solomon has spoken well in his song of Songs. She was 'black but comely.' Medium height, smooth dark skin, snapping black eyes, through which glowed the fires of temper and passion, lips with a fullness that bespoke emotion as well as a facility of expression."[22] Mitchell's daughter, Maggie Lena Walker, was to become the nation's first African American female bank official when she became the President of the Consolidated Bank and Trust Company of Richmond.[23] Walker was also the head of the Independent Order of St. Luke, a benevolent organization which grew out of a black mutual benefit society established in 1867 by Mary Prout who had been enslaved.

A seamstress, employed or enslaved by the Carrington family in Richmond, is reported to have "carried dress goods . . . with messages on paper patterns or in eggshells, the 'bewildering pattern skillfully worked' into a message that could be read only by knowing the code."[24] Originally from Princeton, New Jersey, Mary J.R. Richards posed as an enslaved woman during the war to spy for the Union in Richmond, Virginia. She had returned to the United States after teaching in Liberia for four years. In April 1865, she became an instructor of freedpeople in St. Mary's, Georgia following Richmond's surrender to Union forces.[25]

And still another spy was Mary Catherine Windsor who, shortly after the Civil War began, had journeyed from Philadelphia, Pennsylvania to New Orleans to visit her brother. The ship she was on was traveling on the Mississippi River when she saw Confederate forces hiding in the bushes on shore getting ready to attack the craft. Windsor gave the alarm which saved the vessel and after that incident, regularly engaged in similar reconnaissance activities on ships during the war. Her small stature, "not quite 4 feet in height and less than one hundred pounds," sometimes made her difficult to detect.[26]

James McPherson tells the story of another Union spy, the wife of a man who had escaped to Union lines in Virginia. However, in spite of the fact that the woman's actions were as dangerous as and essential to the man's ability to pass information on to Union forces, we never know her name, only that she is Dabney's wife. She becomes an appendage to his heroism: "his wife . . . expressed a great anxiety to be allowed to go over to the other side as servant to a 'secesh woman' [Confederate] . . . The request was granted. Dabney's wife went across the Rappahannock, and in a few days was duly installed as laundress at the headquarters of a prominent rebel General. Dabney . . . was soon found to be wonderfully well informed as to all the rebel plans . . . his reports always turned out to be true . . . How he obtained his information remained for some time a puzzle to the Union officers. At length, upon much solicitation, he unfolded his marvelous secret to one of our officers." His wife was his "marvelous secret." To alert her husband, who watched from across the river, about Confederate troop movements, she had devised an elaborate system of moving items on a clothesline at the rebel headquarters where she was employed.[27]

In another indication of unconscious marginalization of the African American presence, Luis Emilio, a white officer of the African American 54th Regiment of Massachusetts Volunteer Infantry, reported: "A family of ten contrabands came in to us at Graham's on the 29th, reporting but few Confederates in our immediate front, and that they were taking up the railroad iron. Captain Tucker, the next day, with twenty men, went out on a scout, and exchanged shots with the enemy."[28] This group undoubtedly included women. It is to be noted that the African American men are not identified, either. It is also to be noted that Emilio was freer of the taint of racism than most whites during this period. His accounts of the valor and nobility of African American soldiers made a significant contribution to African American history.

The recruitment and support of African American male participation in the Civil War represented another level of female activism. Recognizing the war as a unique opportunity for African American men to secure their manhood as well as full citizenship, African American women lent their wholehearted support to recruitment activities. A few were official recruiters; several unofficially recruited; many lent their support to recruitment activities by writing and speaking in support of black enlistment.

Mary Ann Shadd Cary was an abolitionist, newspaperwoman, suffragist and emigrationist who became the only officially paid female recruiting officer for the Union army when she received a commission from Governor Levi P. Morton of Indiana in August 1864 to raise African American troops. She returned to the United States after having emigrated to Canada to accede to a request from her good friend, Martin Delany[29], to aid in the recruitment of African American soldiers. She also became a paid fundraising agent for Chicago's Colored Ladies Freedmen's Aid Society.

Delany's enlistment of Cary speaks volumes to the confidence he had in her abilities to be a successful recruiter and to his commitment to equal rights for women. She had long been a voice, some might say a caustic voice, for black self-reliance and independence and, to her, the Civil War was a perfect chance for black men to prove their mettle. Physically, she was "rather tall, but of a fine physical organization—wholly feminine in appearance and demeanor—has a well moulded head set upon a rather slender neck, which gives her, when erect or speaking animately, what white folks would say, a very saucy look."[30] Also described as having a "commanding form, piercing eyes, and [a] stirring voice,"[31] she certainly had a rapier wit which she used to attack and condemn anyone, black or white, she considered antagonistic to African American progress. She used this ability to urge African American men to fight for a nation which she felt had heretofore oppressed them.

Like many of the northern African American female participants in the Civil War effort, Cary was a member of a longstanding activist family, the Shadds. While in Canada she had started her own newspaper, *The Provincial Freeman*, which covered every issue that concerned African Americans—self-help, self-reliance, integration, emigration. She compiled and published the memoir of Osborne Perry Anderson, a participant in John Brown's 1859 raid on Harper's Ferry, Virginia [now West Virginia] who escaped capture and later served in the Union army during the Civil War.

After the war she received a law degree from Howard University and taught in the District of Columbia's public schools. She challenged the United States House of Representatives Judicial Committee in 1870 for the right to vote and when she won she became one of the few women to vote in federal elections before voting rights were extended to women in 1920. In keeping with her strong belief in racial self-help and self-reliance, Mary Ann formed the Colored Women's Progressive Franchise Association in 1880 to fight for equal rights.[32]

Unofficial recruiters included Harriet Jacobs who helped to obtain enlistees for the Massachusetts 54th and Josephine St. Pierre Ruffin, who recruited for the Massachusetts 54th and its overflow regiment, the 55th USCT. Ruffin, like Jacobs, was also involved in freedmen's relief activities. As a member of the Sanitary Commission, she repaired and sewed clothes for refugees at Twelfth Baptist Church in Boston.[33] Ruffin and her husband, George L., a legislator and judge, had returned to the United States at the outbreak of the Civil War after expatriating to Great Britain.

Following the war she was an activist in the women's suffrage movement as well as the National Federation of Afro-American Women[34] which merged in 1896 with the National League of Colored Women, Washington, D.C. to form the National Association of Colored Women. She edited the group's magazine, *Woman's Era,* and spearheaded relief efforts for the African Americans, known as Exodusters, who went west to Kansas after the Civil War. Ruffin is described as "one of the handsomest women in Boston, her regular, commanding features, abundant black hair . . . and olive complexion making a noticeable and pleasing appearance."[35]

Sattira Douglas, wife of the famous Chicago abolitionist H. Ford Douglas who was serving in the 95th Illinois Regiment of Infantry Volunteers,[36] wrote to the *Weekly Anglo-African* in June 1863 in support of the recruitment of African American soldiers. "Now is offered the only opportunity that will be extended, during the present generation, for colored men to strike the blow that will at once relieve them of northern prejudice and southern slavery. If they do not now enroll themselves among those other noble men who have gone forth to do battle for the true and right, it will only prove the correctness of the aspersion indulged in by our enemies, that we are unworthy of those rights which they have so long withheld from us, and that freedom would not be appreciated by us, if possessed."[37] She was a regular contributor to the paper.

In addition to aiding the military as soldiers, spies and recruiters, some African American women performed other heroic deeds as well. One woman walked 200 miles disguised as a man.[38] Women like Eliza Ann Preacher Turner, the wife of Bishop Henry McNeal Turner, who was the chaplain to Company C, 1st United States Colored Infantry (USCI), accompanied their husbands into dangerous territory. William H. Brown, a private in the regiment, reported on a Fourth of July celebration in Roanoke Island, North Carolina where he was stationed. He noted that "our most worthy and industrious chaplain, H.M. Turner, came along with his little wife by his side, who by the way, appears to be a noble woman." Since he mentioned that Turner "goes with us every where in cold or heat, battle or sickness," it can be assumed that Eliza Ann also endured some of the same discomfort.[39]

The wives and children of Robert and John Smalls were with them when, in 1862, they steered the Confederate steamboat, the Planter, to Union lines in Charleston, South Carolina, providing the Union with a major victory and supplying the African American community with ammunition in their struggle to prove the worthiness of the black man to participate as an equal in the conflict. Robert Smalls served five terms in the South Carolina House of Representatives during Reconstruction. After their escape, his wife, Hannah, became active in relief work. She was the treasurer of the Ladies' Fair of Beaufort, South Carolina which aided refugees on Edisto Island, South Carolina.

Amy Spain was lynched in 1865 in Darlington, South Carolina (in front of the courthouse, no less!) for shouting, "Bless the Lord the Yankees have come!" Although the lynchers may have missed the symbolism, she was hung from the sycamore tree where monthly auctions of enslaved Africans were held. Of course, it is ironic that slave auctions would be held before a "seat of justice." It is said that Spain "heroically heard her sentence" and that she "declared she was prepared to die" for principle.[40]

While on a southern speaking tour in 1867, with a stop in Darlington, Frances Ellen Watkins Harper gave a more poignant, detailed account of the atrocity: "about two years ago, a girl was hung for making a childish and indiscreet speech. Victory was perched on our banners. Our army had been through, and this poor, ill-fated girl, almost a child in years, about seventeen years of age, rejoiced over the event, and said she was going to marry a Yankee and set up housekeeping. She was reported as having made an incendiary speech and arrested, cruelly scourged, and then brutally hung."[41] Harper did not mention Spain's name and the picture in *Harper's Weekly* made her appear to be middle-aged but both sources are undoubtedly referring to the same incident. At least it is hoped that they are the same. Otherwise, Darlington has an especially unsavory history concerning African Americans.

Colonel Thomas Wentworth Higginson, white officer in the African American 1st South Carolina Volunteers, told of Fanny Wright, the wife of one of his soldiers and the company's laundress, who escaped from enslavement to her husband's camp with two of her children, one of whom had been shot dead in her arms. He also recounted the daring exploit of a seventy-year-old enslaved woman who led the escape of herself and twenty-two children and grandchildren by floating forty miles down the Savannah River on a rickety flatboat to freedom behind Union lines. Higginson observed that "my young lieutenants did not have to teach the principles of courage to this woman's grandchildren."[42] Two of this extraordinary woman's grandsons, with the last name of Miller, were members of Higginson's regiment.

In recounting the story of the massacre of about 400 African American and 200 white soldiers and African American civilians, including women and children at Fort Pillow, Tennessee by confederate soldiers, William Wells Brown told the touching story of a young wife who had, in spite of the danger, gone to the battlefield to retrieve the body of her husband. She found him alive under several corpses, only to be killed herself, along with her husband, by returning rebel soldiers the day after the slaughter.[43]

A white private in the Sixteenth Army Corps and an eyewitness to the Fort Pillow slaughter gave a report to his commanding officers of another incident during the episode. "He saw a black woman, who was wounded during the action, shot through the head and killed, by one of the rebels." This occurred after the battle when the Union battalion had surrendered so her murder was a deliberate act.[44] No more information is given about the woman such as why she was there or her name. Naturally, Fort Pillow became a rallying cry for African American soldiers who sought to revenge the outrage.

Those women who actively participated in military operations placed their very lives on the line for freedom. Knowing full well the consequences, they submitted to their fate. None of the women—the soldiers, spies, recruiters and other heroes—were background support players. They operated on the front lines as change agents and warriors.

NOTES

1. William Still, *The Underground Railroad* (New York: Arno Press, 1968, 1872), 297.

2. C. Peter Ripley, ed., *The Black Abolitionist Papers, Volume V: the United States, 1859-1865* (Chapel Hill: University of North Carolina Press, 1992), 220-221.

3. James Henry Gooding, *On the Altar of Freedom: a Black Soldier's Civil War Letters from the Front* (New York: Warner Books, 1991), 29.

4. Luis F. Emilio, *A Brave Black Regiment: History of the Fifty-fourth Regiment of Massachusetts Volunteer Infantry* (New York: Bantam Books, 1992, 1894), 41.

5. Samuel Sillen, *Women Against Slavery* (New York: Masses and Mainstream, 1955), 51.

6. Sarah Bradford, *Harriet Tubman: the Moses of Her People* (New York: Citadel Press, 1994, 1886), 96.

7. Charlotte Forten Grimke, *Journals of Charlotte L. Forten Grimke* (New York: Oxford University Press, 1988), 442.

8. Darlene Clark Hine, et al., eds., *Black Women in America: an Historical Encyclopedia* (Bloomington: Indiana University Press, 1993), 1179.

9. Margaret Busby, ed., *Daughters of Africa* (New York: Ballentine Books, 1992), 77; Gerda Lerner, *Black Women in White America* (New York: Vintage Books, 1972), 328.

10. Bradford, 137. Gerda Lerner, in *Black Women in White America*, page 327, gives the date of this letter as July 25, 1865, perhaps because the tone implies

that the war was still going on. I have used Bradford's date because the book was written closer to the dates mentioned.

11. Ibid., 142.

12. Susie King Taylor, *Reminiscences of My Life in Camp With the 33rd United States Colored Troops* (New York: Arno Press, 1968, 1902), 34-35.

13. Ibid., 26.

14. Ervin Jordan, Jr., *Black Confederates and Afro-Yankees in Civil War Virginia* (Charlottesville: University of Virginia, 1995), 269.

15. Robert Jones, *Fifty Years in the Lombard Street Central Presbyterian Church, Philadelphia* (Philadelphia: Edward Stern & Co., Inc., 1894), 71.

16. *Philadelphia Tribune*, 22 February 1913.

17. Benjamin Quarles, *The Negro in the Civil War* (New York: Da Capo Press, 1989, 1953), 225.

18. Jordan, 285.

19. Ibid., 284.

20. Michael Lee Lanning, *The African American Soldier: From Crispus Attucks to Colin Powell* (Secaucus, New Jersey: Birch Lane Press, 1997), 59.

21. Ibid., 195.

22. Wendell Phillips Dabney, *Maggie L. Walker and the Independent Order of St. Luke: the Woman and Her Work* (Cincinnati: The Dabney Publishing Co., 1927), 25. Dabney does not say that Mitchell was a spy or that she helped Van Lew, although he does say that Van Lew was known as a "Union spy." He also says that Mitchell and her husband, William Mitchell, "a handsome young mulatto butler" were "numbered among the possessions of Mrs. Van Lew."

23. Jordan, 285.

24. Sylvia G. Dannett, *Profiles of Negro Womanhood, 1619-1900* (New York: M.W. Lads, 1964).

There is some confusion between Mitchell and Bowser. Harriet Peterson's article on Mary Elizabeth Bowser in *Notable Black American Women* says that she worked for Van Lew; Jordan attributes this to Elizabeth Draper Mitchell. In fact, Jordan gives information on both women and says that Mitchell worked for Van Lew. Frank Wuttge, Jr., who led the successful effort to dedicate a tree in Mary Elizabeth Bowser's honor in 1977 says that Bowser was the spy who worked for Van Lew, that she was the wife of a Philadelphia abolitionist from the well-known Bowser family, and that she was responsible for information which led to Jefferson Davis' capture. [Letter from Frank Wuttge, Jr., President, Civil War Memorial Committee, West Farms Soldiers' Cemetery, Bronx, New York *in* New York Public Library - Schomburg Center for Research in Black Culture, Microfilm R-4135 no. 32]

25. *Freedmen's Record*, 2 (April 1867).

26. Hallie Q. Brown, *Homespun Heroines and Other Women of Distinction* (NY: Oxford University Press, 1988, 1926), 108-109.

27. James McPherson, *Marching Toward Freedom: Blacks in the Civil War 1861-1865* (New York: Facts on File, 1991), 42-43.

28. Emilio, 275.

29. Martin Delany was a physician, nationalist and emigrationist. During the Civil War he was a major in the Union army and a sub-assistant commissioner of the Freedmen's Bureau during Reconstruction.

30. *Frederick Douglass' Paper*, 9 November 1855.

31. Brown, 94.

32. Hine, *Black*, 225.

33. Rayford W. Logan and Michael R. Winston, eds., *Dictionary of American Negro Biography* (New York: W.W. Norton, 1982), 535.

34. Brown, 151-152.

35. L.A. Scruggs, *Women of Distinction: Remarkable in Works and Invincible in Character* (Raleigh, North Carolina: L.A. Scruggs, 1893), 148.

36. He was passing as a white man. Douglas died in 1865 from the effects of the malaria he had contracted while in the army.

37. *Weekly Anglo-African*, 20 June 1863.

38. Jordan, 85.

39. *Christian Recorder*, 22 July 1865.

40. *Harper's Weekly*, 30 September 1865.

41. William Still, *The Underground Railroad* (New York: Arno Press, 1968, 1872), 768.

42. Thomas W. Higginson, *Army Life in a Black Regiment* (New York: Collier Books, 1962), 234-235.

43. William Wells Brown, *The Negro in the American Rebellion* (New York: Citadel Press, 1971, 1867), 246-247.

44. Ira Berlin, ed., *Black Military Experience* (New York: Cambridge University Press, 1982), 541.

CHAPTER 4

Supporting Themselves: Nurses, Laundresses, Cooks & Entrepreneurs

The Civil War caused great deprivation to a people who, to begin with, had very little. African American men were oftentimes absent from their families because they had enlisted in the armed forces or they had been conscripted as soldiers or menial laborers. Therefore, African American women had to do whatever was necessary to sustain themselves and their families. Many of them toiled as nurses, laundresses, cooks and manual laborers for the government in exchange for rations. They maintained farms and plantations after slaveowners ran away. A great many resorted to using a certain business acumen to supply goods and food to soldiers.

The United States War Department issued an order on January 16, 1864 permitting all general hospitals under their jurisdiction to hire African American women as cooks or nurses. They were to be paid ten dollars a month and receive one ration.[1] Chrissie Chase, who had been enslaved, probably became a nurse under General Ulysses S. Grant due to this directive. She moved to Wickford, Rhode Island after the Civil War. In another instance, George Clary, a white army surgeon, noted that a doctor from another hospital had visited his camp "and selected 10 girls and four men to assist as nurses, etc." in a new hospital he was setting up in an abandoned hotel in New Orleans.[2] It is to be assumed that the women were happy to have this type of employment when the alternative was field work or no work at all.

Harriet Tubman, although she is noted for adopting assertive or combative roles usually reserved for men, ministered to the needs of wounded troops as a nurse. "I'd go to the hospital, I would, early every morning. I'd get a big chunk of ice, I would, and put it in a basin, and fill it with water; then I'd take a sponge and begin. First man I'd come to, I'd thrash away the flies, and they'd rise, they would, like bees round a hive. Then I'd begin to bathe the wounds, and by the time I'd bathed off three or four, the fire and heat would have melted the ice and made the water warm, and it would be as red as clear blood. Then I'd go and get more ice, I would, and by the time I got to the next ones, the flies would be round the first ones black and thick as ever."[3] She also made medicinal concoctions from herbs which she gave away gratis to sick soldiers.

Susie King Taylor, the wife of a 1st South Carolina Volunteer (33rd USCI), nursed soldiers who had been isolated in the camps due to illness because "I was not in the least afraid of the small-pox. I had been vaccinated, and I drank sassafras tea constantly, which kept my blood purged and prevented me from contracting this dread scourge . . . "[4] Fortunately, she never contracted any of the diseases common to camp life, such as cholera, malaria, typhoid, pneumonia, measles and diarrhea. Taylor's ability, like Harriet Tubman's, to use herbal remedies had long afforded African women a place of respect in the African American community, especially among the enslaved.

Sister Lydia Penny, a nurse and fugitive who had escaped enslavement from Memphis, Tennessee, gave service in a variety of concrete ways. She entered Union lines and received employment as a cook when the Union came near to Memphis. She met and married her husband, Thomas, a soldier, there. James H. Payne, Quartermaster Sergeant, 27th USCI told her story.

> Thomas Penny . . . re-enlisted in the service, and joined the Fifth USCT, at Camp Delaware, Ohio. Sister Penny said that she felt it to be her duty to go along with her husband, not merely on account of the love she had for him, but also for the love she had for her country—that the cause which nerved the soldiers to pour out their life-blood was her cause, and that she felt it to be her Christian duty to do all she could for the liberty of her afflicted and down-trodden race. This good woman is called by those who are acquainted with her, 'the mother of the army.' She well deserves the name, for she has been in the service ever since this rebellion broke out, or very nearly as long. Sister Penny says that

she is not tired of the service, nor does she think of leaving the field until the last gun is fired and peace is declared, and every slave is freed from captivity. Many of our officers and men who were wounded at the battle of Deep Bottom will never forget the kind deeds of Sister Lydia Penny, who went among them and administered to their wants as they lay weltering in their blood on the banks of the James, near Jones' Landing. There she could be seen, the only woman present, like an angel from above, giving words of cheer, and doing all in her power to relieve the suffering of the wounded and dying.[5]

Sallie Daffin, fully employed as an American Missionary Association (AMA) teacher with posts in Norfolk, Virginia and Wilmington, North Carolina, helped teach wounded soldiers to read and write while she nursed and wrote letters for them in such places as the hospitals in Portsmouth, Virginia and the Colored Soldier's Hospital in Wilmington. She saw her activities as a relief worker, educator and newspaper correspondent as a part of her overall mission to help her people in any way she could.

Jane was a laundress who traveled with Company K of the Thirteenth Regiment of the Connecticut Volunteers.[6] The women who were left on an abandoned plantation in Harrisburg, North Carolina "take in washing from the city and appear to be industrious," according to white Union doctor, George Clary.[7]

Rose worked as a laundress for white officers in General Egbert L. Viele's headquarters in South Carolina. She and her seven children had been manumitted by her master and common-law husband, James Garrad, on his death shortly before the Union army took Hilton Head. Afraid that Garrad's relatives were planning to disregard his will and sell her and her children, she fled to Union lines. A correspondent for the *Anti-Slavery Advocate* said, "I am told by those that know Rose, that she is a fine-looking, intelligent woman. She is very black, but her figure is perfect, and in her neat mourning dress and bonnet, unless her face is seen, she might be mistaken for as haughty a dame as South Carolina can produce. Her chief attraction, however, is her conversation, which is marked by intelligence respecting the objects of the war, and many other subjects connected with it."[8]

Other nameless laundresses elicited a comparable admiration from a white soldier who wrote home: "I was talking with a colored woman and her *almost* white daughter . . . When the war first broke out she was living in N. Orleans, and her Master, fearing for the safety of the city sold them both to go up the river some 80 miles. She brought $1000 and her handsome daughter brought $1750." When they were liberated by Union soldiers, they "came up here soon after to cook and wash for the Officers. After the Officers left, they built them a little shanty . . . They take in washing for a living and have a little yard where they raise vegetables."[9]

William Summerson told of his and his wife's harrowing escape from enslavement in Charleston, South Carolina—she hid in a barrel and they walked three miles in a swamp with water up to their knees—but he never tells her name. They worked in Port Royal, he as a servant to a Captain Elwell and she as a laundress to officers in the camp. She also did sewing for General David Hunter's wife.[10]

Harriet Tubman taught Sea Island freedwomen how to do washing for Union soldiers and built a washhouse for them out of her own earnings. She relinquished the receipt of the army rations to which she was entitled as a government employee because it made the freedwomen suspicious of her. Instead, she made pies, gingerbread and root beer at night to sell.[11]

In an unprecedented action, laundresses in Jackson, Mississippi formed themselves into a union and in June 1866 formally petitioned the mayor of the city for the right to set equitable prices for their labor.

> Whereas, under the influence of the present high prices of all the necessaries of life, and the attendant high rates of rent, while our wages remain very much reduced, we, the washerwomen of the city of Jackson, State of Mississippi, thinking it impossible to live uprightly and honestly in laboring for the present daily and monthly recompense, and hoping to meet with the support of all good citizens, join in adopting unanimously the following resolution: Be it resolved by the washerwomen of this city and county, That on and after the foregoing date, we join in charging a uniform rate for our labor, that rate being an advance over the original price by the month or day the statement of said price to be made public by printing the same, and any one belonging to the class of washerwomen, violating this, shall be liable to a fine *regulated by the class.* We do not wish in the least to charge exorbitant prices, but desire to be able to live comfortably if possible from the fruits of our labor.

The petition went on to give the set prices: $1.50 per day for washing; $15.00 per month for family washing; $10.00 per month for single individuals.[12] This attempt at empowerment and self-sufficiency was probably not successful, given the era, but it shows that the women knew the value of their work to the white community and it illustrates the collective agency and resistance of the women.

The entrepreneurial skill that some African American women exhibited during the war was also alluded to by Susie King Taylor. The "first colored troops did not receive any pay for eighteen months . . . A great many of these men had large families, and as they had no money to give them, their wives were obliged to support themselves and children by washing for the officers of the gunboats and the soldiers, and making cakes and pies which they sold to the boys in camp."[13] Horatio Eden told of how his "mother ran away from the Edens [slaveowners] with other negroes & took me to Paducah. She made pies for the negro union soldiers and I peddled them for her."[14]

It was, apparently, as cooks, however, that African American female entrepreneurialship was prized because the fare the troops received was often so meager and unpalatable that they had to scavenge for foodstuff on their own to supplement the diet offered by the army. Consequently, they welcomed what they could buy from the women. "One wounded soldier who had previously abhorred blacks was so pleased with the culinary skills of an elderly Afro-Virginian woman that he informed his family that blacks were not so bad after all."[15]

Corporal John Midgley, another white Civil War diarist, told of being wounded and captured by the Confederates. He relayed a very stark picture about the provisions given to the prisoners: "Our rations were still confined to corn bread and water; once I had a bone with very little meat on it and my comrades fairly begged me to give it to them when I was through with it, on my doing so it was passed from one who would gnaw it, to another and so on and finally Nero, a colored nurse brought in a stone and one of the boys crushed the bone and ate it."[16] Luckily, for him, he was able to buy food from African American vendors. "We purchased from colored girls and boys apple and blackberry turnover pies . . . We bought our extra eatables from Aunt Doshia, a fat colored woman who used to steal in."[17]

The diaries and letters of Civil War soldiers abound with references to food because they felt the lack of home-cooked food keenly. They made comparisons of food and they wrote longingly of favorite foods. George Clary, a white Union surgeon, extolled the virtues of his Thibodaux, Louisiana cook. "Our cook makes nearly every morning very light flour cakes fried which we have not yet got tired of with syrup or honey. She also makes very good pumpkin pies, bread puddings, etc . . . [She is] the woman who was the servant of General Twiggs. She has been with Company K ever since we left the Custom House through thick and thin.

I have lately adopted her for the benefit of the hospital in general and myself in particular - her name is Eliza . . . "[18]

Clary showed even more admiration a few months later, describing her as "the fair Eliza. She is large, tall, and strong, and has accompanied the Regt. through fire and flood and storm and smoke. She . . . with flour and yeast powder makes very good biscuit . . . Eliza was a house servant . . . and is a very good one of her kind." [19]

Horace Henry Messenger, a white army substitute for a white Greenwich, Connecticut man who paid Messenger to take his place, wrote to his daughter from Drewry's Bluff, Virginia: "This land that we are on is raised a part of it by the blacks now that was on it when the army come on here. They raised potatoes and peanuts and sell them to the boys here but the boys are not allowed to go to their ground. There is oranges here but we can't get them only as we buy them."[20] Though he does not make it explicit, women were probably raising most of the potatoes and peanuts because their men had been impressed into military service. The reference to oranges most likely implies that some type of official fraud was going on with the army stores because Messenger tells his daughter, "Do not let any body see this," immediately after mentioning the oranges. The practice of paying substitutes was often done by those who could afford it but it eventually caused resentment among lower class whites, especially when the draft was instituted.

Soldiers also felt they were unduly exploited by the white sutlers [merchants] who charged exorbitant prices and cut off their lines of credit when the men could not pay. They sought out African American vendors. Charles B. Haydon, a white Union soldier whose battalion was stationed near Washington, D.C., confided in his journal, "The Irish women who come around camp to peddle are the stingiest people I ever saw without exception. The niggers sell at a much more reasonable rate." In a later entry, he said: "A little black boy came from a house nearby & brought us some very good pies & other eatables which he sold at a fair price."[21]

Orrin Cook, another white Union soldier, said to his diary: "Got out of food and went foraging. Got an infinitesimal pie and two corn cakes from an old negro woman."[22] In another entry he said, "Induced a mulatto woman . . . to accept a greenback dollar for two pies."[23]

Another venerated cook was sixty-five-year-old "Aunt Charlotte" from Newbern[24], North Carolina who was hired by the Sanitary Inspector for the Department of North Carolina for six dollars a month after her white owners fled their plantation. "Many a sick and wounded soldier . . . had reason to bless the culinary accomplishments of this venerable contraband cook, and to praise the alacrity with which, in times of their greatest need, she exerted her skill to save them from suffering." The article, in the August 16, 1862 *Harper's Weekly*, went on to praise "Aunt Charlotte"'s managerial skill which contributed to her success as a cook. " . . . She possesses no mean administrative abilities. She reminds one of an old merchant, habituated to a regular, systematic life, with ability enough to keep all surroundings subordinate to that system . . . 'Aunt Charlotte' has many virtues that ennoble her position. And in the industrious performance of her duties in life . . . she might safely be held up as an example to many who pride themselves on purer blood and a higher scale of existence."

Another woman who bore the objectified label, "Aunt," was Margaret who, traveled with the 3rd USCI in Virginia. She is referred to, by the white major of the regiment, as a "trained cook"[25] so her cooking must have been very good. The use of "Aunt" as a form of address by whites for older black women was considered respectful.

Mrs. Fairfax was referred to as the "chief cook and bottle washer" of the Fifth Army Corps, Army of the Potomac. She is often seen, hands folded demurely in front of her, in a picture of the unit's headquarters at Harrison's Landing, James River, Virginia but rarely is her name given. Little is known about her but it can be assumed that she was from the area. Her value to the officers, as a cook, can be inferred from the fact that she figures relatively prominently in a picture featuring white officers.

One young woman in Kentucky who was employed as a cook in a hospital had to be rescued from recapture by soldiers at her camp. Her former owner, with the connivance of military authorities, came to the camp to take her back into enslavement. "This girl had been away from her master, who is and always has been a noted rebel, for more than six months. She ran away on account of his cruelty. The owner of the girl, with the guard went to the camp, seized the girl, and, amid her cries and frantic appeals for protection, were taking her away. She fell upon her knees, and begged the guard to shoot her upon the spot, saying her master would whip her to death if he got her away. This was too much for the endurance of some of the inmates of the camp, and they interfered and took the girl away from the guard, dressed her in boy's clothes, and secreted her."[26] She was able to escape as a result. Because Kentucky had not seceded from the Union, the slaveowner presumably had the right to retrieve his "property" although he was a notorious Confederate sympathizer. The young woman's services as a cook to the camp and the fact that they knew her personally no doubt played a large part in the soldiers' response to her situation.

Although the dehumanization of African American women as objects of derision is as apparent in the diaries, journals and reminiscences of white Civil War soldiers as it was in white society in general, the entries indicate that their entrepreneurialship was appreciated, even if backhandedly. Of course, the diarists were writing about their own experiences and perceptions so that African Americans, especially women, were incidental to their observations. They carried their racial and gender attitudes to the front.

In addition to nursing, washing and cooking, refugee women demonstrated other skills as well. The white superintendent of the NFRA's Industrial School No. 1 in Washington, D.C., H.M. Barnard, wrote in her report to the agency that the women attending the school showed an industriousness far exceeding her expectations. "These women who have learned the use of the sewing machine in this school, have been able, with some assistance from the school, to purchase machines, and are now working them, and doing a good business for themselves . . . The women show a desire and willingness to learn, which, considering their former condition and age, is truly surprising. Many of them having been field hands know nothing of the use of the needle . . . During the year seven hundred and twenty-five women have received employment, and two thousand six hundred garments have been made by them. A large proportion of these have earned at least a change of clothing for themselves and many of them for their children."[27] The women were paid for their efforts in clothing. The school also had a laundry but the female workers were paid in cash.

Captain T.E. Hall, white Superintendent of Freedmen at Camp Nelson, Kentucky, wrote to the Western Freedmen's Aid Commission asking for "a further supply of clothing and bedding, and also a little money to defray such incidental expenses as transportation, etc." Because the camp housed mostly women and children, he asked that "the clothing . . . be adapted to the wants of women and children." On second thought he decided: "It would be better, perhaps, to send material, as we can have it made up at the 'Home' by the inmates, some of whom are good seamstresses."[28] The home Hall referred to was set up to house refugee women at Camp Nelson after they had been forcibly expelled and many had died from exposure and abuse.

Abisha Scofield, a white AMA worker at Camp Nelson, attested to the unnecessary brutality of the expulsion, contending that the camp commanders misrepresented the women. "The families of the colored soldiers who were in Camp lived in cabins and huts erected by the colored soldiers or at the expense of the women . . . I have witnessed about fifty of these huts and cabins erected and the material of which they were constructed was unserviceable to the Government . . . I believe that they supported themselves by washing, cooking and &c."[29]

The industriousness of the women that Hall and Scofield described is a far cry from the characterization of them as "idle, lazy vagrants, committing depredations, and exercising a very pernicious influence over the soldiers" given by white Lieutenant Colonel John Foley of the 63rd USCI in Memphis, Tennessee. Attitudes such as this allowed the wholesale eviction of African American women and children from camps, and, consequently, their suffering and deaths.

Like African American men, many black women were impressed into service for the army and government. They dug ditches, built battlements and did other types of menial labor. A white Union officer reported on the result of such forced labor as he described a camp at Kenner, Louisiana: "Many of the women are in even a worse condition than the men as regards clothing. From 5 to 16 work daily on the levee, more would if they had shoes. Their rations we issue once a week. They receive 2 qts of meal and 2 lbs of pork for a week."[30] A camp supervisor observed that all the male fugitives and "all women, save those having large families or small children" were employed either working for the government or local individuals in Corinth, Mississippi.[31]

Julia Wilbur, a white abolitionist visiting Alexandria, Virginia, decried the government's actions toward refugee women and children. "Those able to work were hired out immediately . . . at a low rate of wages; little children were *hired* out, that is taken from their mothers and in many instances sent miles away, to be made, to all intents and purposes, little slaves again . . . [Some] of the guard are rough, ignorant and prejudiced men, who take to negro driving naturally, and one of them is allowed to carry a whip and to stand over the women while they are at work in true plantation style, and in several instances women have been beaten by these rough men."[32]

Josephine S. Griffing, white General Agent of the NFRA, condemned the policy of forcibly indenturing African American children as well as the government's attempt to force women to leave their homes and relocate to other areas of the country in order to continue to receive necessary rations. "This apprenticing of children in the slave districts—*except where trades are given*—is in decided opposition to the wishes of the freed people."

Mothers wanted control of their children as well as their own lives so they resisted the indentureships and the forcible removals. " . . . [As] a general rule these mothers of families and old people strenuously oppose . . . that and all measures that look toward this idea of an infringement on their right to *live in society*, and enjoy in common with the poor of white complexion the satisfaction of demonstrating their ability to lay hold of *its* helps to sustain and elevate themselves and their race from the degradation to which it has plunged them while in a state of slavery . . . "[33]

Some of the women did relocate but they were usually young, unmarried females. The April 1866 *American Freedman* carried a typical announcement: "At the request of the Bureau of Refugees, Freedmen, etc., an Employment Bureau has been opened in this city [Brooklyn, New York], to provide employment for refugee freedmen, who are now crowding Washington in great numbers . . . Persons wishing to obtain colored laborers and domestics, will be furnished with circulars, on application to this office." Employers received cheap labor and refugees received a new start. Some freedwomen jumped at the chance but many more were reluctant to leave their families and familiar surroundings.

Luckily, sometimes African American women in the North were available to help to ease the transition for women who did relocate. In addition to being a board member of the interracial Hartford, Connecticut Freedmen's Aid Society, Mehitable Primus and her husband, Holdridge, acted as employment agents for freedwomen who were placed in jobs in the north. Many of the women boarded with the Primuses until they secured employment.

One Waterbury, Connecticut white woman's request to Mrs. Primus for "a girl 13 or 14 years old to take care of a baby and wash dishes" was probably typical. The woman went on to write, "To a good girl I will give her a dollar a week. One that is kind and has a good disposition. I want to take one for one year if she suits me. If not I shall have to send her back of course . . . I have had Irish girls but prefer colored . . . "[34] The Primuses' daughter, Rebecca, was a teacher in Royal Oak, Maryland and she most likely recommended some of the young women to her parents.

Elizabeth Blair Lee, a white southerner whose family remained loyal to the Union, asked her husband, a naval officer, "If you can pick up a good dining room servant, among your contrabands it would be a great benefit conferred on this domicil—We have a small house with two rooms where the man's wife can live if he has one, & she can do the milking & some washing."[35] Their own "servants" had been freed by the

Emancipation Proclamation in January 1863 and most, especially the women, had opted to obtain jobs away from the Lee household.

The Gullah-speaking women of the Sea Islands are an excellent example of African American female assertiveness and survival. They managed the plantations slaveowners abandoned while their men were fighting in the Union army. The women successfully raised cotton, livestock and vegetables for their own use and for sale, attended the schools for freedpeople and wrote encouraging letters to their men.[36]

Several hundred women from the Combahee River area of the Sea Islands formed a colony and made gloves, stockings and raised food for their men in the Union army. They spun yarn in a tin basin and used reeds they cut from the swamps to knit the yarn.[37] One great- grandmother in the Port Royal area of the Sea Islands "cultivated three acres of cotton (a full man's task in old times . . .) besides three of corn and one of potatoes"[38] testifying to the freedwoman's delight in her freedom and self-sufficiency.

Harriet Tubman painted a penetrating portrait of the Sea Island women as they escaped enslavement on the islands. They left on gunboats going to Beaufort, South Carolina so they would be behind Union lines. "Here you'd see a woman with a pail on her head, rice a-smoking in it just as she'd taken from the fire, young one hanging on behind, one hand around her forehead to hold on, another hand digging into the rice pot, eating with all its might; hold of her dress two or three more; down her back a bag with a pig in it."[39] She was depicting strong, resourceful women, much like herself.

However, just as it did with Harriet Tubman and manifold African American males who gave service during the Civil War, the government did not live up to contracts it made with freedwomen. Black women who had been employed by the army had to file formal applications for wages due them. Because of the rampant fraud and deceit practiced by white camp commanders and agents, innumerable petitions for back pay were denied. Laundresses Anna Irwin, Laura Irwin, Rhoda Willis and Milly Humphries applied unsuccessfully in 1866 to the Freedmen's Bureau in Chattanooga, Tennessee for delinquent wages. In spite of a detailed account of their service, they were not compensated.[40] And in another instance, the local superintendent of a refugee camp at Corinth, Mississippi admitted, "Many [of the displaced] have worked from 2 to 12 months, and never received a cent or rag yet as reward—alike as private servants & Government employees."[41]

As camp employees, African American women were prey to the same dangers as soldiers—disease, gun and cannon fire, accidents. As African

Americans, they were subject to the same discrimination as black men. The injustice of their condition, notwithstanding, African American women exploited whatever skills they possessed in order to sustain themselves and their families. Often, this was done in the absence of their husbands, fathers, sons and brothers who were contributing on a different front. They, therefore, had to depend on their own resources and abilities in the face of great deprivation and trial.

NOTES

1. OR, Series III, Volume IV, 32.
2. George Clary Papers, May 25, 1862, Connecticut Historical Society, Hartford.
3. Sarah Bradford, *Harriet Tubman: the Moses of her People* (New York: Citadel Press, 1994, 1886), 97.
4. Ibid., 17.
5. *Christian Recorder*, 7 January 1865.
6. Clary Papers, November 6, 1863.
7. Ibid., May 29, 1865.
8. John Blassingame, ed., *Slave Testimony* (Baton Rouge: Louisiana State University Press, 1977), 362.
9. Nina Silber and Mary Beth Sievens, *Yankee Correspondence: Civil War Letters Between New England Soldiers and the Home Front* (Charlottesville: University Press of Virginia, 1996), 89.
10. *National Anti-Slavery Standard*, 27 December 1862.
11. Dorothy Sterling, ed. *We Are Your Sisters: Black Women in the Nineteenth Century* (New York: W.W. Norton, 1984), 258.
12. Philip Foner and Ronald Lewis, eds., *Black Workers: a Documentary History from Colonial Times to the Present* (Philadelphia: Temple University Press, 1989), 142.
13. Susie King Taylor, *Reminiscences of My Life in Camp with the 33rd United States Colored Troops* (New York: Arno Press, 1968, 1902), 15-16.
14. John W. Blassingame, ed., *Slave Testimony* (Baton Rouge: Louisiana State University Press, 1977), 632.
15. Ervin L. Jordan, Jr., *Black Confederates and Afro-Yankees in Civil War Virginia* (Charlottesville: University Press of Virginia, 1995), 144.
16. Nancy Piccin, "Family's Civil War Artifacts Trace History." *Springfield, Massachusetts Morning Union*, 25 May 1987.
17. Ibid.
18. Clary, November 6, 1863.
19. Ibid., April 2, 1864.
20. Messenger Family Papers, Connecticut Historical Society, Hartford.
21. Stephen W. Sears, *For Country, Cause and Leader: the Civil War Journal of Charles B. Haydon* (New York: Ticknor & Fields, 1993), 45, 134.

22. Guy McLain, et al., eds., *Springfield Fights the Civil War* (Springfield, MA: Connecticut Valley Historical Museum, 1990), 30.

23. Ibid., 57.

24. variously New Bern or Newbern.

25. Ed M. Main, *The Story of the Marches, Battles and Incidents of the Third United States Colored Cavalry* (New York: Negro Universities Press, 1970, 1908), 321.

26. *Liberator*, 24 June 1864.

27. National Freedmen's Relief Association of the District of Columbia, *Fourth Annual Report* (Washington, DC: McGill & Witherow, 1866), 5.

28. Western Freedmen's Aid Commission, *Second Annual Report* (Cincinnati: Methodist Book Concern, 1865), 32.

29. Ira Berlin, ed., *The Black Military Experience* (New York: Cambridge University Press, 1982), 715.

30. Ira Berlin, et al. *Free at Last: a Documentary History of Slavery, Freedom, and the Civil War*. (New York: New Press, 1992), 185.

31. Ibid., 191.

32. *Pennsylvania Freedmen's Bulletin*, 1 August 1865.

33. NFRADC, *Fourth*, 13.

34. Primus Family Papers, Connecticut Historical Society, Hartford.

35. Virginia Jeans Laas, ed., *Wartime Washington: the Civil War Letters of Elizabeth Blair Lee* (Urbana: University of Illinois Press, 1991), 309.

36. Margaret Washington Creel, *"A Peculiar People": Slave Religion and Community-Culture Among the Gullahs* (New York: New York University Press, 1988), 269.

37. Elizabeth H. Botume, *First Days Amongst the Contrabands* (New York: Arno Press, 1968, 1893), 53.

38. Willie Lee Rose, *Rehearsal for Reconstruction* (New York: Bobbs-Merrill Company, 1964), 303.

39. Bradford, 100-101.

40. Berlin, *Free*, 230-231.

41. Ibid., 191.

CHAPTER 5

Working for Our Own Elevation: Refugee Relief Activities

The plight of refugees who fled to Union lines elicited an outpouring of aid and empathy from free African American women who readily turned their attention to the freedpeople thrown into freedom with few, if any, resources. In 1862, at least 400 homeless, penniless fugitives were in Washington, D.C.; 10,000 were there in 1863 with an additional 3,000 in Alexandria, Virginia across the Potomac River from Washington. At the war's end, there were an estimated 40,000 refugees in the District of Columbia.[1] Freedmen's Village in Alexandria, Virginia which was overcrowded with 3,000 refugees in 1863, housed 7,000 by 1864.[2]

Nearly 650 African American women, children, sick and elderly were housed in Fort Norfolk in Winchester, Virginia in 1862. "Of these, half suffered from measles and whooping cough, and deaths easily exceeded births. Wretchedly clothed, they were housed in a warehouse previously used to store guano[3] which was usually filled with smoke because it had no chimneys."[4] The predicament of the freedpeople was heartbreaking but the determination to overcome their situation was heartwarming.

It is interesting to note that the male editors of the *Christian Recorder* did not, initially, favor relief efforts among the displaced because such support might "uphold and encourage Slavery by contributing to their support, in the event that the Government remanded them (the contrabands) to those who might claim them as their property." By March 22, 1862, however, the editors were saying, "the cause is a good one, and deserves special attention."[5]

Their belated endorsement simply gave a stamp of approval to the "special attention" that African American women were already giving the refugees. The plight, especially of the women and children, touched the free women's hearts and the bonds of sisterhood elicited their support. However, black women had long been involved, often as an offshoot of their church activities, in charitable, benevolent, self-help, burial and support societies which aided the infirm, needy and elderly so their assistance to refugees was a logical progression. They had, in addition, played a significant role in raising funds for their churches—sometimes to supplement the pastor's salary, sometimes for building campaigns. In keeping with the multifaceted nature of black female benevolence, other causes besides the refugees received their support as well during the war. For example, the women of Shiloh Baptist Church in New York helped raise money for the *Weekly Anglo- African* in 1862 because it was in a desperate financial crisis. These women also engaged in other charitable work.

Their involvement in anti-slavery, literary, and vigilance groups before and during the war was another factor in their new focus. Sarah Parker Remond was the vice-president of the Salem Female Anti-Slavery Society in Massachusetts, whereas Sarah Mapps Douglass was a member of the Philadelphia Female Anti-Slavery Society. Harriet Jacobs belonged to the Executive Committee of the Women's National Loyal League, an anti-slavery group organized by suffragists Elizabeth Cady Stanton, Susan B. Anthony, and Lucy Stone in 1863.[6] Sojourner Truth also collaborated with this group.

Free women used the networking and organizing skills they had gained in other activities to provide assistance to their needy people. The ladies founded new organizations and expanded the missions of old ones to raise money and produce goods for medical supplies, schoolbooks, clothing and food for refugees. In true womanly fashion, they formed sewing circles, conducted fairs, gave bake sales, and wrote and sold personal narratives to provide material support.

Sometimes they were accustomed to a high level of activism in the shadows of their husbands. The use of "Mrs.," coupled with the husband's first name, and "Miss" reflected the importance of such titles in the African American community. Of course, this was a common practice among the middle class, black or white, but African American women were battling a negative racial stereotype that was not applied to white women. These appellations contested racist notions of African American female inferiority. Unfortunately, however, this practice tends to obscure the identities of the individual women.

Many times, the women were members of prominent families. Elite women tended to be interconnected; they were related to one another by marriage or they belonged to the same churches and organizations. They, therefore, put to service the contacts that these connections provided to solicit assistance and money for relief efforts. Some of the more prominent probably lent their well-known names, if not their actual services, to projects to verify their worthiness. They sometimes belonged to different relief groups at the same time. Some of the associations were longstanding, lasting several years and undergoing title and membership changes. Others were formed to deal with a specific need and disbanded shortly after.

Free women were expected, having had the privilege of freedom, to contribute to the African American community, especially to the newest members of their free community. The women, on the other hand, expected the African American public to support their enterprises because they were working for their own people. They published solicitations for and acknowledgments of donations and services in newspapers and journals. These public displays were appeals to the consciences, purses and ethnicity of the black community.

When necessary, they collaborated with white organizations by forming auxiliaries of national relief associations or becoming members of interracial groups. Sarah Mapps Douglass, for instance, was vice chairperson of the Women's Pennsylvania Branch of the American Freedmen's Aid Commission. Elizabeth Keckley, Frederick Douglass and Sara Iredell [Mrs. Christian] Fleetwood[7] were members of the National Association for the Relief of Destitute Colored Women and Children in Washington, D.C.

Initially, anti-slavery groups individually sought to aid the fugitives in Washington and elsewhere in a very complicated, overlapping effort. Eventually, however, they combined to form large umbrella groups. The National Freedmen's Relief Association of New York, founded on February 20, 1862, joined with other aid societies to become the American Freedmen's Aid Commission. The Port Royal Relief Association became the Pennsylvania Freedmen's Relief Association based in Philadelphia and was a major player in relief work. The New England Freedmen's Aid Society of Boston was another well-known group. In 1863 aid societies confederated into the United States Commission for the Relief of the National Freedmen and in 1865 they became the American Freedman's Aid Union. The Bureau of Refugees, Freedmen, and Abandoned Lands, or the Freedmen's Bureau, came into existence by an act of Congress on March 3, 1865 in response to private philanthropic relief efforts.

In other words, relief organizations were stepping over and on each other in a confusing mishmash of attempts to direct the future of the newly freed refugees. By way of illustration: George Whipple, a white official of the American Missionary Association contended that a letter from another white relief worker, J.P. Thompson, "contains a statement, which, without his so intending it, is being industriously used by the agents of the Freedman's Union Commission, to divert contributions from the American Missionary Association."[8] These groups were in competition with each other for the limited resources allocated to help freedpeople.

African American women operated outside that confusion. Rather, they exercised their networking skills to collaborate with each other in a variety of ways in order to help their brothers and sisters rise to a position which would ensure a viable freedom for all of them. For example, under the auspices of the United States Freedmen's Bureau and the private philanthropic NFRA, Sojourner Truth worked with refugees at the Freedmen's Village in Arlington Heights, Virginia and in the District of Columbia as a fundraiser, counselor, nurse and instructor of domestic skills to refugee women. She is listed in the NFRA's 1865 *Annual Report* as a "Visitor and Distributing Agent, Washington, D.C." Truth interacted with Harriet Jacobs, a leader in relief operations, who was also working in the same locale.

Elizabeth Keckley, another well-known relief organizer, through her own personal contact with Abraham Lincoln's wife, Mary Todd Lincoln, helped to arrange Sojourner Truth's famous meeting with the President in October 1864.[9] Keckley also assisted the well-known public speaker, Maria Stewart, financially, when she came to Washington, D.C. in 1861 to set up a school. She tapped her contacts to provide introductions to important people in Washington for Stewart which eased her adjustment to her new life and city.

Formerly enslaved herself, Elizabeth Keckley was instrumental in founding the Contraband Relief Association (CRA) in August 1862 whose members were African American women. The association later changed its name to the Ladies' Freedmen and Soldiers' Relief Association to reflect its expanded mission and to indicate a change in consciousness about the negative connotation of the word "contraband." Among the 40 founding members were: Elizabeth Keckley, President; Annie E. Washington, Secretary; Mary L. Cook, Secretary; Louisa Slade[10], head of the Visiting Committee; and Jane Le Count Cook.[11] Washington was a teacher in the District of Columbia. Emma V. Brown, Oberlin graduate and founder of a school in Georgetown, was the association's corresponding secretary.[12]

Gracious and dignified, Elizabeth Keckley is famous for her narrative, *Behind the Scenes, or Thirty Years a Slave and Four in the White House*, in which she recounted her life, including being the seamstress and confidante of Mary Todd Lincoln, the President's wife. She was born in Virginia, was sold to a slaveholder in North Carolina, and taken to St. Louis, Missouri where she learned to read and write and where, in 1855, she purchased her freedom and that of James, her son by her white master. She went to Baltimore in 1860, relocating to Washington, D.C. after six months.

Ironically, that same year, Keckley was hired as a seamstress by Varina Davis, wife of Jefferson Davis who was later to become President of the Confederacy. For several years, rumor held that Jefferson Davis attempted to escape capture by the Union army by dressing in women's clothes made by Elizabeth Keckley.[13] Like so many of the women who participated in the Civil War, Keckley was a seamstress who had learned her skill as a result of being enslaved. Apart from teaching, sewing was one of the few respectable and skilled jobs that African American women were allowed to do. It was her skill as a dressmaker which gave her the means to purchase her and her son's freedom.

She said the CRA "was formed for the purpose, not only of relieving the wants of those destitute people, but also to sympathize with, and advise them."[14] In her "Appeal in Behalf of Our People," published in the March 14, 1863 *Christian Recorder*, Keckley reminded more affluent African Americans, "It has been asserted that we, as a people, do not sympathize with this oppressed portion of our race. Let us, my friends, by our benefactions, by words and by acts of kindness, disprove these assertions . . . great obligations rest upon us to do all we can to assist, both morally and physically, those whose lot has hitherto been cast in the dark, rough paths of life . . . Who, in appearing before the Great Judge when life is over, would not rejoice to have done what he could for those destitute brothers and sisters?" This duty, Keckley felt, rightly belonged to African Americans whose condition was better off than the refugees. She argued, "If the white people can give festivals to raise funds for the relief of suffering soldiers, why should not the well-to-do colored people go to work to do something for the benefit of the suffering blacks." It was undoubtedly her own experience of being enslaved, however, which motivated her benevolence toward displaced freedpeople and African American soldiers.

Therefore, Elizabeth "made a suggestion in the colored church, that a society of colored people be formed to labor for the benefit of the unfortunate freedmen. The idea proved popular, and in two weeks 'the Contraband Relief Association' was organized . . . " She

> circulated among the colored people, and got them thoroughly interested in the subject . . . We held a mass meeting at the Colored Baptist Church [Boston], Rev. Mr. Grimes, raised a sum of money, and organized there a branch society. The society was organized by Mrs.[Octavia] Grimes, wife of the pastor, assisted by Mrs.[Sarah] Martin, wife of Rev. Sella Martin. This branch of the society, during the war, was able to send us over eighty large boxes of goods, contributed exclusively by the colored people of Boston . . . [15]

Octavia Grimes, of the Twelfth Baptist Church, started the Colored Ladies' Relief Association; Sarah Martin established the Fugitive Aid Society of Boston at Joy Street Baptist Church. The two groups collaborated to form a branch of Keckley's organization. Twelfth Baptist had splintered off from Joy Street but both churches were highly active in anti-slavery activities, including sheltering and rescuing fugitives. Many members of Twelfth's congregation joined the Massachusetts 54th; their pastor, Rev. Leonard A. Grimes, was a recruiter for the regiment. Several other groups were offshoots of the Contraband Relief Association, including the Young Ladies' Relief Associations in Baltimore and the District of Columbia.

The first annual report of the CRA gave a glowing report of the association's initial year in operation. "We have . . . by our own exertions greatly added to our treasury, and we are happy to say that every effort made by us to obtain funds to alleviate in any way the distresses of our afflicted brethren has been crowned with success . . . " They had hoped, in fact, to increase the scope of their efforts by assisting with much more than the immediate wants of the freedpeople.[16] In this they were successful.

Keckley also sought help from sources other than African American women:

> I suggested the object of my mission to Robert Thompson, Steward of the [Metropolitan] Hotel [New York], who immediately raised quite a sum of money among the dining-room waiters. Mr.

> Frederick Douglass contributed $200, besides lecturing for us. Other prominent colored men sent in liberal contributions. From England a large quantity of stores [and money] was received. Mrs. [Abraham] Lincoln made frequent contributions, as also did the President.[17]

Through Keckley's connection with abolitionists, in particular, Frederick Douglass, they were able to get donations, from even as far away as Europe. In the June 11, 1864 edition of the *Christian Recorder*, the Association acknowledged the "receipt of $112 from . . . the Edinburgh Anti-Slavery Society, the Aberdeen Ladies, and Sheffield Anti-Slavery Societies." Douglass was thanked in the letter for his help in soliciting the funds.

A month after the CRA was formed, the Union Relief Association was established at the Union Bethel Church in Washington, D.C. for the purpose of aiding refugees. Organized on September 10, 1862, African American women dominated the membership. The officers were:

Thomas E. Green, President
Mrs. Susan Tenny, Vice President
James L. Thomas, Secretary
William L. Freeman, Assistant Secretary
Mrs. Margaret Tilghman, Treasurer
Executive Committee:
Mrs. Anna Coakley
Mrs. Anna Dorsey
Mrs. Emily B. Freeman
Mrs. Mary Gooden
Miss Cecilia A. King
Miss Caroline Louden
Mrs. Laura Quinn
Miss Caroline B. Simpson
Miss Elizabeth Smith
Miss Harriet Stewart[18]

Harriet Jacobs was also active in relief operations in the Washington, D.C. area during this time, working under the aegis of Quaker groups and the New England Freedmen's Aid Society. Like Elizabeth Keckley, her compatriot in sanitary work with displaced Africans, Jacobs was a seamstress who had learned her craft while being enslaved. She was famous for the explicit account of her enslavement, *Incidents in the Life of a Slave Girl*, which she published in 1861 under the pseudonym, Linda Brent. She used the fame from the publication of her memoir to solicit funds for her relief work.

Suffering sexual, mental and physical abuse at the hands of her Edenton, North Carolina slaveowners, Jacobs escaped to New York after hiding in an attic for nearly seven years. A white abolitionist purchased her and her children's freedom in 1852. After spending some time in Massachusetts and England, she and her daughter, Louisa, relocated at the outbreak of the Civil War to Alexandria, Virginia where they worked with refugees. They later went to Savannah, Georgia to work with freedpeople.

During the Civil War, Harriet recruited African American men for service in the Union army and she started a school for refugee children. But her most important work was with freedpeople in Virginia and Georgia to whom, because of her own harrowing experience of enslavement, she felt a special attachment. Becoming a major spokesperson for them, Harriet raised money by conducting fairs and establishing sewing circles to produce clothing and medical assistance for the destitute fugitives who were flocking to the Washington, D.C. area. She also helped with the farming at Freedmen's Village in Alexandria, Virginia.

In addition to such strenuous work, Jacobs made time to plead for assistance for "her people" from the larger community. She commented on the condition of the refugees in a letter to William Lloyd Garrison which was published in the *Liberator* in 1862:

> I found men, women and children all huddled together without any distinction or regard to age or sex. Some of them were in the most pitiable condition. Many were sick with measles, diphtheria, scarlet and typhoid fever. Some had a few filthy rags to lie on, others had nothing but the bare floor for a couch . . . Each day brings the fresh additions of the hungry, naked and sick . . . [T]hey know little else than the handle of the hoe, the plough, the cotton-pod and the overseer's lash. Have patience with them. You have helped to make them what they are; teach them civilization. You owe it to them and you will find them as apt to learn as any other people that come to you stupid from oppression.[19]

Unlike Keckley who aimed her efforts primarily at the African American community, Jacobs targeted the white population because she felt they were responsible for the condition of the freedpeople. As her letter to Garrison showed, she attempted to appeal to their consciences.

Sattira Douglas presumed on the longstanding African American activist female network of which she was an integral part by having the Colored Ladies Freedmen's Aid Society of Chicago respond immediately when refugees in Kansas needed help. They shipped needed supplies such as clothing, cooking utensils, food and other essentials, saying "We feel a *very deep* interest in the cause of the freedmen, and hope to be found with liberal hands and hearts, ever willing to administer to their wants."[20]

The Society was established in February 1863 by some of Chicago's leading African American women activists. The organization sponsored lectures and other benefits. Its officers were:

Mary Jones, President
Mrs. James Blanks, Vice-president
Sattira Douglas, Secretary
Mrs. George Lee, Assistant Secretary
Mrs. Henry Bradford, Treasurer
Mrs. Platt, Board of Directresses
Mrs. Sterrett, Board of Directresses
Mrs. Wagoner[21], Board of Directresses
Mrs. White, Board of Directresses

Sattira Douglas was treasurer until she removed to Kansas to teach freedpeople, and Mary Ann Shadd Cary was employed as a traveling agent for fund-raising.[22]

Women in other locations worked tirelessly for refugees as well. Operating in such diverse cities as Leavenworth, Kansas, Nashville, Tennessee and Brooklyn, New York, African American women banded together to aid the suffering freedpeople.[23] Mrs. Mary E. Brown was the president of the Relief Association of Elmira, New York which forwarded a barrel of 114 pieces of clothing to the Union Relief Association of the Union Bethel African Methodist Episcopal (A.M.E.) Church in Washington, D.C. The women of Waters Chapel in Baltimore, Maryland sent two boxes containing 575 pieces of clothing.[24] From Geneva, New York, the Colored Ladies Freedmen and Soldiers Aid Society donated fifty dollars to the AMA for displaced Africans.[25] In addition to at least two other African American relief societies, Boston had a Colored Ladies' Sanitary Commission which sent $500 to displaced Africans in Savannah, Georgia.[26] Women in Worcester, Massachusetts established the Freedmen's Aid Society to assist refugees.[27] The Colored Ladies Society of Syracuse, New York sent a box of contributions to Edmonia Highgate, a teacher in Norfolk, Virginia who was originally from Syracuse.[28]

The First Female Contraband Aid Society of Alexandria, Virginia was a sewing circle established to "furnish aid and comfort" to the freedpeople.[29] Charleston, South Carolina also had a sewing society, the Ladies Patriotic Association, which made clothes for displaced people.[30] The African American women in Springfield, Massachusetts formed a Colored Ladies Aid Society and ran strawberry festivals and other events to support the Union cause.[31]

African American women in New York City gave a gala Grand Calico Dress Ball on February 6, 1862 at Mozart Hall, 668 Broadway, to aid the uprooted persons at Beaufort, South Carolina. They asked for donations of clothing for "the relief of those who in the joy of their new born Freedom, are now appealing to the world for assistance and recognition." The committee consisted of women of "well known character" including,

> Miss C. Bruce
> Mrs. C. Hopewell
> Mrs. J.H. Jackson
> Mrs. E. Odell
> Mrs. E. Parker
> Mrs. L. Shad
> Mrs. P. Williams[32]

They raised $156.31 and numerous articles of clothing which were sent to the Home Committee of the National Freedmen's Relief Association which acknowledged the donation.[33] The ladies emphasized that their donation went "direct to the contrabands, who must know that they have friends of their own race at the North, who are proud to aid them."[34]

In another magnanimous display of charity, benevolence and collaboration, the women of New York contributed $1464 in 1862 to support the Colored Orphan Asylum and Association. The Ladies' Union of Brooklyn and New York played a major role in this effort by holding a bazaar. The list of the members' names in this association, as given in the April 6, 1862 *Weekly Anglo-African*, reads as a veritable who's who of the black elite:

> Mrs. Barnswell
> Mrs. J. Bell
> Mrs. J.W. Bowers

Mrs. Bowser
Mrs. W. Curtis
Mrs. A. Duncan
Mrs. C. Fitch
Mrs. Rev. H.H. Garnet[35]
Mrs. Rev. J.N. Gloucester[36]
Mrs. C. Graham
Mrs. P. Guignon
Mrs. Hall
Mrs. Margaret Jackson
Mrs. R. Jackson
Mrs. J. Jenkins
Mrs. Lambert
Mrs. W. Leonard
Mrs. E. Mann
Mrs. H. Mars
Mrs. J.C. Morell
Mrs. E. Parker
Mrs. J. Peterson[37]
Mrs. Clorice (?) Reason[38]
Mrs. R. Rich
Miss E. D. Richards
Mrs. C. Robinson
Mrs. H. Scott
Mrs. Shadd
Mrs. Dr. Smith[39]
Mrs. B. Stanley
Mrs. E. Stevens
Mrs. E. Symonette
Mrs. Rev. C. Thompson
Mrs. Tompkins
Mrs. C. Topp
Mrs. P. Van Dyke
Mrs. M. Van Stay
Mrs. A. Williams
Mrs. Rev. [Peter] Williams[40]
Mrs. W.J. [Mary Ann Garret Marshall] Wilson

Mrs. E. Parker appears on the Grand Calico Ball Committee and as a member of the Ladies' Union. Also on both lists are Mrs. J.H. Jackson who might be Mrs. Margaret Jackson; Mrs. L. Shad could be Mrs. Shadd; and it is possible that Mrs. P. Williams is the same as Mrs. Rev. Peter Williams.

When the orphanage was destroyed in 1863 during a white draft riot, many of the same women helped to raise money to rebuild it[41] and the Ladies' Union was again instrumental in the success of the endeavor. The Ladies' Union Bazaar Association held a fair and a fund-raising campaign in May 1864 which realized a total of $3239.10 for the benefit of the Colored Orphan Asylum.[42] They used the success of their first fair to solicit aid for the young victims: "We . . . again appeal to a generous public in behalf of the Colored Orphans, and from the ready and liberal response to our last effort in this noble cause, we feel assured we shall not plead in vain . . . " According to the ladies' sentiments, the New York public should give generously because of the shame the "wicked, unprovoked attack of the ruthless and infuriated mob" brought on the city.[43]

Among the participants who either sponsored the fair or gave items and money were prominent African American women from several states, including,

Mrs. E. Bowers
Mrs. Chew[44]
Mrs. Sarah Mapps Douglass
Miss Ada Hinton
Mrs. [Sarah?] Page
Mrs. Charles [Charlotte] Bennett Ray
Mrs. Charles L. Reason
Mrs. Dr. James McCune Smith
Mrs. A.M. Vidal
Mrs. A. Wilson

Again, the social standing of these women can be seen in their connection with some of the leading African American men during this time. Ada Hinton was a member of the family of well-to-do Philadelphia barber, Frederick A. Hinton. She served as the Corresponding Secretary of the well-established Ladies' Sanitary Association of St.Thomas's African Episcopal Church (LSASTC) in Philadelphia.

Although an activist in her own right, Sarah Mapps Douglass was the wife of Rev. William Douglass who pastored St. Thomas' Church in Philadelphia and the sister of the artist, Robert Douglass. Another well-known artist and designer of regimental flags, David Bustill Bowser, was her cousin. Referred to by the Rev. Alexander Crummell as "refined and cultivated,"[45] Sarah was an instructor and administrator at the Institute for Colored Youth (ICY)in Philadelphia. This high school later became Cheyney University. She spearheaded fundraising efforts for refugees at ICY through the formation of a Children's Aid Association and a Mother's Aid Association.

Charlotte Augustus Burroughs Ray was the wife of the famous clergyman, Rev. Charles Bennett Ray who was the pastor of the Bethesda Congregational Church in New York City. She was also the mother of the first African American female lawyer "regularly admitted to the practice of law in any jurisdiction in the United States,"[46] Charlotte E. Ray, who received her law degree from Howard University in 1872.

The women in Philadelphia were equally as active on behalf of their suffering people. The Ladies' Sanitary Association of St. Thomas's African Episcopal Church (LSASTC) first organized itself in April 1863 as an auxiliary to the United States Sanitary Commission. The women's prominence in their community allowed them to be significant fundraisers for relief purposes so that other groups were prompted to seek them out as subsidiaries. In 1866, for instance, they became auxiliary to the Women's Central Branch Freedmen's Relief Association of Pennsylvania after that society actively sought their association.

Philadelphia's African American elite[47] was reflected in the roster of the LSASTC. The individual women were already recognized for their benevolent and charitable activism, especially through their churches. As the editor of the *Christian Recorder* said in an addendum to the group's public thank-you to its donors published in the paper, "The . . . Association is under the especial control of ladies who are well-known to all our citizens for true Christian sympathy and devotion to the needy."[48] The detailed annual report[49] outlining their activities for 1865 listed as members,

Mrs. L. Reddon, President
Mrs. John Chew[50], Vice President
Mrs. Thomas Dorsey[51], Treasurer
Miss Emma L. Jackson, Secretary
Miss Ada Hinton, Corresponding Secretary
Mrs. F. Sebastian, Purchasing Committee
Mrs. Burton, Purchasing Committee

Mrs. Abell
Mrs. Anderson
Miss Lizzie Anderson
Mrs. Bias
Miss Emeline Curtis
Mrs. M.V. Dickerson
Miss Mary Dorsey
Mrs. Doyer
Mrs. Givens
Mrs. Louisa Goins
Mrs. Mary Goins
Miss Sarah Harris
Mrs. Hawkins
Mrs. Harriet Henson
Miss Lucy Henson
Mrs. Layton
Miss Maria Le Count
Mrs. Lozier
Mrs. Emeline Peer[52]
Mrs. Seville
Mrs. Harriet Smith[53]
Mrs. Sneeds
Miss Lucy Taylor
Mrs. Van Brackle
Mrs. Vidal

Harriet Smith and Mrs. Vidal were related by marriage, with Stephen Smith's wife's niece being married to Ulysses B. Vidal. Mrs. Bias was a family member of the well-known abolitionist and temperance worker, James J.G. Bias, if not his wife, Eliza. There is an Elizabeth Bias who was a patron of the Home for Aged and Infirm Colored Persons in Philadelphia. They were probably related. Lucy Taylor was also a patron of the Home. Mrs. T.J. Bowers[54] was the president at the organization's inception but she is not listed in the 1865 annual report. Other names associated with the very successful fair the organization gave in December 1864 (this time to aid soldiers) are missing as well: E. Boddy, Mrs. Gibbons, C. Miller, Mrs. Minton, E. Drummond, C. Christianson and L. Galloway. These women had contributed to the organization before 1865.

The Ladies' Sanitary Association aided African American soldiers in addition to focusing much of their altruism on the refugees in Port Royal,

South Carolina. "Our labors . . . have extended far and near, to the needy in Hospitals, Camps, and elsewhere, and we have received much encouragement from the gratitude manifested by the recipients of our aid." They hoped, through their relief work, that "war may no longer invade the land, and that justice and right towards every man shall henceforth be the motto adopted by this Nation." They understood the importance of the Civil War to the African American community.

The Association collected $1,226.75 for refugees at a fair on December 19, 1864, in spite of inclement weather. They gave goods, clothing, money and food "for the benefit of the sick and wounded in Christian Street Hospital." They aided individual soldiers like Jacob Purnell, 1st Sergeant of Company C, 127th U.S. Colored Infantry, who wrote to thank them "for relieving the wants of a poor Soldier." Other soldiers had their transportation home paid for by the society and the families of soldiers were given financial aid. One hundred dollars was donated to the campaign to erect the Lincoln Monument and $50 was given to the Cooper Shop Refreshment Saloon to "comfort to the sick and weary soldiers and sailors of the Union Army and Navy." Boxes of supplies were sent to Savannah, Georgia and Alexandria, Virginia.[55]

On February 26, 1865, the Ladies' Union Association of Philadelphia reordered itself into an organization which ministered to the needs of freedpeople after initially being established as an African American soldiers' relief society on July 20, 1863. They reformed themselves "with the view of working in behalf of the Freedmen, who, by the Providence of God through the late war, have bursted the fetters which bound them for so many years, and whom it is now our duty and privilege to assist . . . "[56]

The reconstituted organization "sent to different parts of the South, boxes containing articles of bodily comfort, and also the means of mental improvement to the amount of $950.00." In addition, they performed such services as paying the passage home for a stranded freedwoman and purchasing shoes for destitute soldiers. The members included:

Miss Ellen Black
Mrs. Lizzie H.S. Bowser
Miss M.V. Brown, Recording Secretary
Mrs. Elijah Davis, Treasurer
Miss Emily Davis
Mrs. Elijah Hunt
Miss Carrie R. Le Count, Corresponding Secretary
Miss Amelia Mills, President

Miss A. Morgan, Vice President
Mrs. Edith Press

Charles Bolivar, the "Pencil Pusher," supplied another member's name in the January 13, 1914 *Philadelphia Tribune*: Mrs. Henry L. Phillips.

Lizzie Bowser, listed above, had a very successful table at a fair the society gave on May 15, 1865 which sold paintings donated by several renowned artists, including David Bustill Bowser, obviously a relative. David Bowser had been commissioned by the Contraband Relief Association in Washington, D.C. to design a flag for the 1st U.S. Colored Infantry which was presented on August 13, 1863.

The corresponding secretary, Caroline (Carrie) Le Count, was a noted public speaker. She "made many public appearances here [Philadelphia] and elsewhere in reading and recitation. She was popular after a fashion and was for many years in demand as an entertainer."[57] Le Count was an 1863 graduate of the ICY and it was her lawsuit in 1867 against the Philadelphia streetcars which helped to finally, after many years' effort on the part of the black community, outlaw discrimination on public transportation in the city. She was also the fiancee of martyred Octavius Catto, a Civil War veteran, who was killed in white rioting in October 1871 as he campaigned in Philadelphia's African American community for the Republican Party. She identified his body. Later, she was the principal of a public school in the city named after Catto.

Even children were active in relief endeavors. The Pennsylvania Freedmen's Relief Association reported that a "poor little colored child, Edith Webb [from Philadelphia], collected penny by penny, ten dollars, which she sent to us."[58] As an adult, Edith continued her activism, becoming, along with Lucy Adger and Caroline Le Count, a member of the First Presbyterian Church's Ladies of the Sinking Fund.[59]

The children in Sarah Mapps Douglass' school, the Institute for Colored Youth in Philadelphia, were equally as altruistic because they "formed a society . . . calling it the Children's Aid Association. Twenty names have been enrolled, each child paying three cents weekly. A lady gave us a whole piece of nice calico, which the children are making up most enthusiastically for the little orphans in Tennessee. Another society has been formed among the mothers, meeting weekly at the House of Industry in Catharine Street. Most of them are very poor, yet twenty of them gave their names, promising to sew once a fortnight for the freedmen, and engaging to pay five cents weekly. They call themselves the Mother's Aid Association. Over two dollars were collected at their first meeting, which was a very animated and interesting one."[60] These organizations were no doubt established at the instigation of Douglass who was a longtime activist in the African American community but they show that the desire to help freedpeople cut across all class lines.

The women in Philadelphia did not just attend to the needs of freedpeople and soldiers. The sick and elderly, especially women, also received their attention. An interracial enterprise, Philadelphia's Home for Aged and Infirm Colored Persons, was founded in the midst of the Civil War in September 1864 at 340 South Front Street. The institution was moved in 1871 to Belmont and Girard Avenues in the city and renamed the Stephen Smith Home in honor of one of its main African American benefactors.

The women on the Board of Managers made up the Committee of Management for the Home. This Committee was responsible for the "general supervision of the internal arrangements of the Home" and was composed solely of women, as mandated by the Home's bylaws. Only male members of the Board of Managers could belong to the Committee on Property and Finance and "have charge of the real estate and financial affairs of the Home." In other words, women were to stay in their place and leave the "real" work to the men.

African American women, however, were overwhelming supporters and participants in this benevolent move to succor "respectable" indigent and aged African Americans. Many of the patrons probably realized that given the right circumstances, they could be in the same predicament. The Matron of the home was Miliscent Parvin. Other women on the very lengthy list included:

Sarah T. Allen
Anne Alston
Mary Bacon
Sarah Bacon
Elizabeth Bias
Henrietta Bowers[61]
Mary D. Brown
Caroline Burton
Elizabeth S. Burton
Caroline W. Carter
Elizabeth Cole
Elizabeth M. Cooper
Harriet Cooper

Sarah Mapps Douglass
Betsy Freeman
Mary Frisby
Eliza C. Gibbons
Elizabeth Harris
Priscilla H. Henszey
Mary J. Hopkins
Elizabeth Horner
Alice Hudson
Fanny Jackson [Coppin]
Mary Jackson
Rachel T. Jackson
Anne T. Jeanes
Mary Jeanes
Ann Jess
Helen Johnson
Rachel Johnson
Margaret Jones
Rachel W. Jones
Ann Laws
Grace Mapps
Rachel W. Moore
Mary Ann Morris
Elizabeth Parker
Elizabeth W. Parrish
Sarah Parrish
Susan M. Parrish
Sarah Phipps
Hannah W. Richardson
Mary Shaw
Catharine Simpson
Rebecca Simpson
Sarah Ann Sleeper
Sarah Smith
Lucy Taylor
Elizabeth White
Lydia White
Rebecca White
Ann B. Williams[62]

Mary Ann Campbell, wife of Rev. Jabez Campbell of Mother Bethel A.M.E. Church, was also a member. Lydia White, who appears on the list with other prominent names, "managed a Free Labor Store, where nothing was sold that grew or was made in the Southland. That was heroism, because the cost was considerably greater than in the general stores."[63]

It is worth noting that some of these same women were engaged in another benevolent venture, the Home for Destitute Colored Children, located on Woodland Avenue below 46th Street in Philadelphia. Mary D. Brown, Eliza C. Gibbons and Mary Jeanes were life members of the organization which oversaw the Home. Jane L. Johnson, who was the president of the Soldiers' Relief Association, was also a life member.[64]

Hannah Gray, a laundress and seamstress from New Haven, Connecticut, left a similar legacy. At her death in 1861, she bequeathed her New Haven home to be used for "indigent colored females." The congregation, undoubtedly primarily the women, of the A.M.E. Zion Church took care of the home after she died. At the turn of the century, other African American women, the New Haven Women's Twentieth Century Club, took control of the home and expanded Gray's legacy. Although she was not wealthy, Hannah contributed her own money and led fundraising projects for fugitives who had managed to escape to Canada.[65] She gave particular financial assistance to Hiram Wilson, a white agent of the American Anti-Slavery Society, who worked with refugees in Canada, corresponding with Wilson and visiting him in Canada West to see how his efforts were proceeding.[66]

So as not to be outclassed by the ladies in Philadelphia, Susan Paul Vashon helped organize a series of sanitary relief bazaars in Pittsburgh, Pennsylvania in 1864 and 1865 which raised thousands of dollars that were used to nurse sick and wounded soldiers and house refugees.[67] Her activist husband, George, was the first African American graduate of Oberlin College.[68] He had taught in Haiti as well as a white school, New York Central College in McGrawville, New York. Her grandfather was the Rev. Thomas Paul who started the Joy Street Church in Boston. The church conducted a school for African American children in its basement which educated many of Boston's black elite.

In December 1863, African American women in Richmond, Virginia, "having long heard the cries and sighs of the freedmen, women and children of the South, and the many cries of our soldiers, met at the A.M.E. Church . . . to form a society titled, 'The Freedmen's Relief and Soldier's Aid Society.'" They conducted festivals and solicited funds.[69] The officers were:

Miss Charlotte Carter, President
Miss Julia Wilkinson, Vice President
Miss Nancy Outland, Secretary
Miss Margaret Goff, Assistant Secretary
Miss Amy Coleman, Treasurer.

These ladies' must have been quite young since they are all "Miss."

Shortly after the surrender of the Confederacy in 1865, women in Beaufort, South Carolina met at Bethel A.M.E. Church to establish the Ladies' Fair of Beaufort to "aid the destitute Freedmen on Edisto Island and other places in South Carolina." They asked the public to aid them "in alleviating the condition of their suffering brethren." They constituted a twenty-member committee of managers and elected the following officers: Sarah Bram, President; Mary Still[70], an educator, was chosen as the Vice President; Mrs. Hannah Smalls, whose husband, Robert, was the famous *Planter* captain and Reconstruction legislator, was the Treasurer; and Jenny Lynch, Secretary. They authorized agents in Newport, Rhode Island and Oberlin, Ohio to solicit funds in their name.[71]

Even African American women abroad worked for the relief of freedpeople. A seamstress, Ellen Craft, from London, raised money for southern freedpeople and sent "bundles of clothing made by her own hands"[72] back to the United States. She was a member of the Ladies' Auxiliary of the British and Foreign Freedmen's Aid Society.

Craft, whose father was, typically, also her white owner, had fled enslavement in Clinton, Georgia in 1848 in a very celebrated escape. To effect their flight, Ellen posed as a white slaveowner while her darker-skinned husband, William, pretended to be her servant. They went to Boston but had to relocate to Great Britain with the passage of the Fugitive Slave Law of 1850. In London, they were active in the anti-slavery movement, extending their hospitality to other anti-slavery workers like Sarah Parker Remond who stayed with them while she was a student at the Bedford College for Ladies. During the Civil War Remond campaigned for British support for the Union.

Interestingly, Ellen Craft's own mother, Maria Smith, was among the freedpeople living near the headquarters of General James Wilson in Macon as a result of General William T. Sherman's march through Georgia. Ellen had not seen or heard from her mother since the Crafts had escaped enslavement in 1848. She sent money for Smith to come to London in October 1865.[73] The Crafts returned to the United States in 1869 and set up a school in Ways Station, Georgia.

Enslaved or newly-freed African American women tended to network and organize informally to aid themselves and other refugees. These women had made new lives for themselves and their families after being displaced as a result of the Civil War. Once free, they took on the task of advising and helping more recent refugees. One woman on Edisto Island, Sea Islands, South Carolina said proudly that she had "striven and got enough to give seven gowns" to the newcomers.[74]

Edward S. Philbrick, a white speculator from Boston who ran a very profitable (for himself) enterprise in Port Royal, South Carolina, commented on the cooperation among the women on his plantation: "It is a common practice among [the women] to hire each other to hoe their tasks, when sickness or other causes prevent them from doing it themselves, so that most of the tasks of the lying-in women are taken care of by sisters or other friends in the absence of their husbands."[75]

Harriet Jacobs depicted the networking that went on and the concern the women in the camps felt for their own people. "We are now collecting together the orphan children, of whom there are a great number, owing to the many deaths that have occurred of late. In justice to the refugee women, I am bound to testify that I have never known them, in any one instance, [to] refuse to shelter an orphan. In many cases, mothers who have five or six children of their own, without enough to feed and cover them, will readily receive these helpless little ones into their own poor hovels."[76]

The Civil War spurred Annetta M. Lane of Norfolk and Harriet R. Taylor of Southampton to form the Grand United Order of Tents in 1864 or 1865. Enslaved themselves, the women created their benevolent association to aid fugitives. Their organization became the first African American female lodge to be chartered in Virginia after the war.[77]

A devout Christian and a member of Bethel A.M.E. Church in Baltimore, Mary Prout started a secret benevolent association, "an old-time fraternal society: a thought, a vision, for mutual help and benefit to a benighted people" in 1867 for the purpose of providing health and burial insurance and other aid to African American Civil War veterans and freedpeople. The organization expanded under Prout's direction to Norfolk, Portsmouth, Richmond and Petersburg, eventually evolving into the broader-missioned Independent Order of St. Luke, led by Maggie Lena Walker.[78]

Mary Prout had Annie Dickerson, "one of the pillars of Bethel Church in Baltimore," as a shining example of black female activism. Prout, who taught in the church's day school, was Dickerson's assistant. Dickerson "took under her care and instruction all of the new female converts and indoctrinated them in the duties they owed to their God and to their church." She also started "a beneficial society, in which the children paid a small stipend per month and when they died she headed the procession to the graveyard."[79]

Prout and Dickerson were compatriots of another of Bethel's activist women, Annetta Toy Jordan, who was president of the church's Mothers' Association. The association aimed its philanthropy at needy African Americans in the Baltimore area. During the winter of 1866, "upwards of 500 families have been relieved and thirty cords of wood distributed" by the society.[80]

The National Freedman recorded that "Four orphan asylums have been founded, at Memphis, Helena, and Natchez, the first attempt of this kind having been made by 'Aunt Maria,' a colored woman, who collected a considerable number of orphans on President's Island, near Memphis, and still, assisted by Miss Mitchell, has the care of them."[81] "Aunt Maria" is apparently only important as an object lesson because there is no other information given in the article which humanizes her. The use of the ubiquitous 'Aunt" is a further dehumanizing objectification.

In addition to their relief, educational and missionary work, the Daughters of Zion, a mutual benefit society of Avery A.M.E. Chapel in Memphis, Tennessee, saw to it that church members received needed health care in the segregated city. They hired a physician, S.H. Toles, in 1867 "to provide free medical care to all ailing members of Avery Chapel." To support their activities, they "pooled their meager resources, solicited voluntary contributions from the congregation, and sponsored a series of fund-raising events such as fairs, picnics, and balls." They also, under the direction of their president, Martha Ware, and their secretary-treasurer, Jeannie Beckford, controlled the city's freedmen's hospital fund.[83]

The annual reports of the National Association for the Relief of Destitute Colored Women and Children in Washington, D.C. acknowledged the participation of African American women in their relief efforts. The 4th annual report in 1867 related that the Association had received in February 1867 a donation of 47 pairs of stockings knit by the "Freedwomen of Washington, D.C." In March 1867, they received an additional 30 pairs. In 1868, the Association related that the parlor of their new home was "handsomely furnished with the money raised for that purpose by Mrs. Madison, (a colored lady of this city) and her friends last year."[84] This interracial group counted among its members several prominent African Americans, including Elizabeth Keckley, Sara Iredell Fleetwood, and Frederick Douglass.

Nevertheless, class boundaries did intrude somewhat on the aid work of African American women. "Junius," writing from Brooklyn in the December 26, 1863 *Christian Recorder*, chided the members of a local association for being too busy with their fair to help the wives and children of four members of the 14th Rhode Island Colored Heavy Artillery. He said in scathing denunciation, "Think of it; four women . . . with young children dependent upon them, their husbands in the army. They are shivering with cold, without the necessaries of life, making application to a Society, whose purpose is to assist the colored soldiers, and who, it is reported, have collected hundreds of dollars, yet will not give these poor women a dollar. It is not a sufficient plea, that the money collected are for the contrabands; there is not a man or woman who has contributed to the fund, that would object to helping these soldiers wives, out of the money in the society, though given to the contrabands south. These colored men and women in the tobacco factories, will not object, that a part of the $57 contributed by them, should be given to so noble a purpose." The women were taken care of, but by other African Americans in the community. The class issue is alluded to when Junius refers to the working class factory workers who have sacrificed in order to contribute to the freedpeople.

Caste distinctions, notwithstanding, African American relief organizations made a major contribution to the alleviation of the suffering of displaced freedpeople. In addition, just as the aid association in Brooklyn did (even if they failed to do their duty in the instance that Junius cites), many of the societies combined their refugee aid projects with undertakings designed to assist and succor African American soldiers. They also offered help wherever it was needed in the African American community as well.

NOTES

1. Dorothy Sterling, ed., *We Are Your Sisters: Black Women in the Nineteenth Century* (New York: W.W. Norton, 1984), 245.
2. Ervin L. Jordan, Jr., *Black Confederates and Afro-Yankees in Civil War Virginia* (Charlottesville: University of Virginia, 1995), 86.
3. bat or seabird droppings used as fertilizer
4. Jordan, 87.
5. *Christian Recorder*, 22 March 1862.
6. Darlene Hine, et al., eds., *Black Women in America: an Historical Encyclopedia* (Bloomington: Indiana University Press, 1994), 629.

7. Christian Fleetwood was a Congressional Medal of Honor recipient for his service in the 4th USCI during the Civil War. Sara L. Iredell graduated with honors from the Institute for Colored Youth in Philadelphia and was a teacher in Washington, D.C.

8. *American Missionary*, 12 (April 1868), 83.

9. Nell Irvin Painter, *Sojourner Truth: a Life, a Symbol* (New York: W.W. Norton, 1996), 203-204.

10. Wife of William Slade, a Washington businessman and later a clerk in the United States Treasury Department.

11. C. Peter Ripley, ed., *The Black Abolitionist Papers, Volume V: the United States, 1859-1865* (Chapel Hill: University of North Carolina Press, 1992), 251.

Jane Le Count Cook was the widow of the Presbyterian minister, John F. Cook.

12. *Christian Recorder*, 11 June 1864.

13. Jordan, 148.

14. *Christian Recorder*, 14 March 1863.

15. Elizabeth Keckley, *Behind the Scenes: Thirty Years a Slave and Four in the White House* (New York: Arno Press, 1968, 1868), 113-114.

16. *Christian Recorder*, 22 August 1863.

17. Keckley, 114-116.

18. *Christian Recorder*, 4 October 1862.

19. *Liberator*, 3 September 1862.

20. *Christian Recorder*, 12 March 1864.

21. Probably the wife of H.O. Wagoner, a well-to-do Chicago businessman, abolitionist and recruiter of black soldiers.

22. Ripley, 284-287; *Christian Recorder*, 14 March 1864.

23. Bettye Collier-Thomas, *Black Women Organized for Social Change 1800-1920* (Washington, DC: Bethune Museum-Archives, 1984), 26.

24. *Christian Recorder*, 14 March 1863.

25. Joe M. Richardson, *Christian Reconstruction: the American Missionary Association and Southern Blacks, 1861-1890* (Athens: University of Georgia Press, 1986), 97.

26. Marianna W. Davis, ed., *Contributions of Black Women to America*, vol. 2 (Columbia, SC: Kenday Press, 1981), 58.

27. Nick Salvatore, *We All Got History: the Memory Books of Amos Webber* (New York: Times Books, 1996), 114.

28. Clara M. DeBoer, *His Truth is Marching On: African Americans Who Taught the Freedmen for the American Missionary Association 1861-1877* (New York: Garland Publishing, Inc., 1995), 52.

29. *Christian Recorder*, 21 March 1863.

30. G.K. Eggleston, "The Work of Relief Societies During the Civil War," *Journal of Negro History* 14 (July 1929): 290.

31. Guy E. McLain, et al., eds., *Springfield Fights the Civil War* (Springfield, MA: Connecticut Valley Historical Museum, 1990), 164.

32. *Weekly Anglo-African*, 1 February 1862.

33. *Weekly Anglo-African*, 8 March 1862.

34. *Weekly Anglo-African*, 15 February 1862.

35. Julia, Rev. Henry Highland Garnet's first wife. She was also a relief worker among freedpeople in Washington, D.C. for a time before she died in 1870. He was the pastor of New York City's Shiloh Baptist Church and an emigrationist who was famous for his call to armed resistance for enslaved Africans, "Address to the Slaves of the United States of America." The "Mrs. Tompkins" also listed as a member of this group might be Rev. Garnet's second wife, Sarah Smith Tompkins.

36. Elizabeth, wife of Rev. John N. Gloucester, a Presbyterian minister in Brooklyn and the head of the American Freedmen's Friend Society.

37. wife of John Peterson, the principal of the Colored Public School No. 1 in New York City.

38. wife of Charles L. Reason, an educator who had been the principal of the Institute for Colored Youth in Philadelphia but had returned to New York City in 1855 to teach in the public schools.

39. wife of Dr. James McCune Smith, the physician for the Colored Orphan Asylum.

40. widow of Rev. Peter Williams, pastor of St. Phillip's Episcopal Church, one of New York City's largest African American churches.

41. Benjamin Quarles, *The Negro in the Civil War* (New York: Da Capo Press, 1989, 1953), 242, 246.

42. Broadside, Historical Society of Pennsylvania

43. *Liberator*, 22 April 1864.

44. Maybe Mrs. John C. Chew of Philadelphia.

45. Sylvia G. Dannett, *Profiles of Negro Womanhood, 1619-1900* v. 1 (New York: M.W. Lads, 1964), 79.

46. Hine, 965.

Mary Ann Shadd Cary, who received her law degree from Howard in 1870, is considered the first African American female lawyer but she did not regularly practice law.

47. W.E.B. Du Bois referred to them as the "best families in the city" or the "better class" in *The Philadelphia Negro*.

48. *Christian Recorder*, 4 February 1865.

49. Ladies' Sanitary Association of St. Thomas' Church of Philadelphia (LSASTC), *Annual Report for 1865* (Reel 3, Dorsey Collection, Center for African American History and Culture, Temple University, Philadelphia, Pennsylvania).

50. John C. Chew was a well-to-do barber in Philadelphia.

51. Louise, wife of the famous Philadelphia caterer.

52. Ellis Peer was a confectionary merchant in Philadelphia. This might have been his wife.

53. wife of Rev. Stephen Smith, a philanthropist who was one of the wealthiest African Americans in the nation.

54. Possibly the wife of Thomas J. Bowers, a well known musician who was an organist for St. Thomas' Episcopal Church and a student and member of Elizabeth Taylor Greenfield's musical troupe.

55. LSASTC, *Annual Report for 1865.*

56. Ladies' Union Association, Philadelphia, *Report* (Philadelphia: G.T. Stockdale, 1867), 3.

57. *Philadelphia Tribune*, 18 May 1912.

58. *Pennsylvania Freedmen's Bulletin* (October 1867).

59. *Philadelphia Tribune*, 2 August 1913.

60. *Tidings*,1 January 1866.

61. Henrietta Bowers was a seamstress, according to Charles Blockson, *African Americans in Pennsylvania: a History and Guide.* (Baltimore: Black Classic Press, 1994), 51.

62. Home for Aged and Infirm Colored Persons, *Constitution, By-Laws and Rules and Proceedings of the Second Annual Meeting* (Philadelphia: Merrihew Son, 1866)

63. *Philadelphia Tribune*, 19 July 1913.

64. Home for Destitute Colored Children, *24th Annual Report* (Philadelphia: Press of Lewis and Greene, 1879)

65. McCain, Diana Ross, *Black Women of Connecticut: Achievement Against the Odds* (Hartford, Connecticut Historical Society, 1984), 14.

66. "Letters of Hiram Wilson to Miss Hannah Gray," *Journal of Negro History* 14 (July 1929): 344-350.

67. Hallie Q. Brown, *Homespun Heroines and Other Women of Distinction* (New York: Oxford University Press, 1988, 1926), 134.

68. Oberlin College in Ohio, an abolitionist institution, was one of the first colleges in the country to enroll African Americans and women on the basis of a presumed equality.

69. *Christian Recorder*, 26 December 1863.

70. Mary Still was the sister of the famous underground railroad conductor from Philadelphia, William Still. She also taught in Florida.

71. *Christian Recorder*, 26 August 1865.

72. Quarles, 246.

73. R.J.M. Blackett, *Beating Against the Barriers: the Lives of Six Nineteenth-Century Afro-Americans* (Ithaca, New York: Cornell University Press, 1989), 121.

74. Elizabeth Ware Pearson, ed., *Letters from Port Royal, 1862-1868* (New York: Arno Press, 1969, 1906), 294.

75. Ibid., 56.

76. Ripley, 193-195.

77. Jordan, 70. *In Memoriam of Annetta M. Lane,* published by the Grand United Order of Tents after her death in 1908, does not mention that Lane had been enslaved and it does not mention Harriet R. Taylor.

78. Wendell Phillips Dabney, *Maggie L. Walker and the Independent Order of St. Luke: the Woman and Her Work* (Cincinnati: The Dabney Publishing Co., 1927), 118.

79. George Bragg, *Men of Maryland* (Baltimore: Church Advocate Press, 1925), 55-56.

80. Ibid., 117-118.

81. *National Freedman*, 1 February 1865.

82. Kathleen C. Berkeley, "'Colored Ladies Also Contributed': Black Women's Activities From Benevolence to Social Welfare, 1866-1896," *in The Web of Southern Social Relations: Women, Family, & Education* Eds. Walter Fraser, et al. (Athens: University of Georgia Press, 1985), 181, 190.

83. National Association for the Relief of Destitute Colored Women and Children. *Annual Reports* 1867, 1868, 1877 [In the Historical Society of Pennsylvania, Philadelphia]

Susan King Taylor—teacher, laundress, straight shooter, nurse, historian—in her Women's Relief Corps, Grand Army of the Republic uniform. *(Schomburg Center for Research in Black Culture, New York Public Library)*

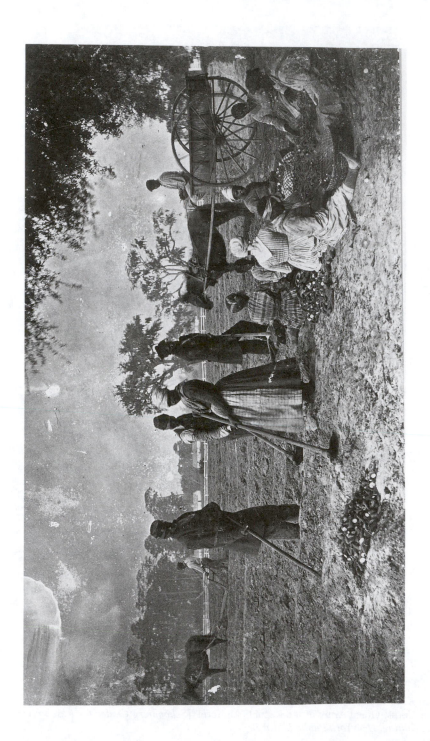

Planting sweet potatoes—James Hopkinson's Plantation, Edisto Island, South Carolina. *(Boston Public Library)*

Cotton crop—Pope's Plantation, Hilton Head, South Carolina. (*Boston Public Library*)

Josephine St. Pierre Ruffin—unofficial recruiter, freedman's relief worker, women's rights activist, editor and African American women's club movement leader. *(Schomburg Center for Research in Black Culture, New York Public Library)*

Mary Ann Shadd Cary—official recruiter, outspoken journalist, suffragist, emigrationist, relief worker, and lawyer. *(National Archives of Canada)*

Laundresses—Drayton's Plantation, Hilton Head, South Carolina. *(Boston Public Library)*

Laundresses—Yorktown, Virginia. (*Schomburg Center for Research in Black Culture, New York Public Library*)

Refugees on barge—canal, Richmond, Virginia. (*Library of Congress*)

Fugitives coming into Union lines—Rappahannock River, Virginia. (*Library of Congress*)

Edmonia Lewis—sculptor. *Schomburg Center for Research in Black Culture, New York Public Library)*

Elizabeth Taylor Greenfield, the "Black Swan"—singer and activist. *(Schomburg Center for Research in Black Culture, New York Public Library)*

Frances Ellen Watkins Harper—orator, poet, writer, and activist. *(Schomburg Center for Research in Black Culture)*

CHAPTER 6

Their Cause Is Our Cause: Succoring African American Soldiers

The Union initially resisted the participation of African American men in the armed forces but were eventually compelled by military necessity to allow black enlistment in the late summer of 1862 with the formation of the 1st Kansas Colored Infantry. General Benjamin Butler then formed the Louisiana Native Guards, made up of free African American men, in September 1862. The 1st South Carolina Infantry was organized a month later by General Rufus Saxton. The famous Massachusetts 54th, the first northern regiment was next in January 1863. The 186,000 black soldiers and 30,000 sailors who participated in the Civil War constituted a significant portion of the African American population. More than one-fifth of all African American males under the age of forty-five served in the Union army. They comprised one-tenth of all Union soldiers and one quarter of all Union sailors.[1] Consequently, many of the women who assisted soldiers through relief organizations had a personal, rather than an abstract, motivation for their benevolence because they were succoring husbands, fathers, brothers, sons and other male relatives and friends.

As soon as African American men were to be officially enlisted in the armed forces, black women formed organizations to give them aid and comfort. Given the climate of racial hostility which existed in the country, African American soldiers' relief associations were, no doubt, established because of the fear and likelihood that white sanitary relief societies would not extend courtesies to black soldiers. For example, Luis Emilio said that due to the animosity of whites in Philadelphia, "Recruiting [of black soldiers for the Massachusetts 54th] there was attended with much annoyance. The gathering-place had to be kept secret, and the men sent to Massachusetts in small parties to avoid molestation or excitement. Mr. Corson was obliged to purchase railroad tickets himself, and get the recruits one at a time on the cars or under cover of darkness."[2]

Like the associations formed to support displaced Africans, the black soldiers' relief organizations were successful because of their massive networking and cooperative nature. The women assisted African American soldiers and the families of troops, nursed the wounded and sick, sent food and other goods, wrote letters for the illiterate and injured, sewed clothes and raised money. They associated with anyone, black or white, whose cause was similar.

Philadelphia, with its relatively wealthy free African American population, had several organizations dedicated to the comfort of soldiers and freedpeople. Fourteen regiments of USCTs were recruited at Camps William Penn and Cadwalader. William Penn was located in Cheltenham, Montgomery County and Cadwalader was on Islington Lane near 20th and Norris Streets. In addition, there was a hospital, Summit, for African American soldiers in the city. "The women played a noble part, and raised large sums for the sick and wounded soldiers, sending committees into the war zone to distribute clothing, dainties and the like."[3]

One organization was the Colored Women's Sanitary Commission, housed at 404 Walnut Street in Philadelphia, which had male, as well as female, officers. Caroline Johnson was the president, Arena Ruffin, the vice president, Rev. Stephen Smith was the treasurer and Rev. Jeremiah Asher held the post of secretary.[4]

The Ladies' Sanitary Association of St. Thomas Episcopal Church in Philadelphia (LSASTC), "believing it a duty we all owe, to assist in quelling this unholy rebellion of the slave power, and sustaining the U.S. Government in establishing Universal Freedom!," gave a fair for sick and wounded soldiers on December 19, 1864 at Concert Hall. The names listed on the flyer[5] identify leading black Philadelphia families:

Mrs. Thomas J. Bowers, President
Mrs. John Chew, Vice-president
Miss Ada Hinton, Corresponding Secretary
Mrs. Thomas [Louise] Dorsey, Treasurer
E. Boddy
C. Christianson
E. Drummond

L. Galloway
Mrs. Gibbons[6]
L. Goines
C. Miller
Mrs. Minton[7]
Mrs. F. Sebastian

Louisa Jacobs, who along with her mother, Harriet, was a leader in relief efforts in the Washington, D.C. area under the patronage of several relief organizations, wrote a letter of grateful acknowledgment to this group. "Accept our hearty thanks for Sanitaries received on the 30th January for sick and wounded soldiers. It is with great pleasure that we acknowledge their receipt; yours being the first colored society which has made us a donation of the kind." Her letter, published in the March 4, 1865 *Christian Recorder*, was an appeal to all African American women to increase their activism.

Louisa used this opportunity to express the motivation behind the activism of women of the LSASTC and other soldiers' relief societies: the sense of duty African American women felt toward the soldiers of their own race. "Your work is a noble one. She who lifts her hand for the elevation of our brave soldiers, sheds a ray of sunlight through some sick and lonely heart."

Recognizing that the fate of African American women was tied to the men of their race, Jacobs expected the women, as the ladies of the LSASTC were doing through their activism, to fulfill their duty as "women":

> Their cause is our cause. By their suffering and death our recognition as a people widens . . . I rejoice that the nation was forced at last to accept the assistance from the men, who, in the beginning of the rebellion, forgetting the wrongs of a life-time, proffered their services to the country. Their patriotism was scorned; but as the storm of war went on, the strength of their arms became a necessity.

If the manhood, and hence citizenship, of African American men could be assured through their valor as soldiers, African American women would also benefit by association:

> And through that necessity has the colored man proved his claim to manhood, his valor commanding respect, even from his enemies

. . . with pride we can point to the fact, that he who was least among men, became a potent help in their dark hour of need. He was not too ignoble to bleed and die, to brave perils and hardships, nor for the honors and emoluments which fall to other men for duties well performed.

However, like many, if not most, African American activists, Louisa Jacobs was compelled to chastise the United States for its continued commitment to white supremacy: "No! the heart of America has yet to grow larger. She sees only the shade of the face, not the merit that stamps the worth of man. He died, (our colored soldier,) for freedom's sake."

Also in Philadelphia was the Soldiers' Relief Association which met on Thursdays at Mother Bethel A.M.E. Church. They placed an ongoing notice in the *Christian Recorder* inviting "all ladies throughout the city and county" to meet with them as they solicit "contributions from the friends of humanity." The committee consisted of:

Jane L. Johnson, President
Esther Armstrong, Secretary
Harriet Bacon
Amelia Brooks
Mary Ann Campbell[8]
Elizabeth Clark
Amelia Howard
Olivia Parker
Sarah Scott
Ann Ware
Emma Williams

Interestingly, the women did not give themselves titles such as "Mrs." or "Miss" as was common during this time. This, no doubt, indicated some measure of class distinction within Philadelphia's African American community. St. Thomas, for example, as opposed to Mother Bethel, was considered the church for the black elite.

Philadelphia had another soldiers' relief organization as well, the Ladies' Union Association (LUA) which was "formed July 20th, 1863 for the Purpose of Administering Exclusively to the Wants of the Sick and Wounded Colored Soldiers." It reorganized on February 26, 1865 to expand its mission to include serving the needs of freedpeople.[9] Unlike many of the other societies, the LUA remained independent of white relief organizations, a fact which spared it an identification with the charges of fraud leveled at some of those groups.

Months in advance of the event, they announced a fair that they were going to be giving on April 17, 1864 at Concert Hall with the appeal: "Feeling that the wants of the soldiers should be attended to by those for whom they are suffering every privation, and doing deeds of valor, we once again earnestly call on the public for assistance . . . we feel that the sacred duty of relieving the sufferings of those who are pouring out their life's blood for the elevation of our race, and the advancement of liberty, should find an echo in every heart, that will make the hands instinctively commence laboring for the cause." The fair made a profit of $360.55 in spite of inclement weather. Two hundred dollars of the proceeds were contributed to the "Penn Relief Association for the benefit of the sick and wounded soldiers."[10]

The Association also "purchased 100 watermelons, 4 baskets of peaches, 4 baskets of citrons, 1 basket of apples, sundry pies, cakes and 6 pounds of tobacco" which were distributed by Amelia Mills, president, Sallie Cole, Sara Louise Iredell [Fleetwood], corresponding secretary, and Emma L. Jackson, vice-president, of the society at Summit Hospital to sick and wounded soldiers in West Philadelphia in August 1864. Interestingly, Emma L. Jackson was also an officer of the LSASTC in 1865. The donation, a very practical and needed contribution, was greatly appreciated by the nearly 500 sick and wounded soldiers.[11]

The LUA was still aiding the hospital in 1865 because they thanked the Ladies' Soldiers' Aid Association of Carlisle in central Pennsylvania for their contribution of $40.00 "for the benefit of the sick and wounded soldiers at the Summit Hospital."[12] By this time, the conditions at the hospital had deteriorated to crisis proportions. There were now "1,200 sick and wounded Negro soldiers [but only] 522 beds, which meant that hundreds of bleeding and dying Negro soldiers, many of whom had lost eyes, arms and legs in defense of the Union were forced to lie on floors and in corridors while awaiting medical treatment."[13] This was what the women of the LUA were anxious to ameliorate.

In addition to the names given earlier, the members of the Association were:

Rebecca Venning, Treasurer
S. Lizzie Brown, Secretary
Mrs. A. Adams
Mrs. Lucy Adger[14]

Mrs. James Aster
Mrs. David Bowers
Mrs. Thomas J. Bowers
Mrs. Joseph Bustill
Mrs. Thomas Davis
Mrs. Henry Johnson
Caroline Le Count
Mary H. Matthews
Mrs. Joseph Wilson[15]

Like the other societies, a great number of the names represented the highest strata of the African American community.

An "observer" remarked in the August 6, 1864 edition of *The Christian Recorder*, that "The Ladies' Union Association deserves the credit and support of the community, as it is laboring successfully for the colored soldiers who have gone from our midst." The association's own report in the same issue details the donations these ladies gave or raised, including one, in a blatant attempt to solicit funds, from "a little girl [who gave] a small box of lint." Surely, if a child could give, adults should contribute, was the thinking.

In 1914, the LUA was still receiving accolades. Charles Bolivar gave them a Mother's Day tribute: "The Ladies Union, who raised money, picked lint and went South, visiting army hospitals with all sorts of comfort and delicacies were likewise mothers."[16] He had said earlier that they "did yeoman service at Camp William Penn, and at army head quarters, delegations going to the front with clothing and other creature comforts."[17]

The Business Committee, led by George Vashon[18], of the State Equal Rights Convention of the Colored People of Pennsylvania, held in February 1865, submitted to that body a resolution which lauded the same organization. This action and the contentious discussion which ensued give a hint of the competition which must have been present between two of the largest relief organizations in Philadelphia—the Ladies' Union Association and the Ladies' Sanitary Association of St. Thomas' Church. The resolution proposed, "of all the many efforts being put forth in the cause of humanity, we recognize none more commendable to the lovers of justice and Christianity, than those of the 'Ladies' Union Association' of Philadelphia, to which this convention tender their warmest thanks, for untiring exertions in relieving the wants of our sick and wounded soldiers, whose suffering can only be imagined but never truly described; and we pledge ourselves to use every influence within our power, to encourage and sustain these ladies in their laudable and benevolent enterprise."

Evidently, however, the participants of this convention were not immune to political and social rivalries because the resolution caused much debate. O.C. Hughes argued for giving the same recognition to other organizations engaged in the same "good cause." Rev. William J. Alston of St. Thomas Church in Philadelphia contended that his church's Ladies' Sanitary Association "had been working, and are now earnestly and persistently, in season and out of season, working for the alleviation of the sufferings of the sick and wounded soldiers." He went on to point out that they had conducted "one of the largest and most successful fairs ever held in Philadelphia, for this cause" and so should be included in the resolution.

William D. Forten, uncle of Charlotte Forten, who authored the resolution, rejoined, however, that unlike the Ladies' Sanitary Association of St. Thomas' Church, the Ladies' Union Association was entirely independent of any white association and that "they were primarily organized for the purpose of relieving the needs of colored sick and wounded troops." He also referred to the fact that "this society had so far sympathized with the objects for which this Convention had been convened, that they had paid their ten dollars and joined the State League." As such, according to Forten, they should be the only ones included in the resolution.

Forten and his supporters lost so the final resolution was amended to include the Ladies' Sanitary Association of St. Thomas Church, the Union Association of Harrisburg and "other similar associations throughout the State."[19] While the minutes of the Convention carry the text of the very long discussion about the propriety of the resolution, there is no mention of the names of the women. However, since many of them were connected by marriage, birth or association to the men at this meeting, it was probably not thought to be necessary to name them since the glory of the women's contributions reflected favorably on the men.

African American women were active on other home fronts also. Several organizations in Norfolk and Portsmouth, Virginia collaborated in 1864 to initiate aid efforts under one umbrella organization, the Ladies' Soldiers' Relief Association. They met at St. John's Chapel in Norfolk and the women of St. Thomas' Episcopal Church were the first to join. Mrs. J.M. Brown and Sallie Daffin were the president and secretary, respectively, of that organization. They called on the African American community, especially the churches "to lend their aid and influence in obtaining funds, and such articles as the necessities of our soldiers demand."[20]

The association's appeal in the August 20, 1864 *Christian Recorder* stated that since African American men "are sacrificing their all upon the altar of freedom" and "experiencing all the fearful horrors of war," women must do their "part in this direction." They were determined to do their "duty to assist in bearing the burden" by giving physical and material aid to the soldiers because while women "are not called upon to enter the field . . . each has a duty to perform equally important." Their efforts gave them "assurance that we, too, have contributed in a measure to the greatest object of our lives." This commitment to black liberation was the overwhelming motivating force for most of the relief groups.

By September 1864, Sojourner Truth was aiding African American soldiers, as well as refugees, in Washington, D.C. under the auspices of the NFRA, as a Visitor and Distributing Agent, and the United States Freedmen's Bureau. Recognizing her own fame and stature, she sold photographs of herself to raise money for travel and other expenses in order to carry on her work. Josephine S. Griffing, white General Agent of the NFRA and a friend of Truth's, acknowledged her contribution, saying that she was "performing important moral and social duties, as well as physical labor for the relief and elevation of her race." Griffing felt Truth, because of her own background of enslavement, had a special rapport with the freedpeople, especially the women, "understanding these people as she does, and naturally drawing them out on subjects they seldom converse upon with others . . . "[21]

In a letter which was published in the *National Anti-Slavery Standard* and the *Liberator*, organs she knew would be interested in reporting on her activities, Sojourner announced, "I am at Freedmen's Village. After visiting the president, I . . . held two meetings in Washington, at Rev. [Henry Highland] Garnet's Presbyterian Church, for the benefit of the Colored Soldiers' Aid Society. These meetings were successful in raising funds."[22] The women, including his wife, Julia, of Rev. Garnet's church, Fifteenth Street Presbyterian Church, were also active in relief work.

In the fall of 1863, before she had gone to the District of Columbia, Truth had organized a Thanksgiving dinner for the 1st Michigan Colored Infantry in Camp Ward, Detroit, Michigan. She collected the donations of food and money and gave a speech at the dinner to the troops.[23] She came back to the east coast to carry on her work.

Lending her sculpting talents to the cause, Edmonia Lewis fashioned a medallion of John Brown and a bust of Colonel Robert Gould Shaw, the white commander who had died along with more than three hundred of the Massachusetts 54th African American soldiers he led at Fort Wagner, South Carolina. She exhibited these pieces in 1864 at the Boston Fair to support the Soldier's Aid Fund.[24] The December 9, 1864 *Liberator* made special mention of Lewis' sculpture of Colonel Shaw. "Among the thousand objects of interest at the Sailors' Fair in Boston was a bust of the hero." The paper went on to quote from another newspaper, "Col. Shaw's family consider it an excellent likeness, and have had it photographed . . . We are sure that many will be thankful to possess a touching and beautiful memorial to one of the ablest in our long list of brave and truthful souls who have gone this early to their reward." Lewis, the paper said, "Undertook to make this likeness of one whom she had never seen, out of grateful feeling 'for what he has done for her race.'"

Edmonia had been successfully defended in 1862 by the lawyer, John Mercer Langston, in a sensational case in which she was accused of poisoning two white female classmates at Oberlin College. She was acquitted but suffered a brutal beating at the hands of white thugs. Langston was an Oberlin graduate who became a recruiter for the Massachusetts 54th Regiment while his wife, Carrie, who had also been an Oberlin student, was instrumental in raising money for a flag for the 55th Massachusetts Regiment. The 55th Regiment was formed after the 54th was filled.

The African American women of Norwich, Connecticut began a Ladies' Aid Society after the 29th Connecticut Colored Infantry was formed in that city. They gave a week-long fair at Breed Hall to raise money to provide for the regiment "every conceivable delicacy that could be imagined, that would bring delight to any one far away from home and longing for its luxuries. There were also useful and needy articles, put up by loving hands, for the brave boys . . . " James L. Smith lauded the women: "Too much cannot be said of the members of the society for their untiring zeal—how they met, through storm and rain—nothing deterred them from their work." After the regiment received the box, E.C. Green wrote to an officer of the 29th, "may I refer you to the pleasure you gave to the ladies of our Soldiers' Aid Society, a year since allowing them to furnish your regiment with a box of hospital supplies, and say to you, if your supplies are at present insufficient, we would be glad to forward another box of similar articles . . . "[25] These women were so anxious to aid the regiment that they begged to be allowed to assist them. Diantha Hodge, representing the ladies of Norwich, presented a flag to the unit as they left for the front and the women gave them a feast when they returned in October 1865.

George E. Stephens, a member of the Massachusetts 54th and a correspondent for the *Weekly Anglo-African*, thanked profusely the Ladies' Soldier's Aid Society of Bridgeport, Connecticut for the "box of goods and delicacies . . . valued at $250" the ladies had sent in November 1863 to the regiment when it was stationed in Hilton Head, South Carolina. The troop, however, had been robbed of the box's contents. Mrs. Jane L. Johnson is mentioned as the society's corresponding secretary.[26]

The Society of Young Rising Daughters of Wilmington, Delaware contributed twenty-three dollars to the Colored Soldiers' Aid Society of that city in August 1864 at the Methodist Episcopal Church. Although, according to a correspondent to the August 20, 1864 *Christian Recorder*, the young ladies endured the scorn of people who did not think they were going to succeed, "they nobly persevered" until they raised the above sum by conducting a fair. In accepting the donation, Daniel Anderson commented that the young women's "acts would have a place in history, and be handed down for the admiration of coming generations yet unborn." The members of the organization included:

Sarah Allen
Susan A. Bostice
Adeline H. Branton
Mary R. Branton
Rebecca Brown
Esther E. Byard
Mary A. Dorsey
Susan(?) Doves
Margaret Elias
Mary E. Hamilton
Adelia Jones
Mary E. Manlapp
Delphine Rice
Rebecca J. Trusty
Rosa E. Trusty
Drusilla Weeb

Soldiers' support organizations existed in the West as well. The Colored Ladies Auxiliary of the Soldiers' Aid Society of Northern Ohio was organized in June 1863 in Cleveland "to promote the cause of our sick and wounded braves." Members included Mary E. Parker, President; Lavinia Sabb, Secretary; Joseph E. Sampson, Corresponding Secretary; and Lucy Stanton Day, wife of the famous abolitionist, William Howard Day, and later a teacher of refugees in the South. It eventually became independent of the Soldiers' Aid Society and did charitable work of its own and with other organizations.

In a letter to the *Weekly Anglo-African*, Sampson, the organization's corresponding secretary, said the women "aided the families of soldiers in our midst, and have sent garments and nourishments to our 5th United States Regiment while sick in the hospital at Camp Delaware, as well as visiting them in person and like ministering angels bathed their feverish brows and moistened their parched lips." A fair raised more than three hundred and twenty-five dollars of which $225 was given to the Sanitary Commission, a national aid society. The remaining $100 was devoted to "other humane purposes." The ladies also gave *Weekly Anglo- African* subscriptions to African American troops at the front. They contributed a valuable pair of vases to a very successful fair held by the Ladies' Sanitary Association of St. Thomas's African Episcopal Church in Philadelphia, showing, as Sampson said, "that the patriotism of our ladies actuates them to cooperate with any enterprise tending to the promotion of a noble end." The Philadelphia group's fair raised more than $1,200.

Sampson wrote the letter in order to champion the work of the organization and to leave a record for history because "if a thing is not told it is never known to any but the receivers." He took this opportunity to "turn darkness into light—by telling you that the ladies of Cleveland are alive to the events of the day, or in other words, are up and doing." Apparently Sampson felt the women of Ohio and other parts west had been slighted. "I am free to confess my jealousy when I read from time to time of the great work that is being performed by the good ladies in almost every city in the East, while so far as newspaper mention goes, apparently we of the far West, occupy the humble seat of do-nothing."[27]

The *Christian Recorder*, however, had given credit to African American women in the West in its May 23, 1863 issue, nearly two years before. "The young ladies of Indianapolis, not willing that their friends, brothers, and lovers, should leave for the seat of war without some public demonstration on their part, gave a donation dinner in the school room. All the delicacies of the season were served up by them, which made the hearts of the volunteers glad to know that they were the recipients of those kind favors, which they promise shall be treasured in their heart of hearts, on the field of battle."

In the same state, Clarissa Hill and Minerva Williams formed a committee to aid the "noble and gallant" African American soldiers from Indiana who had enlisted in the 55th Massachusetts Volunteers, "who are far from home, battling for the rights of their brethren and the cause of freedom."[28] Louisville, Kentucky had a Colored Ladies' Soldier's and Freedman's Aid Society.[29] The city also had "colored soldiers' aid societies, and societies styled Sons and Daughters of the Morning, Daughters of Zion, &c., for relieving disabled colored soldiers, and all other helpless colored sick and afflicted within their reach. They are zealously and efficiently engaged in this good work."[30]

African American women in most other major cities and in many smaller ones, enthusiastically responded to the call to aid black soldiers. Organizations established to lend support to African American servicemen included the Colored Soldiers' Aid Society of Chicago, formed in April 1863 and the Ladies' United Soldier's Relief Association of Portsmouth, Virginia. Hartford, Connecticut had a soldiers' aid society.[31] In Washington, North Carolina, African American women organized a sewing circle to aid the 2nd North Carolina Infantry. Three well-to-do free women from Winchester, Virginia - Marcia Weaver, Mary Strange and Evelina Orrick - contributed food to the Union hospital in the area.[32]

Presenting banners and flags in a public ceremony was a very visible way of showing support for African American soldiers. Women sewed or raised money for regimental flags for their troops. For example, "the noble ladies of New York have made a banner, to be presented" to the 14th Rhode Island Colored Heavy Artillery Regiment in late December 1863.[33] The Colored Ladies' Relief Association provided a state flag to the Massachusetts 54th Regiment, one of the first African American units raised in the north, at a ceremony as they left Boston for the South in May 1863. Massachusetts Governor John A. Andrew presented the flag to the white commander of the 54th, Colonel Robert Gould Shaw. "The Fifty-fourth now holds in possession this sacred charge in the performance of their duties as citizens-soldiers. You will never part with that flag so long as a splinter of the staff, or a thread of its web, remains within your grasp."[34]

The young African American women of the same city gave an American flag to the regiment during the ceremony. Governor Andrew made these remarks: "As the gift of the young ladies of the city of Boston to their brethren in arms, they will cherish it as the lover cherishes the recollection and fondness of his mistress; and the white stripes of its field will be red with their blood before it shall be surrendered to the foe."[35] William Wells Brown noted that, as the unit left Boston, the "sisters, sweethearts, and wives" of the regiment "ran along beside 'the boys,' giving their parting benediction of smiles and tears, telling them to be brave, and to show their blood."[36] By blood, the women meant "nobility." As the first regiment to be recruited in the North, the 54th was looked upon as a test case of the loyalty, valor and honor of the African American community.

Caroline M. Wall Langston, or Carrie, was the wife of John Mercer Langston, a recruiter for the Massachusetts 54th. She led a fundraising effort for a regimental banner for the 55th Massachusetts Regiment which was presented on behalf of the African American women in Ohio. Carrie was aided in her efforts by her friend, Fanny Jackson Coppin, the well-known educator who was then a student at Oberlin College.[37] The heavy silk flag had the inscription, "God and Liberty" on the shields attached to the staff and "Liberty or Death" on the banner.[38]

The women of New Haven, Connecticut raised the money for a flag which was presented to the 29th Connecticut Colored Infantry on January 5, 1864. William W. Grimes, writing to the *Christian Recorder*, was outraged, however, that a white, not a black, man, was chosen to present the flag to the regiment. He expressed his feelings angrily, "In a word, the colored people of Connecticut ought not to complain for a great many of the disadvantages under which they labor, are brought about by their own backwardness; submitting to everything the white men say, without thinking for themselves."[39]

African American women in Philadelphia, under the direction of Mary L. Brown, gave a "soiree dansante" at Franklin Hall on September 16, 1863. The gala was conducted, according to the announcement, "in consequence of the hasty manner in which our 'First Colored Troop [3rd U.S. Colored Infantry],' from Philadelphia, was ordered to the Seat of War, many of their relatives and friends had neither time nor opportunity to wish them a hearty, 'Good Bye.' Desiring to show them our appreciation of their noble patriotism and self-sacrificing spirit which they evidenced, in going forward at the call of their Country to battle, and, if necessary, to die in defence of Liberty and Justice, we wish to send them a handsome REGIMENTAL FLAG! and thereby assure them, though absent, they are not forgotten."[40] Mary Brown, a singer, was a pupil of "The Black Swan," Elizabeth Taylor Greenfield, and the niece of a famous Philadelphia musician and bandleader, Frank Johnson.

The Contraband Relief Association of Washington, D.C. raised the money for a flag for the 1st U.S. Colored Infantry of the United States Infantry in a special campaign for that purpose rather than using money from their treasury. The flag was presented at an elaborate ceremony at the Fifteenth Street Presbyterian Church in the District of Columbia on August 13, 1863, the first anniversary of the Association's founding. Elizabeth Keckley, the President of the CRA, said, "We wished to inspire with zeal and courage those who were to go forth and battle with the enemy, that they might distinguish themselves, not as *cowards*, but as men . . . We felt it to be our duty to do something . . . If these men are to go forth in defence of Union and liberty, surely it is the least we can do to sympathize with, encourage and assist them . . . "

They contracted with David Bustill Bowser[41], a famous artist from Philadelphia, who designed the banner. Bowser used an eagle,[42] a symbol of the Union, on one side of the flag. The other side had a Goddess of Liberty with her foot on the head of a serpent giving a musket to an African American soldier with "a look of deep earnestness on his manly face." The images were to "inspire the hearts of this proscribed race of mankind." Captain James Ferree, a white commander, accepted the flag on behalf of the regiment. "Ladies of the Contraband Relief Association, we thank you; and permit me to say that the colored brother represented on the beautiful flag you have given us, with a musket in his hands, is the emblem of the salvation of the white race."[43]

Further south, the Colored Women's Union Relief Association of Newbern, North Carolina presented a regimental standard to Brigadier General Edward A. Wild's 1st North Carolina Infantry on July 30, 1863 in Boston, Massachusetts. The banner was "made of blue silk, with a yellow silk fringe around the border. On one side the Goddess of Liberty is represented with her right foot resting on a copperhead[44] snake. On the reverse side, a large gilt rising sun, with the word 'Liberty' in very large letters over the sun."[45] The inception of this effort was highlighted in the June 20, 1863 *Christian Recorder*: "the women [have] assembled together at various places for the purpose of presenting a national ensign of freedom to their husbands and sons, for them to fight under triumphantly on the field of battle, in honor of the cause of freedom to their race . . . "

The organization itself conveyed its objective of succoring African American troops by placing their constitution in the July 4, 1863 *Christian Recorder*. "We, the colored women of Newbern, North Carolina, desire to give to the world our object, plans, constitution, and our officers, for the purpose of ameliorating the miseries of our colored soldiers in their struggle for freedom, whatever may be the occasion against oppression." Clearly the signers of this constitution understood the nature of the African American soldier's participation in the Civil War.

The large number of signers and the use of "Mrs.," "Miss," and last names say that Newbern obviously had a well-to-do and active free black population. The document was signed by

Mrs. Mary Ann Starkey, President
Mrs. Hannah Snell, Vice-president
Mrs. Sarah Ann White, Secretary
Mrs. G. Richardson, Assistant Secretary
Mrs. Phillis Henderson, Treasurer
Mrs. L. Newton, President of the Committee
Mrs. C. Blackshere
Mrs. Tamar Bryan
Mrs. Emily Bryon
Mrs. Mary Bryon
Miss Eliza Bunson
Mrs. Caroline Coats
Mrs. Jane Coats
Mrs. P.A. Cook
Miss Hannah Green
Mrs. M.A. Green
Miss Nancy Harris
Mrs. Rosanna Harris
Mrs. Louisa Hicks
Mrs. Juno Jones
Miss Cassy Lawrence
Mrs. E. Lewis
Miss Eliza Lewis
Miss Nancy Lucky
Mrs. Hagar Pitt
Mrs. Hannah Stanley
Miss Katy Stanly
Mrs. Hetty Ward
Mrs. L. Washington
Miss Priscilla Whitfield
Mrs. Rosanna Whitfield
Mrs. D. York

There seems to have been another group of not-so-well-off African American women in Newbern who raised money for a standard for the same regiment. The women had managed to accumulate one hundred dollars for the flag by soliciting donations from the African Americans in the area. The contribution "was almost all in small silver—three-cent pieces, half dimes, and dimes—from the scanty savings of the slave subscribers." According to the August 1863 *Douglass' Monthly*, this was "the first subscription made by slave women in the United States for a flag for colored soldiers." The newsletter gave the transcript of Marian Haight's appeal to the women of Newbern: "Ladies old and young, one and all. I call on you in this time of our great struggle for liberty. We, a portion of us do intend to go forward and try and collect money enough to purchase a decent flag for our colored soldiers and gentlemen for it is [our] good and the good of our daughters that our husbands and sons do enlist to fight our battles and gain our liberty. Therefore, there remains a work for us to do and 'Let us rise and do our part cheerfully. Please give me something to aid us in this matter.'"[46] Their effort was obviously successful because a hundred dollars was a substantial amount from recently freed women who, no doubt, had many other pressing demands on their nickels and dimes.

Two weeks after Union troops occupied Charleston, South Carolina, the African American women of that city presented three flags to the African American regiments in an elaborate ceremony. They also gave flowers to the officers and a white swan fan which was forwarded to President Abraham Lincoln.[47]

Even the women of the notorious Camp Nelson in Kentucky presented a banner. "One woman procured and presented a flag to the 116th Regiment Colored Infantry, in behalf of the women of Garrad County, Ky., and the rebel white people threatened to cut her throat for doing it if she did not leave."[48] The camp was infamous for its abuse of African American women by white soldiers and the surrounding white community. Given the treatment of the women in the camp, in general, the response of the whites was to be expected in the case of the woman who presented the flag to the 116th.

The recipients of aid and flags made public expressions of gratitude not only to acknowledge the efforts of the women but as a public relations stratagem to solicit even more support. These open displays fostered a bit of healthy competition between the women in different cities who vied with each other to see who could raise the most money, give the finest flag or conduct the biggest fair. Sallie Daffin, a teacher of freedpeople as well as a relief worker in Norfolk and Portsmouth, Virginia, publicly recognized Philadelphia's Mother Bethel Sabbath School Association's donation of "a box of clothing, books, papers, &c." which she duly "distributed among the sick and wounded soldiers and sailors, at the Portsmouth [Virginia] hospitals." The acknowledgment was published in the April 1, 1865 *Christian Recorder* and it included an appeal to "friends in the North . . . [to] continue to render us their assistance in this great work for our people."

Daffin also gave a public appreciation from Norfolk's Ladies' Soldiers' Aid Association for boxes received from Philadelphia's Ladies' Sanitary Association of St. Thomas' Episcopal Church and from the Soldiers' Aid Society of Wilmington, Delaware. She highlighted their donations and relayed the "unfeigned and lasting gratitude of many of our brave, wounded boys" that the ladies' "benevolence and charity benefited."[49]

Mary Magnos, President of the Norfolk, Virginia Ladies' Soldiers Aid Association and an instructor of freedpeople, sent a letter to another Philadelphia relief organization, the Ladies' Union Association, thanking them for a box they had sent to Norfolk. "Your box reached me in safety this morning; and I assure you it was thankfully received by us, and I know that it will be received with tenfold feelings of gratitude by the dear sick and wounded colored soldiers now in our midst . . . [It] is a source of great gratification and pleasure to me to be able to do something for our noble and devoted soldiers, who are giving their lives for the cherished liberties that have always been withheld from us by tyrant hands, and are now fighting that we may now enjoy these liberties." The Ladies' Union Association had the letter printed in the August 27, 1864 *Christian Recorder*.

Sergeant Major Thomas R. Hawkins of the 6th USCI wrote to the *Weekly Anglo-African*, thanking "Mesdames [Mary] Magnos and Slith, also to Misses Frances E. Williams, E.[Edmonia] Highgate, and a host of others" of the Norfolk Ladies' Soldiers Aid Association for their aid to African American soldiers.[50] Sergeant Henry S. Hammond of Company B, 3rd USCI wrote from Morris Island, South Carolina to Central Presbyterian Church in Philadelphia: "give my thanks to those philanthropic ladies of your church, and tell them the soldiers of the third U.S.C.T., will cherish the memory of that act of kindness in the hour of danger, and prove themselves worthy . . . "[51] Rev. Henry McNeal Turner, Chaplain of the 1st USCI, took pains to give accolades to Mrs. Henry Cover and the Colored Ladies' Soldiers' Relief Association in

Georgetown, District of Columbia for their gift of $20 and other items. "To say this was noble, would be to use an epithet entirely inadequate. Let the act then speak for itself."[52]

As men, African American soldiers were fighting the collective cause of all African Americans. "They have come forward by thousands, and rallied around the so called 'banner of the free,' hoping that by preserving it from the hands of the enemy to make our beloved country free—what she has so long been called in song and story: 'The land of the free and the home of the brave,'—after two hundred years or more of oppression and injustice, and having not only their rights as citizens, but their manhood ignored . . . "[53] The redemption of their manhood through military service meant the elevation of the race as a whole. African American women, therefore, worked collectively to ensure that their men received the support necessary to do their duty as men.

NOTES

1. William Loren Katz, *Breaking the Chains: African-American Slave Resistance* (New York: Atheneum, 1990), 160-161.

2. Luis F. Emilio, *A Brave Black Regiment: History of the Fifty-fourth Regiment of Massachusetts Volunteer Infantry 1863-1865* (New York: Bantam Books, 1992, 1894), 10.

3. *Philadelphia Tribune*, 2 February 1913.

4. Frank H. Taylor, *Philadelphia in the Civil War* (Philadelphia: The City, 1913), 189. It is interesting that this is the only African American female organization in Philadelphia he refers to in his book, given the more prominent position of three others.

Asher was the pastor of Shiloh Baptist Church in Philadelphia and the chaplain of the 6th USCI of Pennsylvania.

5. Broadside, Historical Society of Pennsylvania.

6. Perhaps the wife of John Gibbons, who owned a carpentry business.

7. Most likely from the family of Henry Minton, famous Philadelphia caterer and restauranteur.

8. Mary Ann Campbell was the wife of Rev. Jabez Campbell who was an elder at Mother Bethel and an editor of the *Christian Recorder*.

9. Ladies' Union Association, Philadelphia. *Report* (Philadelphia: G.T. Stockdale, 1867), 3.

10. *Christian Recorder*, 30 April 1864.

11. *Christian Recorder*, 3 September 1864.

12. *Christian Recorder*, 1 April 1865.

13. John A. Saunders, *100 Years After Emancipation: History of the Philadelphia Negro 1787-1963* (Philadelphia: Free African Society, 1964),79-80.

14. Wife of Robert Mara Adger, a businessman, founder of Benjamin Banneker Institute in Philadelphia and Director of the Philadelphia Building and

Loan Association. Lucy had performed with the famous "Black Swan," Elizabeth Taylor Greenfield's musical troupe.

15. *Christian Recorder*, 4 February 1865; *Philadelphia Tribune*, 28 February 1914.

16. *Philadelphia Tribune*, 23 May 1914.

17. Ibid., 28 February 1914.

18. George Vashon, a lawyer and educator, was the husband of Susan Paul Vashon who conducted sanitary relief bazaars in Pittsburgh, Pennsylvania for sick and wounded soldiers and refugees.

19. State Equal Rights Convention of the Colored People of Pennsylvania, February 8th, 9th, and 10th, 1865, *Proceedings, February 8th, 9th, and 10th, 1865* (Philadelphia: The Convention, 1865), 15-17.

20. *Christian Recorder*, 20 August 1864.

21. National Freedmen's Relief Association of the District of Columbia, *Fourth Annual Report* (Washington, DC: McGill & Witherow, 1866), 15.

22. Bert J. Loewenberg and Ruth Bogin, eds., *Black Women in Nineteenth-Century American Life: Their Words, Their Thoughts, Their Feelings* (University Park: Pennsylvania State University, 1976), 236.

23. Carleton Mabee, *Sojourner Truth: Slave, Prophet, Legend* (New York: New York University Press, 1995), 117.

24. Dorothy C. Salem, ed., *African American Women: a Biographical Dictionary* (New York: Garland Publishing, 1993), 327.

25. James L. Smith, *Autobiography* (Norwich, CT: Press of the Bulletin Company, 1881), 118-119.

26. Donald Yacovone, ed., *A Voice of Thunder: the Civil War Letters of George E. Stephens* (Urbana: University of Illinois Press, 1997), 293-294.

27. *Weekly Anglo-African*, 4 February 1865.

28. *Christian Recorder*, 12 December 1863.

29. Bettye Collier-Thomas, *Black Women Organized for Social Change, 1800-1920* (Washington, DC: Bethune Museum-Archives, 1984), 26.

30. *New York Times*, 13 March 1865.

31. Yacovone, 294.

32. Jordan, 87.

33. *Christian Recorder*, 26 December 1863.

34. William Wells Brown, *The Negro in the American Rebellion* (New York: Citadel Press, 1971, 1867), 148.

35. Ibid., 152.

36. Ibid., 155.

37. William Cheek and Aimee Lee Cheek, *John Mercer Langston and the Fight for Black Freedom* (Urbana: University of Illinois Press, 1989), 393.

38. *Douglass' Monthly* (August 1863).

39. *Christian Recorder*, 20 February 1864.

40. Broadside, Library Company of Philadelphia.

41. Bowser was the cousin of Sarah Mapps Douglass and her brother, Robert, who was also a well-known artist. They were all members of the well-to-do,

activist family, the Bustills. Probably the most famous descendant of this family is Paul Robeson, the famous singer, peace activist and sufferer for principle.

42. The eagle has been, of course, the United States' national bird since 1782; the serpent represented Confederates and their sympathizers.

43. *Christian Recorder*, 22 August 1863.

44. "copperhead" was also used to refer, in a derogatory way, to northerners who supported the South during the Civil War

45. *Christian Recorder*, 4 July 1863.

46. It is possible that the two groups of ladies are the same but the correspondent from the *Independent* as reported in *Douglass' Monthly* is so condescending in telling the story while the *Christian Recorder* treats the women with the utmost respect that it is difficult to see them as the same. Plus, Marian Haight's name is not mentioned in the *Recorder* article. I have a suspicion that the former is motivated by the condescending racial and gender attitudes typical of his day because he uses the ubiquitous "black dialect" and misspellings, etc.

47. Benjamin Quarles, *The Negro in the Civil War* (New York: Da Capo Press, 1989, 1953), 328.

48. Western Freedmen's Aid Commission, *Second Annual Report* (Cincinnati: Methodist Book Concern, 1865), 31.

49. *Christian Recorder*, 26 November 1864.

50. *Christian Recorder*, 20 August 1864.

51. *Christian Recorder*, 20 February 1864.

52. *Christian Recorder*, 27 August 1864.

53. Smith, 97.

CHAPTER 7

Ties of Consanguinity and Love: Teaching Freedpeople

Despite the fact that the white Yankee schoolmarm has come to represent all teachers of freedpeople, many of the African American women active in the war effort devoted their attention to educating newly freed Africans. The most logical reason for the white female as the symbol of Civil War and Reconstruction teachers is that they were in the majority. For example, two-thirds of the teachers hired by the American Missionary Association (AMA), the largest agency providing teachers to the South, were females. Most of them were white but many were African American. Unfortunately, some of the organizations, like the National Freedmen's Relief Association, contributed to the construction of the white schoolmarm symbol by not indicating the race of its teachers. While the omission of a teacher's race was oftentimes due to a commendable desire to avoid racial distinctions, the lack of such information makes the African American women, and hence their contribution, invisible.

A great many sources only mentioned that a teacher was "colored." For example, the *Pennsylvania Freedmen's Bulletin* listed several white teachers and principals, by name, but said simply that a principal in Shelbyville, Alabama was "assisted by two Colored teachers."[1] In another instance the same publication said that a "young colored woman was sent as teacher" to Person County, North Carolina at the request of an "association of African Baptist churches" in the county who were raising money to build churches and schools for themselves. The association was only able to "give the teacher her board and do her washing free of charge; this last being the special contribution of one poor woman to the cause of education among her people."[2] Surely such benevolence, on the part of the teacher as well as the laundress, deserved to be acknowledged by giving the names of the women making such major sacrifices. Despite such indifference on the part of white agencies and the outright racism they encountered, many African American women enthusiastically sought employment as teachers or set up their own schools.

The teachers were influenced by the rhetoric of self-help and moral improvement which had long been a part of African American social thought in the black community. They and those being taught believed education held the key to full citizenship and self-reliance. Lizzie, writing from Lower Morrow, Ohio in the June 24, 1865 *Christian Recorder*, articulated this point when she wrote, "unless we educate ourselves, we must perish in our ignorance." Instructors also knew that the destiny of the freedpeople would be their own fate because white public opinion, and therefore public policy, made very little distinction between classes of African Americans.

Usually freeborn, highly educated, socially connected and already teachers, African American educators hoped to contribute to the process of uplift by acting as intermediaries between a racist system and the newly-liberated people confronting that system for the first time. With true missionary zeal, Sara Stanley, who had attended Oberlin College, said, "my motive is to serve these people, to utter a plea for those who have no voice to plead for themselves."[3] In keeping with the principle of uplift through service, several of the teachers were also active in relief and other charitable ventures. By doing so, they made strong alliances with each other as well as with the African American communities in which they taught.

Most felt that they, as African Americans, would have better success with the freedpeople, especially as role models for proper conduct and self-reliance. According to Sallie Daffin, "how much soever those of other races may sympathize with them, yet none can so fully experience the strength of their needs, nor understand the means necessary to relieve them as we who are identified with them."[4] Edmonia Highgate asserted, "Colored teachers when *imbued* with the right *spirit and properly qualified* [should be] *in the front ranks of this work.*"[5]

Eventually teaching for the American Missionary Association in Port Deposit, Maryland and Chickahominy, James City County in Virginia, Ellen Garrison Jackson of Concord, Massachusetts made a fervent plea in June 1863 to the Association to be in the front ranks: "I have a great desire to go and labor among the Freedmen of the South. I think it is our duty as a people to spend our lives trying to elevate our own race . . . Who can feel for us if we do not feel for ourselves? And who can feel the sympathy that we can who are identified with them?"[6]

Jackson is an excellent illustration of the interconnectedness of the northern free African American community. Before going to Boston, she had been a member of Concord's anti-slavery society. Jackson received a letter of introduction from Mary Brooks of the Concord Anti-Slavery Society to Maria Weston Chapman, a leading white Boston abolitionist. Brooks, also white, referred to Jackson as "a very intelligent girl for one of so few advantages" and mentioned that Jackson won prizes "most frequently in our common schools for superiority of learning."[7]

In Boston, though, Jackson was absorbed into the African American community. She became a member of the activist church, Joy Street Baptist, which was started by the abolitionist Rev. Thomas Paul. The American Anti-Slavery Society first organized in his church. A school for African American children was held in the basement of the church. Susan Paul Vashon, the organizer of sanitary relief bazaars in Pittsburgh, Pennsylvania was Paul's granddaughter. Rev. J. Sella Martin, an advocate of the right of the enslaved to engage in armed revolt and a sometime supporter of emigration, would most likely have been Jackson's pastor at the church because he led the church until 1862. The women of the church, including Rev. Martin's wife, Sarah, organized the Fugitive Aid Society of Boston which collaborated with the women of the Twelfth Baptist Church to form a branch of Elizabeth Keckley's Contraband Relief Association. Jackson was presumably one of the women involved in this group, as was Josephine St. Pierre Ruffin who sewed clothes for refugees at Twelfth Baptist.

Lucy Stanton Day was another educator imbued with the right spirit and proper qualifications who wanted to be in the front ranks of educating freedpeople. The wife of the famous abolitionist William Howard Day and a 1850 graduate of Oberlin College, she said in her application to the AMA: "I wish to engage in this work because I desire the elevation of my race." Day felt she was ideally suited for the work due to "my practical knowledge of labor, my love for, and identity of race."[8] She had had this sense of commitment to her people for a long time, having uttered the biblical injunction in her graduation address from Oberlin, "When I forget you, Oh my people, may my tongue cleave to the roof of my mouth, and my right hand forget her cunning."[9] Lucy practiced what she preached by becoming an instructor of freedpeople, although not for the AMA who rejected her application.

Day, who was very light-skinned, recalled an incident from her childhood which contributed to her reverence for education. She had attended the local white school in Cleveland, Ohio, until a white Baptist minister pressured the school to dismiss her. "She never forgot his coming into the classroom, pointing at her, and saying aloud, 'Everything is all right but one, and that is that little dark face.'" As a result of this incident, her stepfather constructed a school for African American children at his own expense in the city.[10]

Rebecca Primus of Hartford, Connecticut enthusiastically left very comfortable middle class surroundings to be sent to Royal Oak in Talbot County, Maryland by the Hartford Freedmen's Aid Society in December 1865. She set up a school there "under the auspices of the Baltimore Association—an organization formed solely for the moral and educational improvement of the colored people of that state." The school was partially funded and maintained by the African American community of Royal Oak.

Josephine Booth, a friend from Hartford who was also teaching freedpeople in Oxford, Maryland, expressed what she saw as the mission of African American teachers. "I have found the people friendly and hospitable so far, and my coming among them with plain manners and a desire to benefit them I think will meet with success. And above all I shall endeavor to impress upon them their moral and religious obligations. Let us Rebecca who have had the advantages of knowledge and Christian culture lift up the standard of Truth and Peace . . . "[11]

Although similarly constrained by contemporary class distinctions, Rebecca was less sanctimonious, however. The well-read and articulate teacher fit in well with the people she was serving, finding them human, humorous and engaging, albeit different. In fact, she married Charles Thomas, her landlord during her stay in Royal Oak and a commissioner of her school, when he became a widower. Thomas had been enslaved but had managed to acquire property and apparently some education. The couple lived in Hartford after their marriage.

Rebecca's school began with ten day and 26 evening students but quickly increased to seventy-five; a Sabbath School had between 50 and 60 members. The students, adults as well as children, made rapid progress. So soon out of enslavement, most could not read "but they are industrious, & hopeful of the future, their interest in the school is unabated & many of them deny themselves in order to sustain it." In two years' time, "many learned [the alphabet,] & also to read in 'Sheldon's First Reading Book' quite well, now they're using 'Hillards Third Reader', can spell well, study

Geog. & Arith. & are learning to write. The children can make figures rapidly & write upon slates legibly."[12]

Primus had been a teacher in Hartford's segregated schools. In her new post, she pushed the African American residents of the Royal Oak community to build a school house which was completed in October 1867 with the help of people in Hartford. She did much of the fundraising. At the opening of the new school, the African American community raised an additional $100 to support the school and voted to name it Primus Institute after Rebecca.[13] Although much of the history of the school, especially information about Rebecca, has been lost by the Royal Oak community, the building is apparently still standing, having last been used in the late 1960's. Many of the older residents remember attending the now deteriorating two-room school as children.[14]

Her mother, Mehitable Primus, was very active in the campaign to raise funds as well. Charles Thomas thanked Mrs. Primus on behalf of "the denizens of our little village" for "the action you have taken in prospering the cause of education with us—I refer to your donation of funds for assistance in erecting our model school-house. This benevolent act, my dear madam, is, and will be cherished by the many who are deriving the benefit of the same." It is apparent, however, that her future son-in-law was trying to impress Mrs. Primus with his erudition, especially when he referred to her daughter. "The lady-like deportment, sterling ability, and real personal worth of your highly esteemed daughter, late in charge of our flourishing school has been particularly spoken of by our white friends, and she has left us with many regrets."[15]

Rebecca recognized what a hardship it was for these newly freed people to erect and sustain the school but it was a point of pride to her for them to be self-sufficient. This was especially true since she could see that already, freedom meant exploitation and pseudo-enslavement for them. "Although the whites are mostly secesh (secessionists) here they all give colored men and women employment. The greatest difficulty is they do not pay sufficient wages and if the people will not accept their terms they send off and get 'contrabands' as they are here denominated, to work for them so that it takes the labor right out of these people's hands and they are obliged to submit. I hope there will be justice, impartial justice, given to the colored people one of these days . . . " Rebecca made a distinction between the African Americans in Maryland and the refugees in the District of Columbia. "The freed men, women, etc. in Washington are a different class of people from those in this state I am told."

The only hope for African Americans was through the exercise of the franchise, according to Primus. "I'm glad there is so much sympathy manifested in behalf of the Colored man's rights, and I hope the subject will continue to be agitated throughout the country by our smart and intelligent colored men as well as white, until these rights which are so unjustly withheld from us now, have been obtained." Primus did her part, as a woman, by preparing freedmen for the "intelligent" exercise of their rights. She placed the responsibility for securing rights on African American men but felt that the attainment of rights would benefit all African Americans.

A picture of what life was like for northern African Americans who went South to teach can be gleaned from Primus' well-written, insightful and humorous letters to her family back in Hartford. Her letters also mention several African American teachers who are largely absent from historical sources. On arriving in Baltimore on her way to Royal Oak she stayed at an African American house, "a pleasant boarding place with a very agreeable family and on a delightful street—it is the rendezvous for the colored teachers under this society." One of the new teachers was "a colored lady - almost white - from Canada"; she did not give her name.[16] Rebecca was amazed at the number of African Americans in Baltimore. Of course, coming from Hartford with its relatively small African American population, Baltimore must have seemed like a wellspring of black culture and life.

The records of white funding and sponsoring agencies also give an idea of what the experience of black teachers was. AMA records, for example, are replete with documents attesting to the discrimination and violence the African American instructors endured, and challenged. Other organizations also record the racial problems African American teachers faced. Black educators were segregated and given inferior accommodations by the officials of white organizations. They were discriminated against in traveling accommodations and insulted on southern streets. Whites hostile to black education attacked teachers and burned schoolhouses.

At the very least, African American teachers expected the organizations they worked for and the people hired by those groups to be relatively free of racism. They saw racial discrimination as inconsistent with the "Christian" principles these agencies supposedly espoused. Sara G. Stanley complained to William Woodbury about her white supervisor, W.S. Coan, who she felt held "peculiar, secession, pro-slavery, anti-Christian, negro hating principles, and malign prejudices" and who took pleasure in advocating the inferiority of 'negroes' and the necessity of social distinctions, with special application to colored missionary teachers." She went on to point out the special nature of the AMA's work among freedpeople. "You will please understand Professor, that I am not advocating a social unity of the races in New York or New England. I fully apprehend the distinctions of Society, and at the North Mr. Coan would have an incontrovertible right to select his own circle of acquaintances, and without any detriment to any persons or any things; but here, in the missionary field, it is different. He has no right to pursue any course that will militate in the slightest degree against the Cause he professes to serve."[17] Edmonia Highgate penned a postscript concurring with Stanley's complaint.

Stanley again complained to George Whipple, another white AMA official, this time about the white matron, Fannie Gleason, who had refused to return to the AMA house in Norfolk until the African American instructors housed there, including Stanley, were removed. She commented facetiously, "If we could entirely set aside the fact of individual responsibility, we might, in consideration of her former surroundings, and the fact that her intellectual training has not perhaps been as thorough and extended as some others of us, pass by this expression of her feelings with indifference. But as the character of nations, communities, societies depend upon the character of individuals composing them, there can be Truth, Honesty, Equity, in the whole, only as these qualities inhere in individuals."[18] Clearly, Sara Stanley was not cowed by the racism she encountered. She continued to call to task whites who violated her sense of racial justice.

Apparently, the AMA did not remove Gleason from her post because in 1868 she was successful in preventing an instructor, Phebe Henson, from living in the AMA house in Norfolk. Henson was from New Bedford, Massachusetts, but had been born in Norfolk. Writing to an AMA official, Gleason admitted, "I do not quite like the idea of having colored teachers in our family; we tried the experiment here in 63 and 64 [she's referring to the incidents with Stanley and other instructors] and it was not a success . . . I do not like to mix up the two races. Perhaps you will say I'm prejudiced to color. I will take them separate without mixing."[19] She must have felt very comfortable expressing such feelings to the agency which employed her and she must have been correct since there is no record that she suffered any repercussions.

Another white AMA teacher, Mary Reed, also felt comfortable acknowledging her racism. She wrote to the Association that she was "willing to teach freedmen but did not wish to eat and sleep with them, including teachers."[20] Like Gleason, Reed assumed she had the right to discriminate against African Americans. Segregationists were to use the same personal preference of association argument to deny African Americans access to public accommodations later, spurring the 1960s Civil Rights Movement.

In 1868, Stanley wanted to hold her wedding to a white man at the Mobile, Alabama AMA house where she boarded. The white AMA official in Mobile, George A. Putnam, objected to having the wedding at the house ostensibly for fear of the reaction of whites in the community. Naturally, the AMA felt the sting of Stanley's disapproval. She wrote to the Association's secretary, J.R. Shipherd, alerting him to the problem. "As an officer of an Association established upon the principle of human Brotherhood, God being no respecter of persons, you see the matter in the light of simple right and justice, rather than that of unchristian prejudice . . . The injury Mr. Putnam purposes doing me would be far greater than any injury caused to others by a contrary course. Something is due me in the matter as a woman simply. Your delicacy of perception will at once show you how my character would be compromised by a refusal to be allowed to be married in the house where I have lived, and to be required to skulk away as if I were committing a crime . . . My marriage at this house I consider as an act of common justice . . . "[21] She married Charles A. Woodward in the home of a friend, however, but not before challenging the AMA to do the right thing: "I expect to be married and leave for the North early next week but I wish first for you either to avow or disavow Mr. P[utnam]'s acts."[22] The Association sidestepped the issue when they ruled that no AMA teacher could be married until she resigned her commission so that Stanley, if no longer employed by the AMA, would not have been able to use their facilities.

White AMA teachers at a refugee school at the infamous Camp Nelson, Kentucky circulated a petition which was forwarded to the Association asking for the removal of seventeen-year-old E. Belle Mitchell Jackson, a new teacher at the school, because they did not want to share quarters with her. John G. Fee, a white abolitionist and the superintendent of the camp, had hired Jackson and supported her stay in the face of white opposition. "A chaplain to one of the regiments, whose home was down in Maine, together with some army officials also boarding at the hall, protested against this young woman's eating in the common boarding-hall. All the lady teachers (white) sent there by the American Missionary Association and the Freedman's Aid Society, refused, with two exceptions, to come to the first tables whilst the young woman was eating. She was, in person, tidy, modest, comely . . . A major, whose home was in Illinois, and the steward, whose home was in the same State, came to me and suggested that I remove the young woman . . . I said, 'I will suffer my right arm torn from my body before I will remove the young woman . . . [She] is fitted for her position; she is modest and discreet; she is a Christian, and as such Christ's representative: What I do to her I do to him.'" In spite of such strong and righteous support, Jackson was removed and Fee was demoted.[23]

Jackson was eventually hired by the AMA to teach at the Missionary Free School of Color in Lexington, Kentucky in 1865. She also attended Kentucky's interracial Berea College[24] in 1867 with which Fee was associated. Her husband was a trustee of the college. She is best known, however, for her part in founding the Colored Orphan Industrial Home in Lexington in 1892.

Lucy Stanton Day's application to teach for the AMA was rejected allegedly because she was the sole support of her seven-year-old daughter. This criterion did not exclude white female applicants from positions with the AMA, however.[25] Dorothy Sterling gives another possible reason for Day's rejection—the fact that the Association may have been reluctant to offend the famous abolitionist, William Howard Day, although he had evidently abandoned his wife, leaving her and their child without support before she finally divorced him. In due time, Lucy Stanton Day went to Mississippi in 1871 without the support of agencies like the AMA and taught in the public school systems.[26]

Another Oberlin-educated woman, Mary S. Patterson Leary, a widow, was also refused a post by the AMA. Again, the reason given was that she had a child. Obviously, in spite of her background, just as in Day's case, the Association did not see fit to apply the criteria for employment equitably to African American and white women because there were white women with children who were hired as matrons by the organization.

Leary was the widow of Lewis Sheridan Leary who joined and was killed in John Brown's raid on Harper's Ferry. She later married another believer in armed resistance, Charles Langston, the brother of John Mercer Langston. To honor other African revolutionaries, they named their two sons, Dessalines and Nathaniel Turner. Their daughter, Carrie, was the mother of another revolutionary, this time in the field of poetry, Langston Hughes.

Clara Duncan, an orphan who had worked as a domestic to pay her way through Oberlin, complained from Norfolk, Virginia in a December

1864 letter to William Woodbury, the white superintendent of the Norfolk AMA schools, that a white woman, Mrs. Brown, hired by the Association needed to be removed because of her racist conduct. She insisted that there is "the absolute need of a change" since the woman has "no interest in the cause [she] is not the best person to have charge of a Mission House."[27] Sallie Daffin made the same complaint about the woman, apparently to no avail.

Not only were Blanche Harris and Pauline Freeman[28] discriminated against in the steamboat on the way to their posts in Natchez, Mississippi but they endured the racism of white Association teachers while in Natchez. They were segregated from white teachers and given inferior accommodations on the steamboat and the AMA official [Rev. Sela G. Wright] accompanying them did not defend what they saw as their basic civil rights. In fact, Wright contended to the AMA that the agency had made a mistake in sending African American teachers South and that the young ladies' presence on the trip, not the racist incident, made it "unpleasant for all of us."[29] The women had, of course, protested their treatment.

Later, an AMA official in Natchez insisted that Harris move from the home of an African American woman she was boarding with to the AMA Mission House. She asserted in a letter to George Whipple that she preferred to live with African Americans because "our influence would be greater." If she went to the Mission House, "I would be obliged to room with two of the domestics, and that I must not expect to eat at the first table, and might come in the sitting room sometimes. My room was to be my home." Unwilling to live under such conditions, she rented rooms from another African American family.

Her letter reported that while the white officials wanted to remove the African American teachers from Natchez, "the colored people seemed equally determined to have us remain, and they would support us." The African American community was concerned that the new school for freedpeople the AMA was building would not have African American educators. The teachers were told by Wright that "although he brought us down we could not compare with the white ladies. One of the ministers, Baptist, wished to know if we had lost our knowledge coming down here."[30]

African American teachers endured physical violence as well as the emotional assaults engendered by racism. Whites threatened to burn Edmonia Highgate's school in Lafayette Parish, Louisiana in 1866. "There has been much opposition to the school. Twice I have been shot at in my room. My night scholars have been shot but none killed. The rebels have threatened to burn down the school and house in which I board . . . "[31] Martha Hoy's school in Trappe, Maryland was burned in April 1866. Another teacher, a Miss Dickson, was attacked in the same town. Hoy was immediately posted to Burkittsville, Frederick County, Maryland after her school was burned. She wrote of her new school: "Most of the colored people are very poor here, but they are industrious and hard-working, greatly desirous that their school should be maintained . . . "[32]

Ellen Garrison Jackson was attacked by whites in Port Deposit, Maryland as she taught night school for freedpeople. She fought back physically and verbally until the whites resorted to only verbally insulting her.[33] That was fine with her. Jackson and another educator, Miss Anderson, brought a suit against the Philadelphia Baltimore and Washington Railroad in 1866 for its segregated waiting rooms in Baltimore, noting "It will not benefit us merely as individuals also but it will be a standpoint for others."[34] They had been thrown out, bodily, from the waiting room. Anderson is probably Matilda C. Anderson, formerly of Brooklyn, New York who was teaching in Edesville, Kent County, Maryland.

Jackson felt that African American women were obligated to fight for racial equality because black men had done their part in securing the freedom of enslaved Africans. "Our soldiers went forth with sword and bayonet to contend for right and justice. We [women] could not do that. But we contend against outrage and oppression wherever we find it."[35]

Like so many of the African American teachers hired by agencies such as the AMA, Jackson was assigned to an isolated school in Port Deposit, Maryland and given meager supplies and equipment. And like other black educators she suffered the everyday petty indignity of racial injustice in the South. Nevertheless, she committed herself to the struggle, not just in education, but in all phases of African American life.

In letters to her family back home in Hartford, Connecticut, Rebecca Primus, teaching in Royal Oak, Maryland, mentioned Jackson and Anderson's lawsuit as an example of the racism many teachers encountered and the African Americans in Maryland endured. Miss Dickson[36], teaching in nearby Trappe, Maryland was "stoned by white children, and repeatedly subjected to insults from white men, in passing they have brushed by her so rudely she says 'as to almost dislocate her shoulders.' She says she tries to bear it patiently. I feel real sorry for her, her position is truly an unenviable one. The whites are very mean there I'm told. White children take colored children's books from them and otherwise misuse and ill-treat them." Primus recounted other racial incidents as well, including murders of African Americans in the area.[37]

Mary Osbourne records an attack on a teacher in Vienna, Maryland: " . . . a colored lady, teaching at Vienna, in this county,—sent out from Philadelphia,—was met on the street by two men, one of whom struck her a blow in the face so violent that it prostrated her, and she lay on the ground for some time before she recovered sufficiently to seek her house . . . It would really be amusing, if it were not so despicable, to see the petty meannesses the people here will descend to, to show their abhorrence to a 'colored teacher.'"[38] So much for the vaunted southern male chivalry a la *Gone With the Wind.* Also note, like so many other accounts written by whites, the "colored teacher," even though she is a colleague of Osbourne's, is not important enough to be identified by name. Rather, she is simply objectified as a racial symbol.

In spite of the fact that they had to contend with rampant racial discrimination in the organizations which hired them and from the whites they encountered in the south, the African American educators of freedpeople persevered and resisted. Blanche Harris remarked at the end of a long letter complaining to George Whipple about the racism she faced in her work with the freedpeople: "Sometimes we get discouraged and think we had better resign, and then we know that we must suffer many things . . . but we know and feel that there is plenty of work to be done and feel willing to sacrifice much to see our race elevated."[39]

The outspoken feminist and abolitionist, Maria Stewart, became one of the oldest teachers when she taught, then in her sixties, in Washington, D.C. during the Civil War. Like Rebecca Primus, she was a native of Hartford, Connecticut. In a testimonial, Rev. William B. Jefferson of the Third Baptist Church in Washington related that Stewart "came to Washington during the late war, without friends or relatives, to lend a helping hand toward educating her race. She taught Sabbath school for the Church of the Epiphany . . . in the morning, and in the afternoon for the Church of the Incarnation, on Twelfth Street, and after this for Trinity Parish on Ridge street . . . "[40]

Considered the first American female lecturer and political writer, Stewart came to Washington after suffering financial and personal setbacks in her life. She had begun her short-lived speaking career in 1832 in order to support herself as a result of being cheated by unprincipled white executors out of the provisions of her well-to-do husband's will. By 1835, she had given up public speaking, probably as a result of the negative reaction of conservative African American men, who, like many white men, considered public speaking by women improper. She struggled throughout her remaining years to make ends meet.

She came to Washington, D.C. in 1861 after teaching in New York City and Baltimore. Stewart disclosed in her memoir "Sufferings During the War," that Elizabeth Keckley whom she had known in Baltimore gave her necessary assistance to sustain herself as she set up a school in the city. She mentioned another instructor, M.F. Kiger, who was teaching in Washington at the same time.[41] Mary F. Kiger was a native of D.C. who taught at an African American school at 24th and F Streets in the city.[42]

Another teacher in the District of Columbia was the up and coming Sara Iredell Fleetwood. Fleetwood, a native of Pennsylvania, graduated from the Institute for Colored Youth in Philadelphia and Oberlin College. She taught in Frederick, Maryland before relocating to Washington to teach in the public schools there. In Philadelphia, she was active in the Ladies' Union Association, a soldier's relief organization, and in Washington, she was involved with the National Association for the Relief of Destitute Colored Women and Children. After the Civil War, she married the Civil War veteran and Congressional Medal of Honor winner, Christian Fleetwood, who was also an activist. Sara eventually graduated from the Freedmen's Hospital Nursing Training School in D.C. and devoted the remainder of her professional life to the field of nursing. She was also heavily involved in the National League of Colored Women, a club movement which focused on the needs of African American women.[43]

Imbued with a missionary spirit, then, African American women actively pursued positions from agencies like the AMA, the American Tract Society of New York, the American Baptist Home Missionary Society, the Pennsylvania Freedmen's Relief Association, to name a few of the most active. The African American founded and led African Civilization Society which sought "to prove the complete fitness of the educated negro . . . to teach and lead his own race"[44] by hiring only African American instructors was also quite active. This society established six schools for African Americans from 1864-1867 and employed 129 teachers and assistants. Most of the African American teachers of freedpeople ended up working for white organizations, however, while some conducted private free or fee-based schools. Numerous teachers were supported or sponsored by several local organizations at a time and they moved from post to post as the need arose.

Many of the educators were already self-supporting or contributing financially to their families when they chose to seek relatively low-paying employment as teachers of freedpeople.[45] The meager pay given by relief organizations was a test of the African American instructors' commitment because the wages were considerably less than what they could have made in the north. The AMA paid between $15 and $25 a month, making a distinction as to gender with males receiving higher salaries; the American Freedmen's Union Commission paid from $20 to $30 based on experience.[46]

The white Commissioners of the schools in Washington, D.C. voted in January 1866 to pay white teachers in white schools $60 a month and African American teachers in black schools $37.50, "provided that the commissioner is satisfied of the competency of the teacher and that the use of a building be obtained without cost to the Board." In April, it was decided to pay all female teachers, regardless of race, $37.50 a month; in August the pay of female teachers and African American male teachers was raised to $45 per month. In September, the pay of white male teachers was increased to $75 monthly. By 1868, the same inequity in pay persisted with white male teachers in white schools receiving $75 a month, black male teachers in black schools collecting $50, female teachers of either race being paid $50 and assistants receiving $35.[47] No reason was given for the disparity but it can be assumed that the usual presumption of white supremacy was in operation.

The insufficient pay was especially difficult for most of the African American teachers because they were often required, through circumstances, to provide for themselves and contribute to their families. Racial oppression against African American males meant that they often did not have access to properly compensated employment so that African American women worked outside the home through necessity. This was often true in the case of the teachers.

The case of Matilda C. Anderson of Brooklyn is an example of that exigency. She asserted, "If my circumstances should allow me to do so, I would heartily engage in this work without compensation. But being poor and dependent upon my own exertions for a livelihood, I regret that I cannot serve from motives of pure benevolence . . . "[48] Anderson is probably the "Miss Anderson" who brought a suit, along with Ellen Garrison Jackson, against the Philadelphia Baltimore and Washington Railroad for its segregated waiting rooms in 1866. She was sponsored by the NFRA as a teacher in Edesville, Kent County, Maryland.[49]

Sara Stanley is another example. She wrote to the AMA in 1864, "possessing no wealth and having nothing to give but my life to the work, I therefore make this application to you."[50] In a follow-up letter, she explained that her circumstances necessitated asking for wages for the cause she had committed herself to: "The salary you are accustomed to give I would be compelled to ask for, my friends not being in sufficiently affluent circumstances to enable me to teach gratuitously."[51]

Later, after being hired by them, Sara Stanley had to write several letters to the AMA asking for back wages which were owed to her. On June 27, 1865, she wrote:

> I wrote to you in the latter part of May . . . asking for the salary due me, and informing you that I had been solicited to take charge of a school in which the pupils were required to pay for their tuition. Presuming those letters failed to reach you, I wish to state that receiving no direction from you I considered it best to agree to the proposal of the people, and have now a very flourishing and interesting school. I will doubtless receive from it a sum sufficient to pay my board, rent of the school room, and all incidental expenses of the school . . . Please send me the salary due me for the months of March, April, May and June. I am compelled to be a little importunate about the money, as my board bill falls due before the payment of the pupils' monthly fee.[52]

Still in dire financial straits, July 10, 1865 found her writing again because "my pecuniary affairs are such that it will cause me serious embarrassment" if she did not receive the money. And on August 1, 1865, she wrote again reminding the AMA of its debt to her.[53]

Financial concerns affected Mary Weston Fordham, also. A member of an elite free family, Fordham conducted a school in Charleston, South Carolina during the Civil War. In spite of the fact that she was arrested for teaching African Americans, due to South Carolina's laws against educating African Americans, she ran her school for several years before and during the war. Because of the law, she was liable for a "fine, imprisonment, and corporeal punishment." Very literate, Fordham was also considered a creditable poet, as well as an excellent teacher.

She was hired by the AMA to teach in the Saxton School (later Avery Normal Institute) run by Thomas Cardozo in Charleston in 1865. Fordham protested, threatening to quit, when she found that a white instructor with similar skills and duties received a salary of $50 a month, while she received only $25. Francis L. Cardozo (Thomas' brother) wrote a letter of protest to the AMA, asking them to at least raise her wages to $35. "This young lady is a most excellent and experienced teacher." When the association refused, he added five dollars a month to her pay from his own pocket so as not to lose so valuable an instructor.[54]

One unnamed African American teacher opened a school in Person County, North Carolina even though the people in that community could only give her room and board. Another woman offered to do the teacher's laundry free of charge as her contribution "to the cause of education among her people." This community was also supporting "many orphan children, thrown upon them by the cruel fortunes of slavery and the war."[55]

The wages were paltry, the labor was arduous, the classes large and the hours were long, but the rewards were apparently worth it. Sallie Daffin said the four dedicated African American teachers in Norfolk, Virginia "who exercise all their energies in behalf of our much injured and long-oppressed race . . . [have] their labors repaid by the interest manifested by their pupils."[56] A 1860 graduate of Philadelphia's Institute for Colored Youth and a native of Philadelphia, she was one of those educators.

Clara Duncan, originally from Pittsfield, Massachusetts, declared from Norfolk, Virginia: "I came here because my heart and soul were in this work and I am prepared to give up everything, *even life*, for the good of the cause and count it no hardship but an honor and blessing to me."[57] Sara Stanley echoed the same sentiment. "My duties are laborious and exhausting. I teach from nine o'clock until four and then two hours in the evening school for adults . . . It is wearying work to the teacher, but admirable for the cultivation of grace and patience."[58]

While stationed in Natchez, Mississippi, Blanche Harris had a very difficult schedule. She taught regular school from 8:00 a.m. to 2:00 p.m., at 3:00 p.m. she had a class of adults and after that she conducted a night school. One afternoon a week there was a prayer meeting; another afternoon, a sewing school; and a singing school. Still, Harris said, "I have become very much attached to my school; the interest they manifest in their studies pleases me."[59]

The December 15, 1865 *Pennsylvania Freedmen's Bulletin* carried a letter from William F. Mitchell to Joseph E. Rhoads, the Secretary of the Pennsylvania Freedmen's Relief Association, which described the arduous teaching and learning schedule of one young woman in Nashville, Tennessee. "The primary school is in the charge of Emily C. Bird, a colored girl, who received the limited education that she has, in the first school organized by our Association in the southwest. This young woman, besides teaching five hours per day, recites to Wilmer Walton, the principal, two or three times a day. She desires to devote her whole time to study, but we need her services just now, and the good work she is doing for the little children under her charge will aid rather than retard her education."

In spite of continuing racial violence in Maryland, Mississippi and Louisiana, Edmonia Highgate continued teaching because she could clearly see the value of her work. "I have a very interesting and constantly growing day school, a night school, and a glorious Sabbath School of near one hundred scholars. The school is under the auspices of the Freedmen's Bureau, yet it is wholly self supporting. The majority of my pupils come from plantations, three, four, and even eight mile's distant. So anxious are they to learn that they walk these distances so early in the morning as never to be tardy. Every scholar buys his own book and slate etc."[60]

Originally from Syracuse, New York, Highgate's mother, Hannah, and two sisters, Willella and Caroline, also instructed freedpeople in the South. Her parents had been enslaved so that she felt a special bond with the freedpeople she taught. Those links were strengthened when her brother, a soldier, was killed in the battle at Petersburg, Virginia in 1865.

A product of a New York state normal school, Edmonia left a higher-paying principal's position in Binghamton, New York to teach freedpeople in Mississippi and Maryland, in addition to Louisiana. Her application letter to the AMA emphasized that she knew "just what self denial, self discipline and domestic qualifications are needed for the work" and that she had such qualities to "labor advantageously in the field for my newly freed brethren." She felt her background entitled her to be given important teaching posts. When Highgate objected to remaining in a post in Darlington, Maryland, saying, "I do not conceive it to be my duty to stay here in the woods and teach thirty-four pupils when I have an opportunity of reaching hundreds," she was given a position more to her liking in New Orleans.[61]

Interestingly, Edmonia Highgate, along with Frances Ellen Watkins Harper, spoke at the 1864 National Negro Convention in Syracuse to urge continued African American support for the Civil War and to speak in favor of Abraham Lincoln's reelection. Clara Duncan also attended but did not speak. Women had rarely addressed these August meetings.[62] Perhaps that is why Highgate gave a speech nuanced, probably facetiously, by the gender norms of the day. "Miss Highgate said she would not be quite in her place, perhaps, if a girl as she is, she should tell the Convention what they ought to do; but she had, with others *thought* about what had been proposed and those thoughts she would tell them."[63] She was certainly not retiring or submissive in other areas of her life, as her career attests.

She spoke a few days after being sent home from Norfolk because she had suffered a mental collapse as a result of her taxing work among the freedpeople. Sallie Daffin reported her breakdown in the October 8, 1864 issue of the *Christian Recorder*. "Yesterday Miss E.G. Highgate left here for her home in Syracuse, N.Y., in care of Miss C.C.[Clara] Duncan, being afflicted with that terrible malady, 'aberration of mind.' There is no teacher who will be more universally missed than Miss H.—Her efficiency in the missionary field has been proved in numberless instances. Our laborers are falling rapidly in the field." Nevertheless, Edmonia Highgate was back to work teaching freedpeople in the South by March 1865. She used the period of rehabilitation to seek donations for the AMA's efforts to educate freedpeople.

One of the greatest rewards for the teachers was the eagerness with which African Americans embraced education because it proved that they were ready for citizenship. The teachers spoke of the thirst for knowledge that the refugees displayed. Charlotte Forten used the motivation of her students to debunk the notion of black inferiority and laziness: "I find the children . . . eager to learn . . . and many make most rapid improvement. It is a great happiness to teach them. I wish some of those persons at the North, who say the race is hopelessly and naturally inferior, could see the readiness with which these children, so long oppressed and deprived of every privilege, learn and understand. I have some grown pupils . . . who take lessons in the evenings . . . I never saw any one so determined to learn."[64]

Charlotte Forten's Philadelphia family had a proud heritage of activism. Her grandfather, James Forten, was a wealthy sailmaker and Revolutionary War veteran who was heavily involved in anti-slavery activities as were her parents, Robert and Mary. Her uncle was Robert Purvis, also wealthy, who devoted his time and money to such organizations and activities as the Philadelphia Vigilance Committee and aiding fugitives. Charlotte married the activist minister, Francis Grimke, in 1878 and together they continued to fight for civil rights for African Americans.

Forten, a poet and educator before she went south to work with refugees, lived for a time with another activist family, the Remonds of Salem, Massachusetts. She was particularly close with Sarah Parker Remond who was also active in anti-slavery work and who agitated for support for the Union in Great Britain. Charlotte had been acknowledged as something of a poet by many in her abolitionist circles. William Wells Brown said, "Were she white, America would recognize her as one of its brightest gems."[65] Her poetical subjects invariably reflected her anti-slavery and anti-oppression leanings. She continued to correspond with abolitionists after she relocated to Port Royal, South Carolina, writing letters about her experience which were published in the *Liberator*, a leading abolitionist newspaper.

Charlotte represented the Pennsylvania Freedmen's Relief Association as a teacher at Port Royal from 1862 to 1864. Like her poetry, her instruction stressed African American history by including information about the black experience in her curriculum. "Talked to the children a little while to-day about the noble Toussaint [L'Overture]. They listened very attentively. It is well that they should know what one of their own color could do for his race. I long to inspire them with courage and ambition (of a noble sort), and high purposes."[66] She said, "the children are well-behaved and eager to learn."[67] Forten also grew to appreciate, if only from the distance of class, the rich culture of the Sea Islanders.

Mary Magnos, who, in addition to teaching was the president of Norfolk, Virginia's Ladies' Soldiers Aid Association, reported proudly, "When I first opened my school I found the children exceedingly ignorant. Not having had the advantage of any teaching at all, there were only two out of thirty that knew the first letters of the Alphabet. But they are exceedingly anxious to learn. During the short time I have been teaching them they have all learned the alphabet and many of them are reading small pieces in the Freedmens Primer. They attend punctually and never absent themselves except in case of sickness."[68]

Sallie Daffin's adult students in Norfolk, Virginia had the same appetite for learning, "I have a class of adults some of whom, three weeks ago, did not know a letter of the alphabet, but are now spelling"[69] In November 1864, she was writing enthusiastically, "Our evening school has been organized, and bids fair to be a success. Nearly three hundred persons have been enrolled already, and others are coming in."[70] Some of the women she instructed started a sewing circle to provide clothing for the poor in their community. Later, she held a teaching post in Wilmington, North Carolina where, like Forten and Magnos, she taught wounded soldiers to read and write while she nursed and wrote letters for them at a nearby hospital for African American soldiers. And, she was a regular correspondent to the *Christian Recorder*, signing her letters simply "Sallie."

Fanny Jackson Coppin, the first African American woman to head an institution of higher learning in the United States, the Institute for Colored Youth, started an evening school for freedpeople while a student at Oberlin College. She said: "It was deeply touching to me to see old men painfully following the simple words of spelling; so intensely eager to learn."[71] Coppin had been enslaved until an aunt purchased her freedom while she was an adolescent. She had to work as a domestic in order to pay a tutor before she could attend the Rhode Island State Normal School. Because of her own experience, Coppin knew the value of an education for freedpeople.

Susie King Taylor's experience mirrored Coppin's. She, too, knew how important education was to and for African Americans. At a mere fourteen years of age, she had escaped enslavement in Savannah, Georgia by fleeing to Union lines in 1862. Her desire to learn to read and write led her to gain those skills by any means possible. She took lessons surreptitiously from two free women in Savannah—Mary Woodhouse and Mary Beasley—, a white playmate and the son of her grandmother's white landlord.

Taylor taught African American soldiers in her husband's regiment, the 1st South Carolina Volunteers (33rd USCI), and freedpeople on St. Simon's Island, Georgia. Of the soldiers she said, "I taught a great many of the comrades in Company E to read and write, when they were off duty. Nearly all were anxious to learn."[72] In addition, she established a school on the island. "I had about forty children to teach, beside a number of adults who came to me nights, all of them so eager to learn to read, to read above anything else."[73]

Isabella Gibbins[74], an instructor in Charlottesville, Virginia who had also been enslaved herself, reported on the number of freedpeople eager to learn. "The schools are filled but the children still come to see if they can be admitted. I have sixty-three pupils . . . We have some grown scholars in the school and they work hard to learn all they can."[75] She taught for the New England Freedmen's Aid Society.

M.A. Parker, a teacher in Raleigh[76], North Carolina, said: "It is surprising to me to see the amount of suffering which many of the people endure for the sake of sending their children to school . . . They are anxious to have the children 'get on' in their books, and do not seem impatient if they lack comforts themselves. A pile of books is seen in almost every cabin, though there be no furniture except a poor bed, a table and two or three broken chairs."[77]

Sara Stanley remarked on this desire for education in her official report to the AMA from her post in St. Louis, Missouri: "I commenced school with fifty four scholars, which in two weeks increased to seventy five. The whole number at present is one hundred and the average attendance nearly eighty. All the pupils can read using McGuffey's series of readers from the First to the Fifth. I have organized classes in Geography, Grammar, and Mental Arithmetic; they have entered upon these studies, which are entirely new to them, with great avidity . . . I can assume no merit for this advancement, it is owing almost wholly to their own efforts . . . "[78]

A white superintendent of education in North Carolina reported on one school under his supervision which illustrated the ardent aspiration for education newly-freed Africans demonstrated. "Side by side, commencing their alphabet together, and continuing their studies until they could each read the Bible fluently, sat a child of six summers, her mother, grandmother, and great-grandmother, aged 75 years, the representatives of four generations in a direct line."[79]

It is clear that African American educators saw their own fate as tied to their less fortunate brothers and sisters, although many, like white philanthropists, believed they were bringing "civilization" to a people in need of upliftment. For instance, Charlotte Forten felt the freedpeople in Port Royal, South Carolina, who were so different from the middle class African Americans she knew in the North, were, in fact, her "own people" and that her "heart [sang] a song of Thanksgiving" that she was given the opportunity to work with them.[80] Her experience with racism in the North, regardless of being well-to-do and highly educated, convinced her that whatever happened to them affected her.

Light enough to pass for white, "having a slight admixture of negro blood in my veins,"[81] Sara G. Stanley volunteered to teach freedpeople for the AMA. Proud of her African heritage despite a difference in station, she felt she was bound to the refugees by "ties of consanguinity and love" and that "socially and politically they are 'my people'"[82] Stanley served in Norfolk, St. Louis, Louisville and Mobile for the AMA.

Freeborn in New Bern, North Carolina, Sara was the daughter of a teacher, John Stuart Stanley. She taught in Cleveland, Ohio after graduating from Oberlin College in 1856. William Wells Brown was probably referring to her as "a teacher in one of the day schools [in Cleveland], [whose] education places her in the front ranks of her profession." Brown was citing her as an example of "the intelligence, industry and respectability of the colored citizens" of Cleveland.[83]

Blanche Harris was a member of an activist family which recognized the importance of education for black women as well as men. She grew up in Monroe, Michigan and graduated from Oberlin College in 1860. Other members of her highly educated family also taught freedpeople. Her sister, Frankie[84] who also attended Oberlin, taught with Harris in Natchez, Mississippi. Blanche taught for the AMA in Norfolk, Virginia where she was the principal of a school staffed by Edmonia Highgate, Sallie Daffin and Clara Duncan. She also taught in North Carolina and Tennessee.

Newly liberated African Americans wanted to control their own lives and managing their own schools was an indication of their independence. Many preferred African American teachers for their schools. The residents of a refugee camp in Murfreesboro, Tennessee quickly supplied the teachers of their day, Sabbath and evening schools with rations from their own supplies after military officials eliminated their allocations of food.[85] This action not only showed their self-reliance but their commitment to education as well.

In an early 1864 complaint about the callous treatment of African American refugees in a settlement near Fort Albany in Virginia, Louisa Jane Barker, the wife of a white chaplain, mentioned that in addition to supporting themselves without the government's help, the inhabitants of the community willingly and enthusiastically agreed to pay for the services of an instructor for their children. Barker, however, did not give us the name of "well-educated mulatto woman engaged to take the school as soon as a building could be proposed."[86] We will perhaps never know because before the school could come to fruition, the village was destroyed by Union forces under orders from General Christopher Augur in order to force the dwellers into a camp under the control of the Union army.

Many of the schools for freedpeople were financially sustained in some way by the freedpeople themselves. Freedpeople bore "more than half the expense" of the total cost of the 120 schools under the supervision of the Pennsylvania Freedmen's Relief Association.[87] The New York branch of the Freedman's Union Commission passed a resolution in mid-1867 which called for "some plan [to] be adopted by which the people for whose benefit [schools] are established should bear a share of the pecuniary burden of their support." They formed a committee to come up with a plan to bring this to fruition.[88]

General S.C. Armstrong, white Freedmen's Bureau Superintendent at Fortress Monroe, Virginia related, "Several new schools have lately been opened in the rural districts, under the auspices of the Association, in all of which the teacher's salary only is paid; the parents of the schoolchildren having agreed to furnish the rest. The freed people entered, as usual, into the obligation with great readiness . . . "[89]

The Freedmen's Bureau Superintendent of Education in North Carolina reported in 1867 "that many instances had come under his notice where teachers of a self-supporting school had been sustained till the last cent the freedmen could command was exhausted, and where these last had even taxed their credit in the coming crop to pay the bills necessary to keep up the school."[90]

The women in Lexington, Kentucky worked for a year to raise money to establish Howard School in the city in 1866. The school was conducted in a building bought by the African American community and opened with three black teachers and five hundred students.[91]

Another school constructed and maintained by the African American community is the Stanley Institute in Christ Rock, Maryland, a pre-Civil War free African American community in Dorchester County. Built in 1865 and moved in 1867, it is still standing. According to a historical marker placed in front of the building by the Rock Community Improvement League in 1976, it is the "oldest community-owned one-room school-house still intact in Dorchester County." The school "was used continuously until July 1966, as Rock Elementary School for students in grades 1 through 7." Desegregation, no doubt, caused the school to no longer be used. Local residents say proudly that the school was never under the white school board's direction.

African American educators promoted the freedpeople's attempts at self-sufficiency because these efforts reinforced arguments for the readiness of all African Americans for equal rights. Mary E. Watson aided the endeavors of the freedpeople in her school in Darlington, Maryland by lecturing for a small fee and forming an Educational Society in order to support her school financially.[92] She wrote from Darlington on July 1, 1867: "The scholars improve rapidly and are much interested in their lessons. On the 20th we had an examination; the proceeds were for the benefit of the school." She was especially proud that her students did well in arithmetic because it forced "a number of white Marylanders" despite "past and present prejudices" to express "their surprise and satisfaction with the system on which our school was conducted" and that the children's recitations "in arithmetic . . . they thought they had never seen excelled by such small children . . . [By] their manner I was assured that they were among those who believe in the oft repeated assertion of the incapacity of the negro to acquire a knowledge of arithmetic. So these little ones in their humble sphere, made some converts besides causing their parents to thank God and take courage . . . "[93] Watson, a graduate of Rhode Island State Normal School, also served in Norfolk, Virginia and Port Deposit, Maryland.[94]

Martha Hoy, formerly of Brooklyn, raised seventy dollars and six cents at a two-day year-end festival to support her school and the church in Prince Frederick, Maryland. She hung paintings of "Colored Volunteers," "Battle of 54th Mass. Regt," and the "African Prince," mounted a Union flag, spelled out the word "Progress" in cedar boughs and hung the words "PERSEVERE AND ADVANCE" on the walls in order to inspire her students and their parents.[95] Hoy also taught for the AMA in Trappe and Burkittsville, Maryland.

In another demonstration of support for black self-reliance, Harriet Jacobs announced that one of her fairs selling articles donated by friends in Massachusetts and New York had cleared one hundred and fifty dollars. One hundred and thirty dollars of this amount were used for the Jacobs Free School in Freedmen's Village in Alexandria, Virginia. The school had been built by freedpeople in 1863 but whites attempted to commandeer control of it without input from the freedpeople themselves. Jacobs, seeing that the refugees were unused to confronting the system, showed them, by example, how they could retain management of their school. "I wanted the colored men to learn the time had come when it was their privilege to have something to say." She forced the issue at a board meeting and then took the African American trustees to the appropriate government officials to get a legitimate title to the land and school for them. She was instrumental in seeing that the school was paid off and furnished.

Her ultimate goal was to ensure that freedpeople exercised some measure of independence and control over their education was an excellent way to do this. She said, "I do not object to white teachers but I think it has a good effect on the freedpeople to convince them their own race can do something for their elevation."[96] Louisa, Harriet Jacobs' daughter, and Virginia Lawton, from Cambridge, Massachusetts, were hired as teachers in the school. Lawton, "a young colored woman of good education and great worth of character," was sent by the New England Freedmen's Aid Society.[97] Lawton's sister, E. Mariana Lawton, began teaching at the school in 1865.

Jacobs had already challenged the white superintendent of the Village because he had broken up a home she had established for old women and orphan children. She confronted him in front of his superior, the military governor, so that he could see "how unjust he had been to these poor people." He was forced to give her back the rooms she had been using. Jacobs was more than capable of taking on the whites who tried to take control of the school in the Village and of training the African American men in the exercise of their rights.

Agents of the Friends' Association of Philadelphia described the school in June 1864. "We visited a school taught by [Harriet Jacobs'] daughter who has two assistants. There were 280 names on the roll, with an average attendance of 140. While we were in the room the scholars at the direction of their teacher, sang a song of freedom, and the sound of their voices, in the chorus where this thrilling word occurred, might almost quite have been heard as far as the old slave-pen, on the wall of which, until recently, appeared the name of a firm, with the words in large capitals, 'Dealers in Slaves.' There is an evening school of 175 adults in the same building, and in all, 20 schools for emancipated slaves are now in operation in this place, so lately the hotbed of secessionism and pro-slavery feeling."[98]

From the District of Columbia area, Elizabeth Keckley, the leader of a major African American relief organization, stressed how a commitment to education and self-reliance proved her people's readiness for freedom. "The schools [in D.C.] are objects of much interest. Good teachers, white and colored, are employed, and whole brigades of bright-eyed dusky children are there taught the common branches of education. These children are studious, and the teachers inform me that their advancement is rapid. I number among my personal friends twelve colored girls employed as teachers in the schools at Washington. The Colored Mission Sabbath School, established through the influence of Gen. Brown at the Fifteenth Street Presbyterian Church, is always an object of great interest to the residents of the Capital, as well as to the hundreds of strangers visiting the city."[99] Louisa Jacobs and Virginia Lawton are probably among the friends mentioned by Keckley as they were teaching in schools for freedpeople in the capital.

Frances Rollin, along with Mary Weston Fordham, taught for the AMA in Charleston, South Carolina in 1865, after teaching for the Freedmen's Bureau. Like Fordham, Rollin was from a well-to-do Charleston family. And also like Fordham, she was considered one of the "best native teachers" in Charleston. Rollin attended the Institute for Colored Youth in Philadelphia before returning to Charleston to teach. She later married William J. Whipper, a Civil War veteran and Reconstruction state senator in South Carolina. She is the author of a biography of Martin

Delany, *The Life and Times of Martin Robison Delany*, which she published under the pseudonym, Frank A. Rollin, to disguise her gender.

Caroline (Carrie) Groves and her daughter, Phoebe, moved from New York City to Washington, D.C. in 1863 to teach. Groves had been a successful principal in New York before becoming a principal at the Union Bethel A.M.E. Church.[100] R.H. Cain, an A.M.E. bishop, praised Groves' work while condemning the inactivity of the auxiliary which was set up to aid the school. He saw the school as a way to gain more members for his church. "Educate the children in your faith, and you will have your church filled with intelligent members.[101]

Mary Smith Kelsey Peake, whose white-looking husband was a spy for the Union, opened the first school sponsored by the AMA late in September 1861 in Hampton, Virginia near Fortress Monroe for freedpeople. The school was started in Brown Cottage on the grounds of Chesapeake Female College.[102] She taught more than fifty children in her day school and twenty adults in the evening school. An educated free woman, Peake had already been teaching enslaved Africans in the Hampton area, even though Hampton had been burned by confederate troops, when the AMA asked to sponsor her efforts. In July 1861, the area was occupied by Union forces who camped at nearby Fortress Monroe. James McPherson notes ironically that her school was located near where the first Africans arrived in the British colonies in 1619.[103]

Peake had been a longtime activist, having helped to organize, in 1847, the Daughters of Zion, a benevolent society dedicated to aiding African fugitives.[104] She died of tuberculosis in February 1862, a little more than four months after opening her school. The Hampton Normal and Agricultural Institute eventually, in 1868, evolved from her school.

Similar schools were opened in the same area. Lewis Lockwood of the AMA stated that one of these schools was "under the instruction of Mrs. [Mary] Bailey, assisted by Miss Jennings, and James, a bright boy who acts as monitor. They are all colored persons, and Mrs. Bailey is a free woman."[105] A freedwoman, Mary Green, was an assistant teacher in Fortress Monroe, Virginia as was Lucinda Spivery, also newly-freed.[106] Spivery, after receiving more education headed an AMA school in Hampton, Virginia.

Various newly-freed African American women taught on a rudimentary level or assisted instructors. Eventually, some of the females who were educated in the freedmen's schools would also become educators. Lily Granderson, hired by the AMA, had secretly taught other enslaved Africans while she was still enslaved.[107] She was a teacher for the

AMA in Natchez, Mississippi. Given her limited education, Hettie tutored the students in St. Helena Village on Edisto Island, South Carolina until "she could carry them no further" and so turned them over to a more advanced instructor.[108]

Anna Bell Davis and Leannah Powell established the Newtown School for refugees on Cameron Street in Alexandria, Virginia in 1863. Davis, a refugee herself, had received some education while enslaved and began the school while housed in a former slave-pen as a result of being displaced by the war. She ran the school alone in 1865.[109]

Mary Chadwick had learned to read while still enslaved. That experience showed her how important education was. "My master once sent me for a book of Hannah More's. Instead of bringing the whole pile like the rest did, I fetched the one massa wanted. He said why didn't you bring all the books. I said I seed it on the back, massa. He said, 'Who learnt you to read? Bring me the cowhide' and gave me three or four licks on the head." She used her very elementary education to teach in an AMA school in Beaufort, North Carolina while receiving instruction from Association teachers.[110]

Many African American women opened or taught in private schools. The women who established fee-based schools were, of course, exercising their entrepreneurial instincts by capitalizing on the demand for education while providing a needed service. Nancy (Nannie) Waugh Warrick opened a school in the Smothers House at Fourteenth and H Streets in Washington, D.C. in 1861. It was burned to the ground a year later "at the hands of . . . incendiaries, who, even at that time, were inspired with all their accustomed vindictiveness towards the colored people." She then established a private school at L Street, near Sixteenth Street.[111]

Mary Still, sister of the famous underground railroad conductor, William Still of Philadelphia, taught for the AMA in Beaufort, South Carolina and at the Stanton Institute in Jacksonville, Florida from 1865 to 1872. She had directed a private school in Philadelphia from the 1840s to the end of the Civil War. She was also active in freedmen's relief activities and was the vice president of the Committee of Managers of the Beaufort Ladies' Fair of the Bethel A.M.E. Church which was formed to aid freedpeople in South Carolina. Hannah Smalls, wife of the famous Robert Smalls, the captain of the *Planter* steamboat, was an officer of this group also.

Mary Chase established the first day school, Columbia Street School, for Africans who had escaped to Union lines in Alexandria, Virginia in September 1861. The school was located near Wolf Street.[112] She was also active in Elizabeth Keckley's Contraband Relief Association, serving as the organization's corresponding secretary until June 1864.

Very little information was found about the following teachers[113] but they, too, merit further study because they often risked their lives, health and financial well-being to minister to the educational needs of newly free African Americans:

Louisa Alexander, an Oberlin College graduate taught for the AMA at the Saxton School[114] in Charleston, South Carolina. Originally from Mayslick, Kentucky, she also taught in Marietta, Georgia. Celinda Anderson, from New York, was a teacher of freedpeople in Delaware. Lucy Barbour was a teacher in a Washington, D.C. school at Seventeenth and I Streets. She was originally from D.C. J.V. Benjamin taught for the AMA in Port Deposit, Maryland. Amanda Borden taught refugees at the First Select Colored School in Alexandria. Martha Bailey Briggs, of New Bedford, Massachusetts taught in Easton, Maryland and later at Howard University in Washington, D.C. Isabella Briscoe conducted a school in the Georgetown area of Washington, D.C. at Montgomery and Mount Zion Streets. Mrs. Brooks taught, along with her husband, Rev. Thomas Brooks, at the Ninth Street Methodist Church in Louisville, Kentucky. E.J. Brooks taught at the E and Ninth Streets school in D.C. She was a native of D.C. M.E. Brooks, from Maryland, taught at the M Street School in Washington, D.C. Emma V. Brown, who attended Oberlin College with Mary Jane Patterson and Fanny Jackson Coppin, conducted the O Street Grammar School in Georgetown in the District of Columbia. A native of Georgetown, Brown ran her own school in the area before she taught for the New England Freedmen's Aid Society. She was also a member of the Contraband Relief Association. Carolyn Bryant taught for the AMA in Fayetteville, North Carolina. Laura J. Cardozo, from Brooklyn, New York, was an AMA teacher in Charleston, South Carolina. Charlotte Pankus Gordon Carroll established the first school for refugee children in Washington, D.C. in 1861. Carroll had been enslaved in Alexandria, Virginia but was sent to school by her owner. She married David Carroll, a well-to-do church elder in the District of Columbia. Her daughter, Rebecca T. Gordon, assisted her in the school. Mary A. Coakley, a native Washingtonian, taught at the East Street School in Georgetown, District of Columbia. Hannah W. Cole, employed by the NFRA, was the principal of an industrial school in Roanoke Island, North Carolina. Rachel J. Cook was a teacher at the O Street School in D.C. She was a native Washingtonian. Mrs. Corpru taught in the Hampton, Virginia area. Jane

A. Crouch, along with Sarah A. Gray, started a day and evening school for refugees in Alexandria, Virginia in 1861. The school was St. Rose Institute and it was located on West Street between King and Prince. Both Crouch and Gray were natives of Alexandria. Gray later conducted her own private school in the city. Martha Culling was commissioned by the NFRA. Mary Day taught for a short time for the AMA in Wilmington, North Carolina. She was a native of the state. M.C. Deas was an AMA teacher in School No. 2 in Savannah, Georgia. Jane Deveaux, a free woman from Savannah, Georgia, was teaching in a school her mother founded when Union troops captured the city in 1864. The Freedmen's Bureau later hired her to continue conducting the school. Maria Dorster, of Massachusetts, was a teacher at the O Street School in D.C. Harriet Byron Douglass conducted a fee-based school in Alexandria, Virginia, St. Patrick's, which also catered to refugees. It was founded in 1864 and was on St. Patrick Street. Grace Dyson taught at the school at D and Twelfth Streets in D.C. Rosabella Fields was an AMA teacher in Charleston, South Carolina. Laura V. Fisher, from D.C., taught at the M Street School in the District. G.I. Fleet, taught at the 24th and F Streets school in D.C. Annie L. Foote, taught at the O Street School in D.C. Clara Freeman, from Vermont, attended Oberlin and taught for the AMA in Natchez, Mississippi. Sophia Freeman taught for the AMA in Franklin, Tennessee. She was a native of Newark, New Jersey. Mary Garrett, of the District of Columbia, taught at the M Street School in that city. She was originally from Troy, New York. Mary R. Goines taught at the E and Ninth Streets school in D.C. She was a native of D.C. Clara Gowing was a teacher at the First Select Colored School in Alexandria, Virginia. Sarah Greenbrier, of Cleveland, Ohio, was an AMA teacher in Arlington, Virginia. Alice Hall taught in Still Pond, Maryland for the New York Branch Freedman's Union Commission. She was from Lansingburgh, New York. Delonius Harris taught for the AMA in Macon, Georgia. Charlotte Hicks from Albany, New York taught for the NFRA in Anderson Courthouse, South Carolina. Mrs. Hitch was a teacher in Macon, Georgia. Miss E. Hitch taught in Macon, Georgia. Harriet W. Hoffman, from New York, was a teacher of freedpeople. Harriet Holloway was an AMA teacher in Charleston, South Carolina. Adeline Howard taught in Still Pond, Maryland for the New York Branch Freedman's Union Commission. Lizzie R. Hunter, from New York, was an AMA teacher in Charleston, South Carolina. Charlotte Jackson taught for the AMA at the Norfolk, Virginia Night School. Ellen M. Jackson, the daughter of Rev. Nathaniel Jackson of Washington, D.C., was in charge, until her death in 1865, of a day school in the District of Columbia which had been started by Charlotte Pankus Gordon Carroll. Martha L. Jarvis, an Oberlin graduate, taught in Meridian, Mississippi. Cornelia A. Jennings was hired by the Protestant Episcopal Aid Society and the Freedmen's Bureau to teach at St. Mark's Episcopal School in Louisville, Kentucky. Charlotte Johnson was an AMA teacher in Charleston, South Carolina. Kitty Johnson, from New York, was a teacher of freedpeople in Georgia. She taught for the Methodist Episcopal Freedmen's Aid Society. Laura Johnson and her mother conducted a school in Logan County, Kentucky. Miss Jones was a teacher for the AMA at School No. 2 in Savannah, Georgia. C.A. Jones taught at a school at the corners of Seventeenth and I Streets in the District of Columbia. She was originally from D.C. Matilda Jones attended Oberlin College and taught at the Boston School in Washington, D.C. in 1865. She married Rev. S.W. Madden, pastor of First Baptist Church in Alexandria, Virginia. Julia B. Landre was a teacher at Camp Barker in the District of Columbia. Her specialty was music. Mary Caroline Lapene, from New York, was a teacher of freedpeople in North Carolina. Julia Leary was an AMA teacher in Fayetteville, North Carolina. L.V. Lewis and A.M. Thompson opened the Washington Street School for refugee children in 1864 in Alexandria, Virginia. Laura Linsley taught in Oxford, North Carolina for the New York Branch Freedman's Union Commission. Julia Luckett, from Canada, was a teacher at the school on East Street in Georgetown, D.C. Lavinia Martin taught in Macon, Georgia. Lydia McDowell taught for the NFRA in Columbia, South Carolina. C.L. McKinney taught at the Avery Institute in Charleston, South Carolina for the AMA. She was originally from Flushing, New York. Her husband, Christopher, was also a teacher. Harriet E. Mitchel taught for the New York Freedmen's Relief Association at the First National Freedmen's School organized in 1864 in Alexandria, Virginia. Martha Morton conducted a school for indigent children in Logan County, Kentucky. Christiana Nichols, of D.C., was a teacher at the C and Second Streets School in the District of Columbia. M.M. Nickens and M.F. Simms were teachers in a primary school for refugees on St. Asaph Street in Alexandria, Virginia. It was founded in 1864. Mary F. Nickens was a teacher in a refugee school held in Zion Wesley Church in Alexandria, Virginia and funded by the Pennsylvania Freedmen's Relief Association. Josephine Nicks of Natchez, Mississippi worked for the AMA. Miss O'Hear was an AMA teacher in Charleston, South Carolina. Mary Parker taught for the AMA in the Norfolk Night School. Mary Jane Patterson was an Oberlin College graduate who taught in Union Hall, Kentucky, the

Institute for Colored Youth in Philadelphia and the Preparatory High School for Colored Youth [now Dunbar High School] in Washington, D.C. A native of North Carolina, she was the first African American woman to receive a Bachelor of Arts degree. Mary Payne taught for the AMA in Fayetteville, North Carolina. Laura Phenix was a teacher in the Second National Freedmen's School on Wolf Street in Alexandria, Virginia. Miss Porter taught at School No. 2 in Savannah, Georgia for the AMA. Sarah Purvis, of Pennsylvania, taught at the C and South Streets school in D.C. She was probably related to the famous Purvis family of Philadelphia. Mary E. Reed was a teacher in at the E and Ninth Streets school in D.C. and she was originally from the city. Mrs. Robinson taught at the First Select Colored School in Alexandria, Virginia. Margaret Sasportas taught in Charleston, South Carolina for the AMA. Mary Scott taught for the Freewill Baptist Home Missionary Society in her husband's school in Parris Island, South Carolina. Mary Ann Scott was a teacher in Hampton area of Virginia. Amelia Shrewsbury taught for the AMA at Charleston, South Carolina's Avery Institute. Martha Simms was a teacher at the East Street School in D.C. She was a native Washingtonian. Mary Simms started an evening school for refugees in 1863 on Duke Street in Alexandria. There was an M.F. Simms who taught in a primary school in Alexandria; these might be the same person. Charlotte S. Smith, from New York City, was a teacher of freedpeople in St. Augustine, Florida. She was hired by the NFRA. Lizzie Smith taught in Washington, D.C. Her school eventually became the Lincoln Industrial Institute. Georgiana M. Snowden, from New York City, was a teacher of freedpeople in Maryland for the Pennsylvania Freedmen's Relief Association. Her sister was T.B. Snowden who also taught for the Association in Maryland. Anna P. Spencer, originally from New Jersey, taught at the M Street School in Washington, D.C. Sarah Swails, from Elmira, New York, was a teacher of freedpeople in South Carolina. Her husband, Stephen A., a sergeant in the Massachusetts 54th, was the Union Army's first official African American commissioned officer. He also taught freedpeople before going into Reconstruction politics. Anna V. Tompkins, a native of D.C., was a teacher at the Delaware Avenue and H Street school in D.C. Charlotta V. Usher, from Albany, New York, was a teacher of freedpeople. Amanda Wall, from Oberlin, Ohio, taught at Avery Institute in Charleston, South Carolina for the AMA. She also taught in the District of Columbia. Her husband was Captain O.S.B. Wall, a Freedmen's Bureau officer. Her sister-in-law and classmate was Caroline Wall Langston, wife of John Mercer Langston. O.S.B. Wall was

Caroline's brother. Annie E. Washington was in charge of the Boston School in Washington, D.C. when it opened in 1864. She had conducted her own school in the city prior to this. After the Boston School closed in 1868, she worked in the public school system. During the Civil War, Washington was an officer of the Contraband Relief Association. Ella Watson taught in Macon, Georgia. Harriet J. West, from Brooklyn, was a teacher of freedpeople in Maryland for the Friends' Association of Philadelphia. Joanna Weston taught for the NFRA at the Morris Street School in Charleston, South Carolina. She was related to Mary Weston Fordham. Moncuria Weston taught for the NFRA at the Meeting House School in Charleston. Like Joanna Weston, she was related to Mary Weston Fordham. Nancy Williams taught at the Union Town School in Alexandria, Virginia under the auspices of American Baptist Home Missionary Society. Sarah Williams was an AMA teacher in Fayetteville, North Carolina. Anna (Annie) M. Wilson, from New York, was a teacher at the O Street School in D.C. Her father, William J., and mother, Mary Ann Garret Marshall, were also teachers in the District of Columbia, having relocated from New York. Mrs. Wilson was active in the Ladies' Union of Brooklyn and New York. Laura Wilson taught in the Center Street Methodist Church School in Louisville, Kentucky. The students' tuition paid her salary. Catherine Winslow taught for the AMA at Avery Institute in Charleston, South Carolina. Ellen B. Wood started the St. Aloysius' School for Girls in 1863 on Fifteenth Street in Washington, D.C. Wood was originally from Haiti. Her school was fee-based but free for those unable to pay. Alice Woodson taught in the Center Street Methodist Church School in Louisville, Kentucky. The students' tuition paid her salary. There are many more who remain unnamed and unreclaimed.

The African American teachers who took on the challenge of educating the newly freed people were missionaries in the truest sense of the word because they were in the vanguard of educating the black masses, especially in segregated schools. By elevating their brothers and sisters through education, they sought to ennoble and uplift the race as a whole. They, too, were on the front lines in the struggle for black liberation.

NOTES

1. *Pennsylvania Freedmen's Bulletin,* 1 August 1865.
2. *Pennsylvania Freedmen's Bulletin* (August 1867): 3.
3. Ellen N. Lawson, *The Three Sarahs: Documents of Antebellum Black College Women* (New York: Edwin Mellen Press, 1984), 89.

4. Joe M. Richardson, *Christian Reconstruction: the American Missionary Association and Southern Blacks, 1861-1890* (Athens: University of Georgia Press, 1986), 192.

5. Ibid., 196.

6. Dorothy Sterling, ed., *We Are Your Sisters: Black Women in the Nineteenth Century* (New York: W.W. Norton, 1984), 263-264.

7. Letter from Mary M. Brooks to Maria Weston Chapman, Rare Books and Manuscripts Department, Boston Public Library, ms.A.9.2.15.

8. Lawson, 216-217.

9. Ibid., 193.

10. Ibid., 190.

11. Primus Family Papers, Connecticut Historical Society, Hartford.

12. Ibid.

13. *Hartford Evening Press*, 7 November 1867.

14. Personal interviews with Mr. Raymond F. Thomas, Mr. Howard Thomas and Mrs. Carrie Thomas in Royal Oak, May 1997.

15. Primus Family Papers.

16. Julia Luckett, who taught in the Georgetown area of Washington, D.C., was from Canada but it is not certain if she is the woman Rebecca is referring to.

17. Ellen N. Lawson, *The Three Sarahs: Documents of Antebellum Black College Women.* (New York: Edwin Mellen Press, 1984), 86-89.

18. Ibid., 97.

19. Robert C. Morris, *Reading, 'Riting, and Reconstruction: the Education of Freedmen in the South, 1861-1870* (Chicago: University of Chicago Press, 1981), 127.

20. Joe M. Richardson, *Christian Reconstruction: the American Missionary Association and Southern Blacks, 1861-1890* (Athens: University of Georgia Press, 1986), 204.

21. Lawson, 144-145.

22. Ibid., 147.

23. John Gregg Fee, *Autobiography of John G. Fee* (Chicago: National Christian Association, 1891), 181-182. Curiously, Fee does not mention Jackson by name. Jessie Carney Smith's *Notable Black Women* does, however, in an article devoted to the teacher.

24. Ironically, in 1908, the United States Supreme Court ruled that Berea's policy of integration was a violation of Kentucky's segregation laws.

25. Linda Perkins, "The Black Female American Missionary Association Teacher in the South, 1861-1870" *in Black Americans in North Carolina and the South* Eds. Jeffrey Crow and Flora Hatley (Chapel Hill: University of North Carolina Press, 1984), 126.

26. Sterling, 267.

27. Lawson, 246-247.

28. Joe M. Richardson in *Christian Reconstruction* gives her name as Pauline Freeman; Ellen Lawson gives her name as Clara Freeman; Clara DeBoer lists a Clara Freeman but not a Pauline Freeman.

29. Bertram Wyatt-Brown, "Black Schooling During Reconstruction," *in The Web of Southern Social Relations: Women, Family, & Education* Eds. Walter Fraser, et al. (Athens: University of Georgia Press, 1985), 149.

30. Ibid., 238-240.

31. Sterling, 299.

32. *National Freedman*, 2 (May 1866): 148-149. Hoy's school must have been burned in April 1866 because the April 1866 issue of the *National Freedman* lists her as teaching in Trappe while the May issue has her in Burkittsville, apparently as a result of the burning.

33. Richardson (1986), 202.

34. Ibid., 274-275.

35. Sterling, 275.

36. Probably Julia F.P. Dickson from Boston.

37. Primus Family Papers, Connecticut Historical Society, Hartford.

38. *Freedmen's Record* 2 (April 1866):74.

39. Lawson, 240.

40. Marilyn Richardson, ed., *Maria W. Stewart: America's First Black Woman Political Writer* (Bloomington: Indiana University Press, 1987), 95.

41. Ibid.

42. William Loren Katz, ed., *History of Schools for the Colored Population* (New York: Arno Press, 1969, 1871), 263.

43. Darlene Clark Hine, et al., eds. *Black Women in America: an Historical Encyclopedia* (Bloomington: Indiana University Press, 1993), 437-438.

44. Ibid., 463.

45. Linda Perkins, "The Black Female American Missionary Association Teacher in the South, 1861-1870 *in Black Americans in North Carolina and the South*. Eds. Jeffrey Crow and Flora Hatley. (Chapel Hill: University of North Carolina Press, 1984), 126.

46. Ronald E. Butchart, "'We Can Best Instruct Our Own People': New York African Americans in the Freedmen's Schools, 1861-1875," *in African Americans and Education in the South, 1865-1900*. Ed. Donald G. Nieman (New York: Garland, 1994), 43.

47. Katz, 280-281.

48. Ibid.

49. The April 1866 *National Freedman* lists Anderson as teaching in Chestertown, a city a few miles from Edesville. She is also listed as teaching in Morgan Creek, Maryland but this might be the same as Chestertown.

50. Lawson, 78.

51. Ibid., 81-82.

52. Ibid., 116-117.

53. Ibid., 117, 121.

54. Jessie Carney Smith, ed., *Notable Black American Women*, Book II (Detroit, Michigan: Gale Research, 1996), 231-234.

55. *Pennsylvania Freedmen's Bulletin* (October 1867): 6.

56. *Christian Recorder*, 16 April 1864.

57. Lawson, 246.

58. Ibid., 128-129.

59. Ibid., 237.

60. Ibid., 298.

61. Sterling, 294-297.

62. Howard H. Bell, ed., *Minutes of the Proceedings of the National Negro Conventions 1830-1864* (New York: Arno Press, 1969), 15, 25; *Christian Recorder*, 15 October 1864.

63. Sterling, 296.

64. *Liberator*, 12 December 1862.

65. Sylvia G. Dannett, *Profiles of Negro Womanhood, 1619- 1900*, v. 1 (New York: M.W. Lads, 1964), 91.

66. Charlotte Forten Grimke, *Journals of Charlotte L. Forten Grimke* (New York: Oxford University Press, 1988), 397-398.

67. Ibid., 392.

68. Sterling, 267.

69. Ibid.

70. *Christian Recorder*, 26 November 1864.

71. Fanny Jackson Coppin, *Reminiscences of School Life, and Hints on Teaching* (Philadelphia: A.M.E. Book Concern, 1913), 18.

72. Susie King Taylor, *Reminiscences of My Life in Camp With the 33rd United States Colored Troops* (New York: Arno, 1968, 1902), 21.

73. Ibid., 11.

74. Sometimes seen as Gibbons

75. *Freedmen's Record* 3 (June 1867).

76. The 1865 *Annual Report* of the National Freedmen's Relief Association, New York lists a Miss M.A. Parker teaching in Wilmington, North Carolina.

77. *American Freedmen* 3 (April 1869).

78. Lawson, 109.

79. Katz, 369.

80. Lewis Lockwood, *Two Black Teachers During the Civil War* (New York: Arno Press, 1969, 1863), 86.

81. Lawson, 49.

82. Sterling, 263.

83. *Liberator*, 20 November 1857.

84. Clara DeBoer gives Blanche Harris' sister's name as Elizabeth E. Harris.

85. *Pennsylvania Freedmen's Bulletin* 1 (February 1865): 16.

86. Ira Berlin, et al., eds., *Free At Last: a Documentary History of Slavery, Freedom, and the Civil War* (New York: The New Press, 1992), 213.

87. Circular, Pennsylvania Freedmen's Relief Association, Philadelphia, January 15, 1869 [Pennsylvania Historical Society, Philadelphia].

88. *American Freedman* 2 (July 1867): 254.

89. *American Missionary* 12 (March 1868), 49.

90. Katz, 369.

91. Marion B. Lucas, *A History of Blacks in Kentucky* (Frankfort: Kentucky Historical Society, 1992), 239.

92. Sterling, 268.

93. *American Missionary*, 12 (April 1868): 194.

94. Richardson (1986), 197.

95. Sterling, 268.

96. Letter from Harriet Jacobs to Hannah Stevenson of the Teachers Committee of the New England Freedmen's Aid Society, March 10, 1864, Rare Books and Manuscripts Department, Boston Public Library, ms.A.10.1 no. 45.

97. Robert C. Morris, *Reading, 'Riting, and Reconstruction: the Education of Freedmen in the South, 1861-1870* (Chicago: University of Chicago Press, 1981), 111.

98. *Freedman's Friend* 1 (June 1864):4.

99. Elizabeth Keckley, *Behind the Scenes: Thirty Years a Slave and Four in the White House* (New York: Arno Press, 1968, 1868), 143.

100. Butchart (1994), 38-39.

101. *Christian Recorder*, 20 August 1864.

102. Rayford W. Logan and Michael Winston, eds., *Dictionary of American Negro Biography* (New York: W.W. Norton, 1982), 486.

103. Lockwood, iii.

104. Marianna W. Davis, ed., *Contributions of Black Women to America*, vol. 2 (Columbia, SC: Kenday Press, 1981), 276.

105. Benjamin Quarles, *The Negro in the Civil War* (New York: Da Capo Press, Inc., 1989, 1953), 122-123.

106. Ibid., 189.

107. Richardson (1986), 200.

108. Morris, 6.

109. Katz, 288.

110. Ibid., 97.

111. Katz, 203, 263.

112. Ibid., 285.

113. The names are culled from various sources including Butchart, DeBoer, Hine, Katz, Lawton, Lucas, Scruggs, Sterling, *American Freedman*, *National Freedman*, and *Freedmen's Record* and are pretty much limited to 1867 and before to reflect the Civil War period, rather than Reconstruction.

114. Later Avery Institute

CHAPTER 8

Contending Against Outrage and Oppression: Civil Rights Activism

In addition to the outright racial atrocities that could be visited on any African American at any time, were the petty indignities that colored the everyday lives of black people—in retail establishments, hotels, transportation, restaurants, education. African American women felt these affronts keenly and actively fought against them. During the Civil War, they used their husbands', fathers' sons' and brothers' participation as soldiers and sailors in their confrontation with the racial status quo. They also used their gender to illustrate how racism affected "proper ladies," thereby establishing their right to be considered as such.

The physical mistreatment of African American women on the streetcars of some of the nation's major cities during the Civil War spurred the African American community to increase the level of their ongoing activism. The July 30, 1864 *Christian Recorder* reported a mass meeting at the Sansom Street Hall of "some of Philadelphia's best sons and daughters." The meeting was held to protest the inhumane treatment of the city's African American women traveling to minister to sick and wounded African American soldiers in Camp William Penn. "Even old women, whose sons are at Camp Wm. Penn, are obliged to ride on the front platform," meaning that the women were not allowed inside the car to sit but were exposed to the weather by being forced to hold onto the outside of the car. The gathering came up with a set of resolutions, including the following two:

> *Resolved,* That in the sight of the present national struggle, no more shameful sight can be presented to an intelligent, sensitive mind, than that of respectable females standing upon the platform

149

of empty cars, with sons, husbands, brothers beside them in United
States uniform, ready to defend the rights and property of those
railway corporations which treat them thus indignantly and
demand full fare. *Resolved,* That the white citizens of this country
are at this moment arraigned at the bar of retributive justice for
their inhumanity to the people of color, and there is no logical
hope in the mind of any sane man that this trial will close until
justice is done to our outraged people.

An African American woman wrote to the *Philadelphia Press* in
August 1864: "We have in this city three societies[1] of ladies for the relief
of the sick and wounded soldiers." Considering it an outrage that the
women were hampered in ministering to the needs of men who "regardless
of the prejudice they have always encountered in this land of their birth,
have at the call of their country rushed forth to aid in putting down the
rebellion," she said that it was "a stigma upon the city of Philadelphia."[2]
This was true; Philadelphia was well-known for discriminating against
African Americans in public accommodations. Nevertheless, in spite of
incredible activism on the part of the African American community and
the opprobrium heaped on the city from around the country, it was not
until 1867 that the Pennsylvania State Legislature enacted a law
prohibiting discrimination on streetcars. Caroline Le Count, a teacher in
Philadelphia, brought the suit which finally forced the elimination of
legalized discrimination.

The streetcars of the Eighth Avenue Railroad in New York were
ordered in July 1864 by their Superintendent to allow African Americans
"to ride in all the cars (both large and small) of this Company" after Ellen
Anderson had the conductor of one of the cars arrested for assault when
she was forcibly ejected from a streetcar. Anderson, "a
respectable-looking woman attired in deep mourning," was the widow of
Sergeant Anderson of Company F, 26th U.S. Colored Infantry. She
contended that she "was as good as any white people" and she refused to
remove herself from a car reserved for whites.[3] Her case received a great
deal of attention in the black press because every victory meant that
African Americans were one step closer to full equality.

Charlotte L. Brown sued the Omnibus Rail Road Company of San
Francisco in 1863 after being forcibly ejected by the conductor from a
streetcar even though the rail company had rescinded its policy of
excluding African Americans.[4] Also in San Francisco, the wealthy
entrepreneur, Mary Ellen Pleasant[5], successfully fought for passage of an
1863 bill which allowed African Americans to testify in court. She used

this law in 1868 to contest discrimination on the North Beach Railroad Company. Pleasant had been engaging in the struggle for black liberation for a long time. She had been a member of the Chatham (Canada) Vigilance Committee, aided fugitives, allegedly met with John Brown in preparation for his raid on Harper's Ferry, and directed an employment agency for African Americans in San Francisco.[6]

Sojourner Truth also actively challenged discrimination on public transportation. She declared that continuing discrimination in public accommodation was evidence that "it is hard for the old slaveholding spirit to die. But *die* it *must.*" In her sixties, she sought to hasten its death by engaging in several confrontations with conductors. For instance, in the fall of 1865, as she was working with refugees in Washington, D.C., a racist streetcar conductor injured her shoulder when he tried to push her off the car. Truth had him arrested and convicted of assault and battery.[7]

At 5'11" tall, big-boned, dark-skinned with a powerful voice, she was an imposing figure and she used her appearance to advantage. She encouraged fugitive women housed in the Freedmen's Village in Arlington, Virginia to stand up for their rights when kidnappers repeatedly raided the camp and stole African American children to sell in the South:

> The Marylanders tormented them by coming over, seizing, and carrying away their children. If the mothers made a 'fuss,' as these heartless wretches called those natural expressions of grief in which bereaved mothers are apt to indulge, they were thrust into the guard-house. When this was made known to Sojourner, she told them they must not permit such outrages, that they were free, and had rights which would be recognized and maintained by the laws, and that they could bring these robbers to justice. Her electrifying words seemed to inspire them . . . the exasperated Marylanders threatened to put Sojourner into the guard-house. She told them that if they attempted to put her in the guard-house, she 'would make the United States rock like a cradle.'[8]

This would have been an especially important action for Sojourner because while she had been enslaved in upstate New York, she had not only suffered physical abuse as a child but she had experienced the grief of having her own child sold and mistreated. She successfully sued for the return of her son who had been sold illegally one year before the enslavement of Africans officially ended in New York through a gradual emancipation law. Solomon Gedney, knowing that he would have to free Peter [Williams], Sojourner's five-year-old son, in 1827 sold him into permanent enslavement in Alabama. Peter's condition when Truth finally saw her son again, his body scarred from repeated beatings and kickings, no doubt added fuel to her conviction that no mother should ever have to experience the pain she had.[9]

Even though she had been enslaved in New York, Truth had experienced all the horrors of enslavement that the southern African Americans she was now working with had: physical and mental abuse, the sale of her children, backbreaking work and the denial of education. Because she had been initially enslaved by Dutch speakers, English was not her first language. Her English-speaking masters, the John Neelys of Twaalfskill, New York, beat the nine-year-old severely because she could not understand their commands. She bore the scars for the rest of her life.[10] She had only become free in 1827 as a result of a New York law which emancipated African Americans enslaved in the state. Her children, however, had to serve long indentureships after their emancipation. She, therefore, understood that while the immediate needs of the fugitives for clothing, shelter and food had to be addressed, concrete material aid—such as education, employment, land, and citizenship rights—was essential for the newly freed people to help and sustain themselves.

Truth's desire for empowerment and agency can also be seen in the fact of her renaming herself—in discarding a name assigned by someone else in favor of one which reflected, to her mind, her essence. It is the same agency she wished for all African Americans, which is evident in her attempts to help refugees become self-sufficient after the Civil War. Truth initiated a job placement program in 1867 that attempted to secure jobs for refugees and in 1870 she began petitioning the United States government for land in the western territories to be used to settle African American refugees. Her petition the United States Congress stated: " . . . we believe that the freed colored people in and about Washington, dependent upon government for support, would be greatly benefited and might become useful citizens by being placed in a position to support themselves: We, the undersigned earnestly request your honorable body to set apart for them a portion of the public land in the West, and erect buildings thereupon for the aged and infirm, and otherwise legislate so as to secure the desired results."[11] Truth went on a lecture tour to gain support for her project. She later participated in the Women's Rights Movement.

The elderly Harriet Tubman, who gave so much service to the Union, experienced racist treatment similar to Sojourner's in 1865 in Washington, D.C. as she was returning to her home in Auburn, New York. She was forced into the baggage car by the conductor and two other white men even though she had a military pass. Her arm which was injured in the process never fully healed.[12] African American female activists, like Frances Ellen Watkins Harper, used this treatment of "Moses," as Tubman was called, in their campaigns against discrimination. As they did for African American male veterans, they cited Harriet's contributions to the Union to show how race, rather than gender or service, determined the treatment of African Americans.

Harriet Jacobs brought a suit for $5,000 in damages against the Atlantic Navigation Company after she was ejected from one of the company's steamers in Savannah en route to New York. She, along with her daughter, Louisa, had gone to Savannah to teach and work with freedpeople in 1865 after ending her relief activities in Washington, D.C.

The fiery orator and poet, Frances Ellen Watkins Harper, also continued her ongoing activism after the war, lecturing on behalf of freedpeople and working for civil rights for African Americans. Nonetheless, she was dismayed at the lack of progress during Reconstruction and disturbed that the South had not learned its lesson in defeat. She wrote bitterly from Wilmington, Delaware in July 1867: "I am about leaving the unreconstructed States . . . the shadows of the past have not been fully lifted from the minds of the former victims of slavery. We have had a mournful past in this country, enslaved in the South and proscribed in the North . . . I think the former ruling class in the South are not fit to be trusted with the welfare of the whites nor the liberty of the blacks . . . Shall [Robert E.] Lee, with tens of thousands of murders clinging to his skirts, escape the full desert of his crimes . . . Shall Jefferson Davis, with his hands dripping with the blood of Andersonville, and Libby, and Florence[13], breathe the air of freedom . . . "[14]

Like many of the other African American female activists, Harper was involved with the women's suffrage movement after the Civil War. She related the women's struggle for voting rights to the struggle African Americans waged for equality, saying at the Eleventh National Woman's Rights Convention in New York in 1866: "Born of a race whose inheritance has been outrage and wrong, most of my life has been spent in battling against those wrongs." As with most African American women, race was the defining factor, not gender.

She understood clearly that there could be no gender equality for African American women as long as racial inequality existed. "You white women speak here of rights. I speak of wrongs. I, as a colored woman, have had in this country an education which has made me feel as if I were in the situation of Ishmael, my hand against every man, and every man's hand against me. Let me go to-morrow morning and take my seat in one of your street cars . . . and the conductor will put up his hand and stop the car rather than let me ride . . . Aye, in the capital of the nation, where the black man consecrated himself to the nation's defence, faithful when the white man was faithless, they put me in the smoking car! . . . if I want to ride in the streetcars of Philadelphia, they send me to ride on the platform with the driver."[15]

Susie King Taylor was especially disheartened by the racism that continued to flourish after the Civil War. For this veteran, racism, lynchings and discrimination were very hard to swallow. She had expected, as had many other African Americans, that the Civil War would have eliminated discrimination and oppression, especially since African American men had contributed so valiantly to the Union cause. Instead, she found herself confronting insidious and overt racism. She asks in her autobiography,

> I wonder if our white fellow men realize the true sense or meaning of brotherhood? For two hundred years we had toiled for them; the war of 1861 came and was ended, and we thought our race was forever freed from bondage, and that the two races could live in unity with each other, but when we read almost every day of what is being done to my race by some whites in the South, I sometimes ask, 'Was the war in vain? . . .In this 'land of the free' we are burned, tortured, and denied a fair trial, murdered for any imaginary wrong conceived in the brain of the negro-hating white man. There is no redress for us from a government which promised to protect all under its flag . . . No, we cannot sing, 'My country, 't is of thee, Sweet land of Liberty'! It is hollow mockery . . .All we ask for is 'equal justice,' the same that is accorded to all other races who come to this country, of their own free will (not forced to, as we were), and are allowed to enjoy every privilege, unrestricted, while we are denied what is rightfully our own in a country which the labor of our forefathers helped to make what it is.[16]

Taylor saw a man lynched in 1898 in Clarksdale, Mississippi after enduring an uncomfortable segregated train ride from Cincinnati to Shreveport, Louisiana in order to bring her dying son home to Boston. Because the train company refused to sell her a place in a sleeping berth for her son, she was forced to watch him die in Shreveport. Her son's experience made racism all too personal. "It seemed very hard, when his father fought to protect the Union and our flag, and yet his boy was denied, under this same flag, a berth to carry him home to die, because he was a negro."[17]

She also referred to the fact that the African American Civil War veterans that she met in Shreveport did not wear their veteran's buttons because they were afraid they would not be able to get work. At this point in her narrative, she does not mention her own valorous service in support of the Union or the work she was doing with Corps 67 of Women's Relief Corps, auxiliary to the Grand Army of the Republic which she had helped to establish in 1886 in Boston in order to give "aid and comfort in the twilight of their lives" to Union veterans. Rather, she closes her memoir with reiterative words of burning indignation: "Justice we ask,—to be citizens of these United States, where so many of our people have shed their blood, with their white comrades, that the stars and stripes should never be polluted."[18]

Like Susie King Taylor, Isabella Gibbins, an educator of freedpeople who had herself suffered the horrible cruelties of enslavement, was determined that African Americans place the ordeal of enslavement in our epic memory: "Can we forget the crack of the whip, cowhide, whipping-post, the auction-block, the hand-cuffs, the spaniels, the iron collar, the negro-trader tearing the young child from its mother's breast as a whelp from the lioness? Have we forgotten that by those horrible cruelties, hundreds of our race have been killed? No, we have not, nor ever will. O. God help us to love these people."[19] It was probably impossible for Gibbins to be able to love a people who visited such atrocities on her and her people. Nevertheless, she expected African Americans to use the horrendous experience as a stepping-stone for upliftment in the process of developing a racial consciousness that would allow them to overcome the legacy of enslavement.

As wives, sisters and mothers, white women had their relationship to the white male power structure to protect and serve them. African women had no such shelter. The longtime feminist and women's rights activist, Frederick Douglass, clearly understood this as he spoke for African Americans, men and women, at the American Equal Rights Association Convention in 1869:

> I do not see how anyone can pretend is that there is the same urgency in giving the ballot to women as to the Negro. With us, the matter is a question of life and death . . . When women, because they are women, are hunted down through the cities of New York[20] and New Orleans; when they are dragged from their houses and hung upon lamp-posts; when their children are torn from their

arms, and their brains dashed out upon the pavement; when they are objects of insult and outrage at every turn; when they are in danger of having their homes burnt down over their heads; when their children are not allowed to enter schools; then they will have an urgency to obtain the ballot equal to our own. [In response to a voice in the audience which asked, 'Is that not all true about black women?, Douglass said] Yes, yes, yes; it is true of the black woman, but not because she is a woman, but because she is black.[21]

Douglass was referring to the 1863 New York City Draft Riot and a 1868 riot in New Orleans in which 34 African Americans were killed and 119 wounded. African American women were not spared the insane rage of white men and women. They were killed, maimed and made homeless because they were Africans and despite being women. And the fact that some of the women had relatives in the armed forces did nothing to stem the violence.

Douglass, and the rest of black America, received and devoured the horrific details of the disorders from African American newspapers, and there were several white riots between 1863 and 1868. Whites rioted in Detroit in March 1863, killing two people, injuring twenty more and burning more than thirty buildings.[22] Troy, New York and Boston also had draft riots in 1863. Whites resorted to lawlessness in Memphis in 1866, leaving 46 African Americans dead, five black women raped and scores left homeless. Four black churches were burned in May 1866 in Petersburg, Virginia; three of them conducted schools for freedmen. Shortly before these incidents, the barracks housing African American soldiers were burned in Maryland.[23] There was white unrest in New Orleans the same year. Other smaller disorders occurred as white supremacists formed organizations such as the Ku Klux Klan and the White Camellias to forcibly and violently deny African Americans equal rights.

Mrs. Statts, who had gone to New York to visit her son, described one such experience during that city's 1863 white riot to protest the draft: "In the next room to where I was sitting was a poor woman, who had been confined with a child on Sunday, three days previous. Some of the rioters broke through the front door with pick axes, and came rushing into the room where this poor woman lay, and commenced to pull the clothes off from her . . . In a little while I saw the innocent babe, of three days old, come crashing down into the yard; some of the rioters had dashed it out of the back window, killing it instantly . . . One of the mob seized a pocketbook, which he saw in my bosom, and in his eagerness to get it tore the dress off my shoulders. I, with several others, then ran to the 29th street Station House, but we were here turned away . . . I then went down to my husband's in Broome Street, and there I encountered another mob, who, before I could escape commenced stoning me. They beat me severely."[24] Mrs. Statts' story was just one of many.

African Americans did not docilely submit to the atrocities, however. For example, eight African American women on Thompson Street were determined to protect themselves during the riot. "They had filled several boilers with a mixture of water, soap and ashes, a combination which when heated to the proper temperature they called 'the King of Pain.' As William Wells Brown entered the room he saw the huge, tin boilers which were steaming away on an old-fashioned cookstove, filling the room with a dense fog. Encircling the boilers was the octet of Amazons, armed with dippers. 'How will you manage if they attempt to come into this room?' asked Brown. 'We'll fling hot water on them, and scald their very hearts out.' 'Can you all throw water without injuring each other?' 'O yes, Honey, we've been practicing all day.'"[25] These were not fragile, passive women. They knew that their lives depended upon their own resources and resolve.

Over a period of five days, July 13-17, 1863, more than eleven African Americans were killed, hundreds were wounded, thousands were left homeless and destitute during the riots. African Americans also suffered thousands of dollars in property losses; the Colored Orphan Asylum and the Colored Seamen's Home were destroyed. Through their relief efforts, African American women were instrumental in raising money to rebuild the orphanage. It is significant, however, that while the draft of white men into the army sparked the New York City Draft Riot, it was a longstanding fear of black economic competition and anti-African attitudes which were at the root of the carnage.

African American women knew that they were not going to be spared racist treatment because they were females. Rather, their race made them the targets of vicious physical attacks and discrimination. Therefore, they contended against outrage and oppression on whatever front presented itself.

NOTES

1. The Ladies' Sanitary Association of St. Thomas Episcopal Church, the Soldiers' Relief Association and the Ladies' Union Association.

2. Phillip S. Foner, "The Battle to End Discrimination on Philadelphia's Streetcars," *Pennsylvania History*, 40 (1973): 270- 271.

3. *Christian Recorder*, 9 July 1864.

4. Shirley J. Yee, *Black Women Abolitionists: a Study in Activism, 1828-1860*. (Knoxville: University of Tennessee Press, 1992), p. 134.

5. Sometimes known as "Mammy" Pleasant, an appellation she understandable disliked.

6. Darlene Clark Hine, et al., eds., *Black Women in America: an Historical Encyclopedia* (Bloomington: Indiana University Press, 1993), 932-933.

7. Dorothy Sterling, ed., *We Are Your Sisters: Black Women in the Nineteenth Century* (New York: W.W. Norton, 1984), 254.

8. Frances W. Titus, *Narrative of Sojourner Truth* (New York: Arno Press, 1969, 1878), 182-183.

9. Nell I. Painter, *Sojourner Truth: a Life, a Symbol* (New York: W.W. Norton, 1997), 32-35.

10. Ibid., 14.

11. Titus, 199.

12. Hallie Q. Brown, *Homespun Heroines and Other Women of Distinction* (New York: Oxford University Press, 1988, 1926), 64- 65.

13. military prisons

14. Frances Smith Foster, ed., *A Brighter Coming Day: a Frances Ellen Watkins Harper Reader*. (New York: Feminist Press at City University of New York, 1990), 124-125.

15. Ibid., 217-218.

16. Susie King Taylor, *Reminiscences of My Life in Camp With the 33rd United States Colored Troops* (New York: Arno Press, 1968, 1902), 61-64.

17. Ibid., 71-72.

18. Ibid., 59, 76.

19. *Freedmen's Record* 3 (June 1867).

20. Because white enlistment had dropped in the North, a draft was instituted in 1863. Poor whites rioted in New York to protest being conscripted into the army because they could not afford to pay $300 each to get substitutes to serve in their stead.

21. Philip Foner, ed., *Frederick Douglass on Women's Rights* (New York: Da Capo Press, 1992), 87.

22. Donald Yacovone, ed., *A Voice of Thunder: the Civil War Letters of George E. Stephens* (Urbana: University of Illinois Press, 1997), 232.

23. *National Freedman* 2 (May 1866): 149

24. Committee of Merchants for the Relief of Colored People Suffering From the Late Riots in the City of New York. *Report* (New York: George A. Whitehorne, 1863), 16-17.

25. Benjamin Quarles, *The Negro in the Civil War* (New York: Da Capo Press, 1989, 1953), p. 241.

CHAPTER 9

Don't Fret for Me: Resisting By Surviving

One of the greatest forms of resistance to their condition during the Civil War was African American women's mere survival. Far too often the odds, physical as well as mental, were against them. Nevertheless, they were active agents in their own survival and in doing so, African American women insured the collective survival of the black community. They disrupted the southern plantation system by running away, being recalcitrant, engaging in work stoppages, striking and cooperating with Union troops and they attempted to keep families and homes intact. They often suffered great deprivation in the process.

Black women challenged the system of enslavement directly by confronting slaveholders and committing acts which interfered with the plantation system. Savannah was the first enslaved person in Hancock County, Georgia to seize her freedom by fleeing to the Union lines.[1] "Saucy" wives of African American soldiers were imprisoned in Louisville, Kentucky.[2] Their sauciness undoubtedly stemmed from the fact that their husbands' enlistments ensured their own freedom. Mary Fields, Eliza, Mildred, Patsy and Lucinda all seized the opportunity of freedom which their husbands' and fathers' enlistment afforded by leaving the place of their enslavement.[3] A woman asked leave of her mistress to attend a choir rehearsal and escaped to Union lines in Lexington, Kentucky, along with several others, taking a carriage and three horses. In Henry County, Kentucky, Susan fled enslavement with all her children in 1864.[4]

Evidently, white Southerners had deluded themselves into believing that the African Americans they enslaved would care more for their white enslavers than they would for freedom. This was a notion that they had especially assigned to enslaved women. "The masters had expected more than obedience from their slaves; they had expected faithfulness—obedience internalized as duty, respect, and love."[5] Of course, if one enslaves other human beings, it is incumbent on the enslaver to be oblivious to the natural human feelings of the enslaved.

If the diaries and journals of whites in rebel territory are any indication, enslavers were sorely disappointed in the assumed loyalty of the people they enslaved. By way of example, white slaveowner, Mag Bingham, wrote to her brother in 1862, complaining about the recalcitrant behavior of the African women she enslaved: "The boys are not so insolent, the women are inclined to be so."[6] It is instructive that Bingham refers to the insolent females as "women," while the males are referred to as "boys." Resistance obviously forced some measure of respect from the slaveholder.

Mary Boykin Chesnut, wife of a Confederate official, gives us another example. She remarked mournfully in her diary: "The Martins left Columbia [South Carolina] the Friday before I did. And their mammy, the negro woman who had nursed them, refused to go with them. That daunted me."[7] Chesnut, who had been so sure that African Americans were content in enslavement, related in another diary entry a conversation she overheard, "They talked of the negroes wherever the Yankees had been, who flocked to them and showed them where the silver and valuables were hid by the white people. Ladies' maids dressing themselves in their mistresses' gowns before their faces and walking off."[8]

After complaining about African American male insubordination and insolence, the August 6, 1862 *Richmond Enquirer* reported that "negro women, too, are not behind the lords of creation in these acts of impudence. Cases are reported where these wretches have attempted to smack the jaws of their mistresses, and it is not an uncommon thing for them to dress in their mistresses' clothes put on their jewelry and ornaments, and leave them in the face of day . . . The people will thus see what they are to expect when the Yankee and the negro shall obtain the ascendency. Who would not rather die a thousand deaths than submit to such indignities and insults on the part of these black villains?" It is not too much of a leap to see why an unreconstructed, unpunished and unrepentant South would usher in the kinds of racial atrocities which characterized the post-bellum period.

The diaries and logs of enslavers give a more immediate and unembellished depiction of enslavement because the manipulation of history to benefit the socially constructed notions of race which characterize later white renditions of the Civil War is absent. Because they are rationalizing and justifying the oppression of African Americans, white Civil War histories written shortly after the conflict attempt to paint a picture of "happy darkeys" who were loyal to their masters during the conflict. For example, William W. Davis, writing in 1913, just forty-eight years after the war but during a period of major black disenfranchisement, wrote: "The fact is that the Southern slave was well-fed, well-housed, well-treated, and lastly, well-watched and controlled; hence the peace about the slave quarters on isolated plantations when war was raging at no great distance. Many slaves in the white households loved 'their white people' and in return were loved with a sincerity proven by experience."[9]

The narratives and actions of enslaved Africans clearly challenge such an outrageous idea. Certainly there were Africans who did not actively or violently resist enslavement but like all human beings, Africans had a natural desire to be free. And, a crucial element of that desire was a resentment toward whomever and whatever denied such freedom. African American women expressed their resentment against the people and system which prevented their exercising full freedom. Their narratives invariably emphasize the horrors of enslavement, especially the break up of families, sexual and physical abuse, loss of children, things that had a special significance for women.

African American women acted on their belief in their natural right to be free. According to Ervin L. Jordan, Jr., "Afro-Virginian women initiated individual acts of resistance that demonstrated their capacity for ferocity. Poisonings, assaults, stabbings, arson, vandalism, escapes, and murders terrified and astounded Confederate Virginians."[10] He details several instances of defiance. African American women throughout the South engaged in similar acts, a fact which is solidly attested to in the diaries of whites writing during this period.

Mill, an enslaved woman from Memphis, illustrates the type of African American woman most representative of an inherently resistant spirit. She told Laura Haviland, a white abolitionist, about how she came to be free and how she paid her mistress back for the special denial of her womanhood—the loss of her children. As Union soldiers approached the plantation, Mill's owner wants reassurance of her loyalty:

> "Now, Mill, you won't go, will you?"
> "I'll go if I have a chance."
> "Now, remember I brought you up. You won't take your children away from me, will you, Mill?"
> "Mistress, I will take what children I've got left."

"If they find that trunk of money or silver plate you'll say it's yours, won't you?"
"Mistress, I can't lie over that; you bought that silver plate when you sold my three children."

Mill and the other enslaved people left with the Union soldiers, leaving her mistress crying and wringing her hands and bereft of her money, silver plate, food and other goods. There was no equivocating about the nature of enslavement or the nature of the enslaver—Mill understood that to the slaveholder, herself a woman, Mill's children were objects to be bought and sold, like silverplate.

That this white woman was blind to the fact that she had committed a monstrous crime by selling, and profiting from the sale, another woman's children, speaks volumes about the nature of enslavement. Her blindness is possible only because she, like other enslavers, had created a psyche which would allow her to cherish her own children and possessions while selling the most cherished possession a parent has—children. Such a psyche is feasible only if the parents of the children being sold, and the children, have been removed from any possibility of being seen as having an essential humanity by the enslaver. The enslaved are viewed, by the enslaver, as objects devoid of feelings of any kind; they are not parents but chattel with reproductive capability. However, certain principles of humanity are compromised in the enslavement process, not just for the enslaved but also for the enslaver—one cannot believe in one's own humanity while outraging the humanity of other human beings. Objectification allows oppression and the unreconstructed psyche which allowed the objectification of African Americans is the mentality that most southerners carried with them into the period following the Civil War. Further, such a psyche cannot be changed by simple legislation. Rather, it must be re-educated.

When Haviland asked Mill if she didn't think she should have kept the silverplate for herself, she replied, "O no I couldn't touch it. It was part of my poor dear children."[11] Haviland also missed the point—why would Mill want to own something that represents such a monumental loss as her children? Mill's story, then, is the horror of enslavement "writ large."

Some enslaved women were able to extract a measure of physical as well as moral justice. In Virginia, Union soldiers saved a young African American woman as she was being flogged by her mistress. She was allowed to disrobe the slaveowner, thrash her, keep her clothes and leave with the troops.[12] Edmonia, who was enslaved in Richmond, is another example. On her return from an errand she brought back with her Union soldiers who ransacked her owner's plantation. After taking what she wanted from the owner's trunks, Edmonia fled with the soldiers.[13]

A slaveowner, William H. Clopton of Charles City County in Virginia, was whipped by some of the Africans he had enslaved after he was captured by the 1st USCI. The slaveowner was stripped, tied to a tree and flogged, first by William Harris who had been enslaved and abused by Clopton and then, by three African women who had recently been beaten by the slaveowner. A correspondent to the *Christian Recorder* crowed, "Oh, that I had the tongue to express my feelings while standing on the banks of the James river, on the soil of Virginia, the mother state of slavery, as a witness of such a sudden reverse!"[14] The correspondent, George W. Hatton of the 1st USCI, mentioned that this happened close to Jamestown where the first Africans arrived in the British colonies. He also referred to the African American women as "ladies," giving them a status so often denied black women, especially enslaved women.

Enslaved women gave food, slaveowners' valuables, livestock and information to Union forces. Susie King Taylor contended that, "there were hundreds of [women] who assisted the Union soldiers by hiding them and helping them to escape. Many were punished for taking food to the prison stockades for the prisoners . . . One of these stockades . . . was in the suburbs of [Savannah, Georgia], and they said it was an awful place. The Union soldiers were in it, worse than pigs, without any shelter from sun or storm, and the colored women would take food there at night and pass it to them, through the holes in the fence. The soldiers were starving, and these women did all they could toward relieving those men, although they knew the penalty, should they be caught giving them aid. Others assisted in various ways the Union army."[15]

Luis Emilio noted, "Mr. Reuben Tomlinson brought a large supply [of fresh vegetables] for the Fifty-fourth,—a present from the contrabands about Beaufort; and similar welcome gifts, followed from the same source from time to time."[16] African American women, without question, made up a major portion of these benefactors.

They aided Union soldiers who were wounded, sick or lost. A white Union soldier contended: "Many a soldier will remember, how, when he fell out of the ranks during one of those severe marches, and the planter near by scowled and glowered so that he would not enter the rich man's door, some poor 'aunty,' black as the ace of spades, helped him to her own cabin, placed him on her own bed, made him tea and gruel, and nursed him as tenderly as his own sister would have done."[17] Lieutenant Hannibal Johnson of the Third Maine Infantry recorded such help in his diary as he hid in the woods near Columbia, South Carolina after escaping from a Confederate prison camp: "Still in the woods, the women coming to us twice during the day to bring us food and inform us that a guide will be ready at dark. God bless the poor slaves."[18]

Two white Union officers related the story of their escape from a Confederate prison in Columbia, South Carolina and their flight through Confederate territory to Knoxville, Tennessee. They received assistance from the enslaved, especially women, which saved their lives. They indicated that a particularly perilous portion of their journey was through western North Carolina. "The country is ransacked by Rebel details, who plunder the defenceless women and children . . . In traveling over a distance of one hundred and thirty miles, across the mountains, a scene of great destitution prevailed; women performed the duties of men; the children had no shoes, and the country seemed given up to entire lawlessness. The remainder of their journey was executed solely under the guidance of women . . . "[19]

Willard Glazier, a white Union soldier who escaped from Camp Sorghum[20] in Columbia, South Carolina, acknowledged the assistance that enslaved Africans gave to Union soldiers. "It is an established fact that it would have been impossible for our men, held as prisoners of war in the South, to make an escape without the aid of negroes . . . "[21] Glazier and his white compatriot were taken to the home of Aunt Katy near North Edisto River close to Aiken, South Carolina which "was the general gathering place of all in want of assistance. The good old soul gladly roused from her slumber when she learned that Yankees were at the door awaiting her attention. We were welcomed with a hearty 'God bless ye, Massa,' and while she made preparations for our 'creature comforts,' a little boy was sent to ask in her dusky neighbors that they might 'rejoice with her' over the good fortune of having an opportunity to aid friends in escaping from a common enemy."[22] Despite the enslaved's graciousness, Glazier was unable to relinquish his basic objectification of the Africans who helped him, continually referring to them as "darkies," "niggers" and "Sambo" and making fun of their speech and religious practices.

Just as African American men did, black women ran away from the plantations and suffered the same fate as black men when caught. George Clary, a white Union surgeon in New Orleans, noted "A girl came in one morning before light from over the river with her arm cut badly. She said her master threw her on the floor against some crockery."[23] Despite being injured, she still ran away.

A correspondent for the *Boston Transcript* related the following eyewitness account of a fugitive: "As I was standing on the land at Lady's Island, a poor but rather good looking yellow woman came over in a 'dug out,' paddled by herself, from the mainland, and her choking sobs drew my attention, when I asked the reason for her hurry and grief. 'O massa, massa, I have no daughter nor child now; the white man shot my daughter in the back, and took his gun and beat the head off my poor child.' She could say no more; she sank upon the ground from exhaustion, and when she was able to stand we noticed blood running down the right side of her dress; she had been shot right through the body, under the lower rib, and has since died of her wound."[24]

Women often ran away to the military camps to be close to their men and to keep their families together. Those who managed to stay in the camps suffered shortages of food, clothing, housing and medical supplies. Diseases included pneumonia, typhoid, measles, smallpox and diarrhea. As the Western Sanitary Commission said in 1863 in referring to the camps in the Mississippi Valley, half of the African Americans in the area were "doomed to die in the process of freeing the rest."[25] Elizabeth Botume described a refugee camp near Beaufort, South Carolina which had more refugees than the camp could cope with so tents were erected to deal with the overflow. During the "unusually severe" winter, "small-pox broke out amongst the refugees, and their wants and sufferings were indescribable."[26]

Josephine S. Griffing, the white General Agent of the NFRA, wrote about the privation of women in the camps in Washington, D.C. "A large part of the sufferers in this District are the wives, children, and parents of soldiers, who have fought and died in our battles." In true abolitionist fashion, she went on to document severe cases, focusing on the material condition of the women:

Sarah Carter whose husband was "carried off in the Southern army" and who had a five month old baby and no wood;

Dolly Davidge, an old woman whose two sons were in Government service, who had no food or wood;

Nancy Dotson, who had been an army cook, had a blind sister she cared for and neither had food, blankets or wood;

Henrietta Williams whose husband was in the army and who had a sick one-year-old child and no food or wood.

Caroline Young whose husband died in government service and who had three children, one of whom was crippled.

She recounted many cases in detail but she also noted how adamant the women were about staying put until they could reunite with their families.

> An astonishing large number of women, who have been brought here by events of the war, without a husband, have seized with great avidity this opportunity to make for themselves and children a *home*, which they have struggled laudably and well to keep, at an expense that has often periled life and bread . . . The strength of their domestic affection predominates . . . not only in their unwillingness to break up the homes, no matter how comfortless, but in the sacrifice the old are willing to make for their grandchildren and great grandchildren, and the returning devotion that the young and middle aged exhibit in hunting up and returning to, or providing for the old mothers and grand parents they have left behind when they were carried away by the rebels, enlisted in the Union army, or were brought away by the soldiers as wards of the Government . . . [T]hough to all appearance they must feel the keenest want, the sacred ties of relations and *home*, in a dark shanty even, are so sweet to them that they refuse to be separated for so great a boon as good rations . . . [27]

The women were resisting being forced to leave their families to take jobs in other areas and states or risk losing the rations that the government provided. As Griffing said, "These women, the only guardians of their children, feel it to be hard, and an infringement of the right guaranteed by their late freedom, that they must again be broken up and turned over to the probabilities of becoming wanderers and vagabonds, instead of receiving the *little pecuniary aid* necessary to bind together the heretofore scattered family relations, which both instinct and law recognize as the first want in society, church, and state."[28]

But a most poignant picture of the desperate situation many African American women were in can be seen in a letter from Emma Steward to her husband, Solomon, in the 1st South Carolina Infantry: " . . . an administering angel has come and borne my dear little babe to join with them. My babe only live one day. It was a little girl . . . I am now sick in bed and have got nothing to live on. The ration that they give for six days I can make it last but 2 days. They don't send me any wood. I don't get any light at all. You must see to that as soon as possible for I am in want of something to eat."[29]

However, many of the Union commanders drove women and children away from the camps, calling the women, as F.W. Lister, white colonel of the 40th USCI in Bridgeport, Alabama did, "colored prostitutes." Lister maintained that he was trying to "prevent the camp . . . from becoming a brothel on a gigantic scale." Refusing to recognize the legitimacy of the marriages African American soldiers entered into, he decided that "the larger proportion of the enlisted men change their so called wives as often as the regiment changes stations." He acknowledged the possibility that there might have been "some virtuous wives . . . amongst the number so excluded from the camp, but I gravely doubt it." According to Lister, the "immorality . . . required a strong effort to repress it." He was obviously given to strong repressive measures. The inhumane treatment he gave their wives and children, he extended to the African American troops under his command. "It is also true that I keep some of the men hand-cuffed, and only regret I cannot have some of them shot."[30]

The women and children were forced to return to their former owners or were left at the mercy of the elements. In May 1864, Colonel A.H. Clark, the white commander of Camp Nelson in central Kentucky, and Lieutenant George A. Harraford, Post Adjutant, issued the following order to Lieutenant John McQueen, Provost Marshal of Camp Nelson: "Information has reached these headquarters that three of the women which you placed beyond the lines yesterday are back in camp; and the colonel commanding [the notorious Speed Smith Fry], directs that you send out your patrol and arrest them, and confine them in the military prison until they are all collected by themselves, when you will tie them up and give them a few lashes, and expel them beyond the lines the distance heretofore ordered. Also, any negro woman here without authority will be arrested and sent beyond the lines and informed that, if they return, the lash awaits them."[31] So the army personnel took on roles as slave drivers and overseers. The spectacle of soldiers whipping destitute, homeless, defenseless civilian women must have been horrible. Nevertheless, familial ties were so strong that the women and children kept coming. Oftentimes, they had nowhere else to go.

Ira Berlin uses Camp Nelson as the epitome of the brutal treatment meted out to the wives, mothers and children of black forces. "Union military officials . . . refused to care for the soldiers' families. Throughout the summer and fall [of 1864] . . . the women and children were driven from the post, often into the clutches of owners who had received advance notice of the expulsion. A final wholesale eviction, undertaken on a freezing November day, caused such suffering that the ensuing publicity forced military authorities to reverse their policy."[32] About 400 women and children were forcibly removed from their camp because they, like the families in other camps, were considered an unwanted problem for the military. One hundred and twenty of them died of exposure.[33] Of course, the fact that they were enslaved or formerly enslaved contributed to the idea that they deserved such unnecessary and inhumane treatment.

The sacrifices their men made as soldiers made no difference. Rev. H.W. Guthrie reported to the Western Freedmen's Aid Commission, "Of about two hundred women whose names I took, about one hundred and seventy-five have husbands in the United States service; the others have fathers, brothers, or sons; one woman had five brothers in the Union army; another one had five sons in it."[34]

Joseph Miller gave a bitter personal witness to the inhumane treatment of African American women and children at Camp Nelson in a sworn November 1864 affidavit:

> I belong to Company I 124 U.S. C. Inft now stationed at Camp Nelson. When I came to camp for the purpose of enlisting about the middle of October 1864 my wife and children came with me because my master said that if I enlisted he would not maintain them and I knew they would be abused by him when I left . . .

This was, obviously, a typical attitude held by slaveowners in the Southern states, like Kentucky, which did not secede from the Union.

The 1863 Emancipation Proclamation, because it was a military tactic rather than a humanitarian gesture, only freed the enslaved in states which had seceded from the Union.[35] The families of many African American forces remained enslaved in unseceded states until the passage of a March 3, 1865 statute which freed the wives and children of soldiers, regardless of the loyalty of the slaveholders. The 13th Amendment which outlawed enslavement was not ratified until the end of 1865. And because the enslavement of Africans was still legal before these acts, Union commanders felt that the burden of supporting the still-enslaved women and children fell on slaveowners.

Miller's wife and children, therefore, were not freed. Nevertheless, he still enlisted, assuming that his family would be taken care of by the government he was giving service to.

> On my presenting myself as a recruit I was told by the Lieut. in command to take my family into a tent within limits of the Camp. My wife and family occupied this tent by the express permission of the aforementioned officer and never received any notice to leave until Tuesday, November 22 when a mounted guard gave my wife notice that she and her children must leave camp before early morning. This was about six o'clock at night. My little boy about

> seven years of age had been very sick and was slowly recovering.
> My wife had no place to go and so remained until morning. About
> eight o'clock Wednesday morning November 23 a mounted guard
> came to my tent and ordered my wife and children out of camp.

He used imagery which leaves no doubt about the horrendous nature of the crime against his family. "The morning was bitter cold. It was freezing hard. I was certain that it would kill my sick child to take him out in the cold. I told the man in charge of the guard that it would be the death of my boy."

Like other African American men, Miller attempted to use his status as a soldier to argue that the government was obligated to support his wife and children: "I told him that my wife and children had no place to go and I told him I was a soldier of the United States." Nevertheless, the white officer, with no remorse or feeling for a fellow military traveler, resorted to the time-honored, "just following orders" to excuse his inhuman actions. He carried them out with particular relish, however. "He told me that it did not make any difference. He had orders to take all out of camp. He told my wife and family that if they did not get up into the wagon which he had he would shoot the last one of them . . . "

Again, Miller's imagery exposed the enormity of the offense against his family. "When they left the tent the wind was blowing hard and cold and having had to leave much of our clothing when we left our master, my wife with her little one was poorly clad." In a distraught state, he was powerless to help them.

> I followed them as far as the line. I had no knowledge where they
> were taking them. At night I went in search of my family. I found
> them at Nicholasville about six miles from camp. They were in an
> old meeting house belonging to the colored people. The building
> was very cold having only one fire . . . I found my wife and
> children shivering with cold and famished with hunger. They had
> not received a morsel of food during the whole day. My boy was
> dead. He died directly after getting down from the wagon . . . I
> know he was killed by exposure to the inclement weather . . . [36]

He might have added that his son was murdered by white agents of a racist bureaucracy which failed to exercise basic principles of humanity in its treatment of African Americans.

Miller's affidavit was one of many complaints filed by African American soldiers. According to Herbert Gutman, African American soldiers at Camp Nelson wrote about 5,000 letters seeking help for their families in less than a year's time.[37]

Two husbands from Missouri made a request that the military might of the Union army be used to have their wives removed from the clutches of slaveholders who are mistreating their families because the men joined the army:

> Complaint has been made to me [Lieutenant William Deming], by Martin Patterson, of Co. 'H,' 2d Missouri Vols of A[frican]. D[escent]. that he has direct and reliable information from home that his family is receiving ill treatment from James Patterson their master, of Fayette, Howard Co. Mo. He says that his wife is compelled to do out door work,—such as chop wood, husk corn &c. and that one of his children has been suffered to freeze, and has since died. Further complaint has been made by William Brooks that his wife and children are receiving ill treatment from Jack Sutter their master, of Fayette, Howard Co. Mo. He says that they are required to do the same work that he formerly had to do, such as chopping wood, splitting rails, &c.

The men wanted the army to assume the position of protector which would have been theirs had they been allowed to exercise their full rights as citizens. "The said Martin Patterson and William Brooks request that permission be granted to remove their families to Jefferson City."[38]

Another area of contention was the forcible conscription of African American men, especially in southern states, which left families without protection and means. In unseceded Kentucky, African American men "were held for forced enlistment for their master's benefit, and for sale to bounty and substitute brokers." In Louisville, General John M. Palmer ordered "all slave-pens and other private establishments for confining colored persons here are suppressed, and the confined discharged, with an invitation to the able-bodied to enlist, and get the three hundred dollars city bounty themselves. The city bounty, so far withheld from colored recruits, is to be paid to them, as it should be, and those slave owners who pocketed it made to refund."[39] In other words, slaveholders sometimes received the enlistment bounty of the African American men they enslaved and sometimes they forced African American men to act as their substitutes in the army. Many "loyal" or unseceded slaveowners received financial remuneration when their bondspeople were conscripted or used in the service of the Union. These practices were so widespread, common and lucrative that special brokerage firms, much like slave brokering companies, were established to capitalize on the market in black recruits.

White men in the slaveholding states which did not secede may have been nominally pro-Union, but they were, more importantly, pro-slavery; they wanted and expected the system of enslavement to remain relatively intact.

Even free African Americans were not exempt from arbitrary and capricious treatment by military authorities. It is to be remembered that the conscription of white soldiers did not begin until 1863 and when the draft was instituted for whites it was accompanied by riots by whites who protested such impressment. It is also to be remembered that the offers of black men to serve the Union cause as soldiers had been rejected repeatedly. When, however, the government had need of black labor, African Americans were expected to docilely submit to forcible, uncompensated service. Consequently, African Americans complained bitterly, lodging formal complaints or pleas for their release. The displaced Africans knew they were being treated unfairly and indicated this by likening their treatment in the camps and at the hands of white soldiers, officers and agents with being enslaved. The denial, by the government, of the African American's basic right to his or her own person and the forcible separation of African American families were some of the more shameful actions by a government given to treating Africans shamefully.

In September 1862, free African American men in Cincinnati were, without warning, rounded up at bayonet point, placed in jail and compelled to do menial labor for the Union army. Of course, no arrangements for payment were made with the men, because they were being treated as criminals. Their families were therefore left unprotected and without sustenance. It is ironic that at the beginning of the Civil War these men had formed a home guard to support the Union and their own families because they were not allowed to formally join the army as soldiers. After they were mustered out of the "Black Brigade," as they came to be called, late in September 1862, many joined the Massachusetts and Ohio African American regiments which were formed after blacks were allowed to enlist.

The African American men in a camp at Roanoke Island, North Carolina sent petitions of protest to President Abraham Lincoln and Secretary of War Edwin M. Stanton in March 1865. They emphasized that not only they, as men, were supposed to have been freed by Lincoln's Emancipation Proclamation but women as well.

> We are told and also we have read that you have declared all the Colored people free *both men and women* [emphasis added] that is in the Union lines and if that be so we want to know where our rights is . . . [40]

They fully grasped the inequity in their position but were determined to fulfill their obligation, voluntarily, as citizens:

> We Colored people on Roanoke Island are willing to submit to anything that we know the President or his cabinet say because we have got sense enough to believe it is our duty to do everything we can do to aid Mr. Lincoln and the Government.[41]

Citizenship, however, carried certain rights, including the right of providing for their families, being properly compensated for their work, and deciding their own actions.

> . . . we are not willing to work as we have done for Chaplain James[42] and be trodden underfoot and get nothing for it . . . Those head men have done everything to us that our masters have done except buy and sell us and now they [James and his assistant, Holland Streeter] are trying to starve the women and children to death cutting off their rations. They have got so now that they won't give them no meat to eat.[43]

At the end of the war, African Americans were still protesting conditions on Roanoke Island and citing the same agents as the abusers. Soldiers of the 36th United States Colored Infantry stationed near Petersburg, Virginia appealed to the Freedmen's Bureau for relief in May or June of 1865.

> When we were enlisted in the service we were promised that our wives and families should receive rations from the government. The rations of our wives and families have been (and are now cut down) to one half the regular ration. Consequently, three or four days out of every ten days, they have nothing to eat. At the same time our rations are stolen from the ration house by Mr. Streeter [Holland Streter] the Assistant Superintendent at the Island (and others) and sold while our families are suffering for something to eat . . .

Just as they were during the war, African Americans were still quite aware that racism and greed were at the root of the problem:

> The cause of so much suffering is that Captain [Frank] James has not paid the Colored people for their work for near a year and at the same time cuts the rations off to one half so the people have

neither provisions or money to buy it with . . . Some soldiers are
sick in hospitals that have never been paid a cent and their families
are suffering and their children going crying without anything to
eat . . . [44]

Other African American men also vehemently protested against the
callous disregard of their families. Free men in Beaufort, North Carolina
who had been forcibly impressed into military service petitioned the
government on their and the newly-freedmen's behalf: "The undersigned
Colored Citizens of the town of Beaufort in behalf of the Colored
population of this Community in view of the manner in which their
Brotheren oppressed by the military authorities in this vicinity respectfully
petition you as the Head of this military Department for a redress of
grievances. Your petitioners desire to make known to you that they and
their brotheren . . . are indiscriminately impressed by the authorities to
labor upon the Public works without compensation. That in consequence
of this system of forced labor they have no means of paying rents or
otherwise providing for their families. Your petitioners desire further to
express their entire willingness to contribute to the cause of the union in
anyway consistent with their cause as Freemen and the rights of their
families . . . "[45]

An assistant to the military superintendent in Arkansas gave a specific
illustration of this practice of seizing African American men for military
service after he visited a camp for freedpeople on the banks of the
Mississippi River in 1864: " . . . in addition to other inconveniences a
recruiting officer or as they termed them (De Pressers) came among them,
and carried away twenty of the Best men leaving some families without
any men to assist them . . . One Martha Thompson eighteen years old had
a small Babe. When asked where her husband was replied he run away the
first chance and joined the union army. The next question asked was how
she come there. She replied her brother come with her but that the pressers
took him. I enquired how she made a living. She replied that she left her
baby with a neighbor and then went and piled cord wood. She seemed
cheerful and determined."[46]

In the South, Confederate rebels and deserters preyed on unprotected
African American women and children, killing, raping and pillaging. That
was to be expected. What was not expected was that Union soldiers were
sometimes guilty of similar crimes. "The wives of some have been
molested by soldiers to gratify their licentious lust, and their husbands
murdered in endeavouring to defend them, and yet the guilty parties,
though known, were not arrested."[47]

Herbert Gutman lists several atrocities committed by Union soldiers against African American women:

> At Haines Bluff, Mississippi, a white Union Army Cavalryman raped 'a grandmother in the presence of her grandchildren.' White soldiers raped two Fortress Monroe, Virginia, women. Two soldiers seized the father and son-in-law of a woman while two others raped her. Another woman was raped 'after a desperate struggle' in the 'presence of her father and grandfather.'[48]

African American soldiers stationed at City Point, Virginia protested to the head of the Freedmen's Bureau in 1865: "Our families have no protection. The white soldiers break into our houses. Act as they please. Steal our chickens, rob our gardens. And if anyone defends theirselves against them they are taken to the guardhouse for it."[49] The white supervisor of a refugee camp in Memphis contended, "Many soldiers and some officers manifest only bitterness and contempt, resulting among the abandoned, in the violence and abuse of these helpless people, in addition to the injuries heaped upon them by the vicious & disloyal in the community."[53]

A white Union surgeon told of one incident: "The white troops, I am sorry to say, have shown a disposition to insult and quarrel with the colored troops. They think they are degraded by doing duty along side of Negro troops, and they thus show very bad feeling and taste. This morning in a fray of this kind a Negro woman was shot by a white cavalry man. The ball took effect in the arm, and we had to amputate it."[50]

The NFRA's white agent, Mrs. Harlan, made a similar accusation in her March 1862 report on her trip to the South: "The negroes have been treated very badly by the Army. They have deprived them of every chicken, and goose, and turkey, and pig, and everything else having animal life that man could dress and eat . . . " Harlan, who was clearly sympathetic to the plight of freedpeople, also mentioned the sexual abuses that white Union soldiers committed against freedwomen.[51]

On one occasion, however, African Americans punished a white abuser. Captain Hannibal Carter of the 2nd Louisiana Native Guard Infantry arrested J.A. Pickens, the white manager of Raceland Plantation in Lafourche Parish, Louisiana, for "his abuse of women workers on the plantation. [A]mong other misdeeds, he had evicted 'a woman with her suckling babe only because she was a soldiers wife.'"[52] Pickens, a Northerner, had been given the plantation to manage.

The mistreatment of African American soldiers and refugees in the camps did not go unremarked in the African American press. *The Christian Recorder* kept a close watch on the situation and published letters from soldiers in the field and commentary from prominent African Americans about the problem. A soldier signing himself, "Bought and Sold," wrote an angry letter to the newspaper. "I am a soldier, or at least that is what I was drafted for, in the 6th U.S.C.T . . . " His concern was for his family who was "almost starving" at home because his pay of $7 per month was not sufficient to keep them. When he first enlisted, "I felt very patriotic; but my wife's letters have brought my patriotism down to the freezing point . . . " He worried that if the soldiers in his regiment were killed, their families would be in worse shape than before. " . . . Who will take care of their wives and little ones? I am very sure that the Government will not, for it will not take care of them while they are in the service; let alone when they are dead and of no more use." He closed with a plea to the editor which showed his predicament: "Mr. Editor, since I have been in the service I have not received enough money to buy a stamp, or I would have put one on this letter. But if you will publish this I will pay you some day."[54]

A few months later, apparently the same soldier wrote another letter under the signature, "Unknown," which was published in the May 21, 1864 edition of the newspaper. Writing now from Hampton, Virginia, he was even more irate, lambasting the "treachery" inherent in the African American soldiers' treatment: "Our families—hundreds, nay, thousands, of helpless women and children—are this day suffering for the natural means of subsistence, whose husbands and fathers have responded to the country's call . . . We ask no elevation further than our rights as men and natives of the country. Our wives and children are as near and as dear to black men, as the white men's are to them."

Pearl took up the gauntlet in June 1864, writing a letter to the *Christian Recorder* which not only condemned the government for paying African American troops less than white soldiers but for committing other inequities as well. "Now we will see the injustice of the usage of our brave soldiers. 1st. The Government refuses to pay them equal wages with white men, for the great reason—*they are black*—and some have been slaves. Southern chivalry binds them in chains and handcuffs, and the Northern Abolitionist crushes them in black prejudice. Such is American Slavery and justice to our race. 2d. The injustice to our brave boys is—that where the hardest of the fight is, there they are put. They are put in the front to bear the galling fire of the enemy; and they must do it without pay, without the comfort of knowing whether the dear ones at home have enough to support them or not—whether they be starving or begging . . . This great Union that is to unite us and make all free and equal, while it takes a part of its sons, and makes them sweat, and toil, and fight for nothing, another part are elevated by the poor despised African's blood and tears. Such is the injustice done our brothers. God help the poor down-trodden soldier, and save the Union, and make it more free!"[55]

Many slaveholders compelled African American women, children, aged and infirm to leave plantations because their men had enlisted in the Union forces. Colonel H.W. Barry, white commander of the 8th United States Colored Heavy Artillery, wrote to Brevet Colonel W.H. Greenwood, asking him to use his influence to see that the soldiers in his regiment who were recruited from the Paducah, Kentucky area, be paid. Greenwood, in charge of building the military railroad in the area, was using Barry's regiment for labor.

> The enlisted men have not been paid since October 31, 1864 now nearly 10 months. A very large number of the men have families now residing in Paducah, Ky. dependent upon them for support.

Barry recognized that his troops were being treated unfairly because of racism:

> The soldiers having formerly been slaves and recruited at a time when the sentiment in Kentucky was bitterly opposed to the arming of colored troops their women and children were driven from their homes and followed their husbands to the recruiting depot at Paducah Ky. and thereforth became dependent upon the wages of the husband and the soldier to supply them with the necessaries of life . . . [56]

He also knew that his men could not perform their duties as soldiers to the best of their abilities when their attention was distracted through worry about their families.

Those women who remained on the plantation continued to be subjected to the traditional sexual and physical abuse inherent in the system of enslavement. They received particularly harsh punishment from slaveholders in retaliation for the men who escaped to Union lines or who joined the Union Army. The soldiers received despairing messages like the following December 1863 letter from Martha Glover of Mexico, Missouri to her husband at the front: "I have had nothing but trouble since you left

... They [slaveholders] abuse me because you went & say they will not take care of our children & do nothing but quarrel with me all the time and beat me scandalously the day before yesterday ... they do worse than they ever did & I do not know what will become of me & my poor children ..."57

Frances Johnson, gave a graphic personal account of her mistreatment in an affidavit filed at Camp Nelson, Kentucky in 1865:

> I am the wife of Nathan Johnson a soldier in Company F. 116th U.S.C Inft. I have three children and with them I belonged to Matthias Outon Fayette County, Kentucky. My husband who belonged to Mary Outon Woodford Co. Ky enlisted in the United States service at Camp Nelson Ky. in May 1864.

She was well aware that the cruel treatment given to her and other African American women was the result of their men seizing their manhood. She also recognized that the slaveowner knew that mistreatment of the women would cause African American men pain:

> The day after my husband enlisted my master knew it and said that he (my husband) and all the 'niggers' did mighty wrong in joining the Army.

Johnson said she was "forced" to leave but, in fact, her voluntary departure exhibited agency and some measure of control over her own actions as did her decision about whether she was in a condition to work. The slaveowner's "cruel treatment" simply allowed a legitimate excuse: "Subsequent to May 1864 I remained with my master until forced to leave on account of the cruel treatment to which I was subjected." She described, in painful detail, the particularly brutal physical abuse which was inherent in enslavement:

> On Wednesday, March 8th 1865, my masters son Thomas Outon whipped me severely on my refusing to do some work which I was not in a condition to perform. He beat me in the presence of his father who told him (Thomas Outon) to 'buck me and give me a thousand' meaning thereby a thousand lashes. While beating me he threw me on the floor and as I was in this prostrate and helpless condition he continued to whip me endeavoring at one time to tie my hands and at another time to make an indecent exposure of my person before those present. I resisted as much as I could and to some extent thwarted his malignant designs. In consequence of this

whipping suffered much pain in my head and sides . . . I stealthily
started for Lexington about seven miles distant where my sister
resided. On my arrival there I was confined on account of sickness
produced by the abuse I had received from my masters son as
aforementioned.[58]

When Johnson snuck back to her master's plantation back to retrieve her
children:

> [I] went to the cabin where my children were, no one but the
> colored folks knowing that I was present, got my children with the
> exception of one that was too sick to move . . . At daybreak the
> next morning I started for Lexington. My youngest child was in my
> arms, the other walked by my side.

She showed the agents of the slave system in all their brutal inhumanity:

> When on the Pike about a mile from home I was accosted by
> Theophilus Bracey my masters son-in-law who told me that if I did
> not go back with him he would shoot me. He drew a pistol on me
> as he made this threat. I could offer no resistance as he constantly
> kept the pistol pointed at me. I returned with him to his (Braceys)
> house carrying my children as before . . . My sick child was moved
> there during the day. I tried to find some chance of running away
> but Bracey was watching me. He took my eldest child (about seven
> years of age) and kept her as an hostage. I found I could not get
> away from Bracey's with my children, and determined to get away
> myself hoping by this means to obtain possession of them
> afterwards . . . [59]

In addition to depicting the resistance that many Africans engaged in,
Frances Johnson's affidavit illustrated several other important points. She
considered herself legitimately married although her marriage was
probably the result of the March 1865 Adjutant General's order freeing the
wives of enlisted African American soldiers. Johnson also showed that she
was aware of the sexual nature of the sadistic treatment she received and
she considered herself chaste and deserving of treatment normally
reserved for "ladies." Her mistreatment at the hands of "southern
gentlemen" gives us a glimpse of what was to come after the Civil War
when an unpunished South wreaked a particularly violent retribution on
African Americans.

Captain A.J. Hubbard, a white officer of a Missouri African American
unit, wrote to Brigadier General William A. Pile in 1864: "I have received

information . . . that the wives of Simon Williamson & Richard Beasley have again been whipped by their master most unmercifully . . . He refuses to let them go to the Post Office to get their letters, and if any one comes to them and brings them letters and reads them to them he is sure to whip them for it . . . If any thing could be done to relieve their families it would afford me a good deal of satisfaction and relieve them from a good deal of anxiety . . . "[60]

Hiram Cornell, a white Union officer in Missouri, asked for advice from his commanding officer on how to deal with the plight of women. "The wife of a colored recruit came into my Office to night and says she has been severely beaten and driven from her home by her master and owner. She has a child some two years old with her, and says she left two larger ones at home. She desires to be sent forward with her husband; says she is willing to work and expects to do so at home or elsewhere; that her master told her never to return to him; that his men were all gone, and that he could not, and would not support the women."[61]

H. G. Mosee, a recruiter in Indiana, had a solution to the problem. Because he was so outraged by the abuse of African American women and children, he made a request in April 1865 to Secretary of War, Edwin M. Stanton, that he be given military orders to prevent the abuse of African American women and children. "I . . . take my pen in hand to inform you of the hardships and troubles of colored soldiers wives here. It makes my heart bleed to see how they are treated. Some are starving . . ."

He obviously found the term "contraband" objectionable because it designated the freedpeople as property. Mosee also recognized the special situation of the unprotected refugee women: "Those persons are the so called Contrabands. They have made their way to this place [New Albany, Indiana] and no men with them or the greater part of them . . . "

He wanted to be given formal power to aid his people because he believed that official sanction from the government would be respected by the perpetrators of crimes against the fugitives, as would anyone exercising such authority. Having the power to enforce laws concerning the rights of the refugees would also have meant that they had a right to the protection that citizenship offered. An African American man with such power would have reinforced African American rights as well as black self-reliance. "If one colored man had military orders to see after such persons this would be stopped such as kidnaping and carrying soldiers wives and children back into Kentucky and going into their houses stealing what they have." He understood that the law did not protect the women because they were, technically, considered slaves:

And because the colored women have not got a white witness they can't do any thing. They stand and look at their own property but can't get it because they have no white witness or military man to speak in their favor . . . If you will send me such papers I will be pleased to serve for the benefit of the colored population of this place. If ever the poor colored people wanted a Bureau it is here . . . [62]

Not only were the families of formerly enslaved men made to suffer by slaveholders but the families of southern free men who enlisted in the army were also subjected to abuses by local white residents. Colonel William Birney complained to the Bureau of Colored Affairs about such mistreatment in Maryland. "[T]he enemies of the enlistment of U.S. Colored Troops have within the last week resorted to the most inhuman outrages against the families of free men of color who have enlisted: the cornfields of these poor people have been thrown open, their cows have been driven away and some of the families have been mercilessly turned out of their homes."[63]

During the war, the New Orleans police chief issued an order "to arrest all negroes out without passes after half past eight, P.M." which revived an earlier slave code. Its purpose was to harass free and enslaved African Americans. The white correspondent for the *Boston Traveller* visited the prison where African American women were held for violating the order.

> There I saw, in one cell, fifteen feet by twenty feet, fifty colored women and girls packed like so many cattle: there were six or eight wooden berths, with *pine mattresses* and *oak pillows*, for these poor creatures to rest their limbs upon. Of course, the most of them were obliged to stand uprightly, or lie upon the wet flooring of the cell . . .

On his return to the prison he found remaining,

> . . . several likely-looking negro-girls still in the cell, and three mothers. All of these mothers had sons in the Union army, enlisted in the colored Native- Guard Regiment. One of them had *three* sons in one regiment; the other had two sons, her only children; and the only child of the third, a boy of nineteen years, was a sergeant in a colored company. These mothers were all the *property* of rebels . . . 'sent to prison for safe-keeping.'

He related the personal account of a specific African American woman to buttress his story:

> One mother told me she was always treated well until her sons joined the negro regiment, since which time she had been whipped and otherwise sadly abused. She was not allowed so much liberty at home, and her mistress had put her off on a short allowance of food, because she did not prevent her sons from enlisting.[64]

African Americans suffered greatly at the hands of the government and its agents in many ways. Yet the greatest deprivation facing Africans was the infrequent, inadequate or lack of pay given to black troops so that their families underwent extreme suffering because they found it difficult to sustain themselves. The government did not live up to the recruitment advertisement published in the February 16, 1863 *Boston Journal*:

> To Colored Men
> Wanted. Good men for the Fifty-fourth Regiment of Massachusetts Volunteers of African descent, Col. Robert G. Shaw. $100 bounty at expiration of term of service. Pay $13 per month, and State aid for families
> . . .

White soldiers received $13 a month with an additional $3.50 allowance given for clothing. Black soldiers, on the other hand, were paid $10 pay per month, with $3 deducted for clothing. It was not until mid-June 1864 that African American soldiers were authorized to receive the same pay as white soldiers. The unfair treatment and payment were recurring themes in many of the letters, diaries, journals and reminiscences of African American Civil War participants. Free women in the north as well as enslaved and freed women in the south suffered as a result of the inequity.

In a major protest and at much personal cost to their families, in July 1863 the 54th Regiment of the Massachusetts Volunteer Infantry refused their pay, "although many had suffering families. By every mail they received letters setting forth the sufferings of their families."[65] The men in the troop declared, "We need the money you offer; our families are starving because the government does not pay us what it promised; but we demand to be recognized as soldiers of the Republic, entitled to the same rights which white soldiers have. Until you grant that, we will not touch a dollar."[66] They went eighteen months without pay.

John S. Rock, a lawyer from Boston, placed a notice in the June 4, 1864 *Christian Recorder* alerting the "wife and children, father and mother, brother and sister, if living in the United States, and dependent upon any soldier of the 54th, or 55th Massachusetts regiments, or 5th Mass. Cavalry regiment" that they could "receive the necessary information to get the State allowance" by contacting him. He had been a vocal opponent to the wage discrimination against African American soldiers.

The notice reflects the straits the families were reduced to and the importance the African American community attached to the issue of unequal compensation. It was considered an affront to the soldiers' manhood and it was a clear indication that African Americans were not going to be afforded the rights they were valiantly defending on the battlefield.

The government awarded African American soldiers the same wages as whites in mid-June 1864 but the Massachusetts 54th did not actually receive their pay until late September 1864. Rock had another notice placed in the September 3, 1864 *Christian Recorder*, saying, that dependents of the same regiments were "if needy, entitled to a State allowance." He gave the particulars of how to go about applying but cautioned, "These cases are not paid immediately, but are carefully investigated." Nevertheless, "all those who are entitled to an allowance will receive it if they apply for it."

African American women denounced the pay inequities because they and their families were directly and adversely affected. Rachel Ann Wicker wrote to "Mr. President Andrew" [Governor John A. Andrew of Massachusetts] in September 1864 to complain that the denial of equal pay and treatment amounted to a moral outrage.

> I write to you to know the reason why our husbands and sons who enlisted in the 55 Massachusetts regiment have not been paid off. I speak for myself and Mother and I know of a great many others as well as ourselves are suffering for the want of money to live on. When provision and clothing were cheap we might have got along but everything now is triple and over what it was some three year back. But it matters not if everything was at the same old price. I think it a piece of injustice to have those soldiers there 15 months without a cent of money. For my part I cannot see why they have not the same right to their 16 dollars per month as the Whites or even the Colored Soldiers that went from Ohio. I think if Massachusetts had left off coming to other states for soldiers the soldiers would have been better off and Massachusetts saved her

credit. I wish you if you please to answer this letter and tell me why it is that you still insist upon them taking 7 dollars a month when you give the poorest white regiment that has went out 16 dollars.[67]

A white officer of the 54th wrote: "Sometimes we almost despair about our men in the matter of pay and proper recognition . . . These men were enlisted . . . legally under the Act of July 1861, and they should then be paid as soldiers . . . Think of what the men do and suffer; think of their starving families . . . There is Sergeant [Stephen A.] Swails, a man who has fairly won promotion on the field of battle. While he was doing the work of government in the field, his wife and children were placed in the poorhouse."[68] The assertion that Swails' family had been forced into the poorhouse was later found to be untrue[69], however, but the possibility certainly loomed for many in his same situation. Swails' wife, Sarah, eventually taught freedpeople in South Carolina as did Stephen.

George Rodgers of New York wrote to Abraham Lincoln from New Orleans in 1864 to express his personal outrage:

> . . . now I stand in the defense of the country ready and willing to obey all orders and demands that have a tendency to put down this rebellion in military life or civil life . . . [when I enlisted I was told] I would get 13 dollars per month or more if white soldiers got it . . . Here I am in the service 7 months and have not received any monthly pay.

It was the effect on his family and the fact that he could not fulfill his obligations as a husband and father which caused him the most grief:

> I have a wife and 3 children neither of them able to take care of themselves and my wife is sick. And she has sent to me for money and I have no way of getting any money to send to her because I can't get my pay. And it goes very hard with me to think my family should be at home suffering . . . [70]

Colonel Thomas Wentworth Higginson, white commander of the 1st South Carolina Infantry, wrote a letter to the *New York Times* expressing his anger at the treatment his African American troops received:

> Mr. Senator [James R.] Doolittle argued . . . that white soldiers should receive higher pay than black ones, because the families of the latter were often supported by Government. What an

astounding statement of fact is this! In the white regiment in which
I was formerly an officer (the Massachusetts Fifty-First) nine
tenths of the soldiers' families, in addition to the pay and bounties,
drew regularly their 'State aid.' Among my black soldiers, with
half-pay and no bounty, not a family receives any aid. Is there to
be no limit, no end to the injustice we heap upon this unfortunate
people? Cannot even the fact of their being in arms for the nation,
liable to die any day in its defence, secure them ordinary justice?
Is the nation so poor, and so utterly demoralized by its pauperism,
that after it has had the lives of these men, it must turn around and
filch six dollars of the monthly pay which the Secretary of War
promised to their widows?[71]

Higginson engaged in a massive campaign in an attempt to correct the
injustice done to his men.

Susie King Taylor's husband, Edward King, was a member of
Company E in Higginson's regiment which was later called the 33rd
United States Colored Infantry. "I was the wife of one of those men who
did not get a penny for eighteen months for their services, only their
rations and clothing."[72] She also acknowledged that "several uncles, some
cousins . . . and a number of cousins in other companies" [other than
Company E] did military duty during the Civil War.[73] Her father,
Raymond Baker, saw service on a gunboat. She knew firsthand, then, the
suffering caused by the unequal, racist treatment given by the Union army
to its black forces.

She, as a woman, was also not exempt from unfair treatment, in spite
of the loyal and extraordinary service she performed for the Union cause.
"I gave my services willingly for four years and three months without
receiving a dollar. I was glad, however, to be allowed to go with the
regiment, to care for the sick and afflicted comrades."[74] Taylor never
received payment or a pension for her services after the war.

Higginson, however, was apparently an exception to the rule when it
came to white officers. Colonel James Montgomery, of the 2nd South
Carolina Infantry, was more to the mark. He made the following insulting
remarks to the Massachusetts 54th, equating their refusal to accept unequal
pay to mutiny. "I am your friend . . . You ought to be glad to pay for the
privilege to fight, instead of squabbling about money. A great many of you
are fugitive slaves, and can by law be returned to your masters. The
government by its setting you free has paid you a thousand dollars bounty
. . . You want to be placed on the same footing as white soldiers. You must
show yourselves as good soldiers as the white . . . You are a race of slaves.
A few years ago your fathers worshipped snakes and crocodiles in Africa.

Your features partake of a beastly character . . . It is mutiny to refuse to take your pay, and mutiny is punishable with death."[75] The 54th was made up of primarily free northern African American men who had never been enslaved and the regiment had proven itself repeatedly on the battlefield. The African American press exposed Montgomery's affront.

Signing herself, Mrs. John W. Wilson, so there would be no mistake about her marriage's legitimacy, a Detroit, Michigan wife wrote angrily in 1865 to Edwin M. Stanton, Secretary of War. "John Wesley Wilson [her husband] has not received any pay from the government for nine months and it leaves me completely destitute. I have no support except what I earn by my own labor from day to day. The relief fund that I have been receiving has been cut off through prejudices to color and it leaves me completely destitute of means for my support. Michigan has no respect for her colored soldiers or their families . . . "[76]

Rosanna Henson of Mt. Holly, New Jersey wrote to Abraham Lincoln in 1864, "Sir, my husband, who is in Co. K. 22nd Reg't U.S. Colored Troops (and now in the Macon Hospital at Portsmouth with a wound in his arm) has not received any pay since last May and then only thirteen dollars. I write to you because I have been told you would see to it. I have four children to support and I find this a great struggle. A hard life this! I being a colored woman do not get any State pay. Yet my husband is fighting for the country . . . "[77]

A soldier, Sergeant William Walker of the 3rd South Carolina Infantry and an ex-slave, led a protest against the unfair pay and harsh treatment by white officers in November 1863. He cited his destitute wife and family as a part of his defense for his actions. Nonetheless, in one of the most shameful episodes of the Civil War, he was convicted of mutiny[78] and shot to death, in spite of the fact that the government had reneged on its promise to pay African American soldiers the same wages and bounties as white soldiers.

Walker's case was a signal to the African American community that it could not expect fair play from a government and a nation which still considered them to have "no rights a white man is bound to respect." Even service as a soldier did not indemnify African American men against overt racist treatment. Walker's case also reinforced the disparate and unequal treatment given to those considered "contrabands." Because he had been freed by Union forces when they took over the Port Royal area of South Carolina, Walker was considered confiscated property. Regardless, he enlisted as a soldier rather than serve as a laborer. He was certainly considered a soldier, however, when it came time to mete out a punishment for his dissent—execution by firing squad.

He maintained in a statement made during the court-martial proceedings, that "on the promise solemnly made by some who are now officers in my regiment, that I should receive the same pay and allowances as were given to all soldiers of the U.S. Army,—[I] voluntarily entered the ranks." He went on to claim that not only was the pay unequal but the management of African American soldiers was much more severe and harsh. "The treatment that has been given to the men of the 3d Reg't S.C. Vols. by a large majority of their officers . . . has been tyrannical in the extreme, and totally beneath that standard of gentlemanly conduct which we were taught to believe as pertaining to officers wearing the uniform of a government that had declared a 'freedom to all' as one of the cardinal points of its policy."[79] Such a defense should have seemed reasonable except that Walker, as an African American man and because he was considered a "spoil of war," was denied the right of legitimate protest.

In a further shameful governmental response, not only did his wife not receive the back pay which was finally, in 1864, granted to African American troops, but she was denied his pension when she applied in 1894.[80] This was typical because many African American women and children did not receive their husband and father's pensions because marriage between enslaved Africans was not recognized as legal. Although a bill was passed in July 1864 which provided pensions for the wives and offspring of formerly enslaved African American soldiers, it only applied to those who came from the states which had seceded from the Union. This meant that the wives and children of the soldiers in the southern states which did not secede - Kentucky, Missouri, Delaware, Maryland and West Virginia - were not eligible for their pensions. As late as 1901, Commissioner Evans of the Pension Bureau was singling out this law as "an open invitation to fraud, perjury, and misrepresentation . . . and it should be repealed."[81] Of course, he was rationalizing the denial of pensions to the wives, mothers and children of black Civil War soldiers and veterans.

In some instances, a portion of the pay owed to African American men serving in the military was deducted to offset the government's cost of providing for the many African Americans who swarmed to Union military installations. In one case, General John E. Wool, commander of Fortress Monroe in Virginia issued an order which stated: "The Quartermaster will furnish all the Clothing. The departments employing these men, will furnish the subsistence specified above [$10, rations and clothing], and as an incentive to good behaviour, (to be withheld at the discretion, of the Chiefs of the departments, respectively) each individual of the 1st Class, will receive, two (2) dollars per month; and each individual of the 2nd Class one (1) dollar per month for their own use. The remainder of the money valuation of their labor, will be turned over to the Quartermaster, who will deduct from it the cost of the Clothing issued to them, the balance will constitute a fund to be expended by the Quartermaster under the direction of the Commanding Officer of the department for the support of the women and children, and those that are unable to work . . . "[82]

Five dollars per month were deducted from the "wages of the able-bodied employed in the public service in Washington and Alexandria" for "the support and relief of the women and children who had escaped . . . from the rebel territory," according to M.C. Meigs, white Quartermaster-General, in a November 1864 report to Edwin Stanton, Secretary of War. Meigs gave accolades to white Lieutenant Colonel E.M. Greene since "the result has been highly successful and creditable to the intelligence and judgement of the officer in charge."[83] This meant that, oftentimes, the laborers and soldiers did not receive any pay whatsoever.[84]

White soldiers were not assessed such a cost even though many poor whites also flocked to the camps or begged for and received assistance from Union officials. Rev. Henry McNeal Turner, the chaplain of the 1st USCI, wrote from Goldsboro, North Carolina: "Thousands of poor white people are coming in town daily and drawing rations. Women come from forty miles off, travelling for days, to and from the town, to find something to eat. Others take advantage of this benevolence on the part of the Government, to traffic, and satisfy their roguish ambition by whining for rations, and then speculating with them."[85]

Elizabeth Blair Lee, a southern white woman whose father, husband and brothers supported the Union, reported in a letter to her husband in August 1863 that her brother, Frank Blair, a Union officer, "had as many white people in [his] wagon train as Negroes when he left Jackson [Mississippi]; his empty wagon were filled with white women & children who begged for his protection—."[86]

To dispel the myth of craven, begging freedpeople, T. Morris Chester, a Civil War correspondent, took pains to point out that whites received greater assistance than blacks. He documented in a June 12, 1865 dispatch to the *Philadelphia Press* that the whites of Richmond drew substantially more rations than African Americans:

White men	950	Negro men	104
White women	3,825	Negro women	1,200
White children	5,085	Negro children	1,840 [87]

Such detailed documentation was expected to counteract the negative stereotype which was fast becoming a part of white public opinion and which persists to this day..

In 1867, the Daughters of Zion of the Avery A.M.E. Chapel in Memphis, Tennessee hired their own doctor, S.H. Toles, to provide medical care to church members because the African American community was denied equal access to the public hospitals. Dr. Toles, in turn, documented the Freedmen's Bureau's partiality toward the city's poor white community at the expense of the African American population because "poor whites had received twice the aid the colored people had." Not only was the African American community taxed for public services which whites were granted, there were special taxes borne by the community for aid that they received. All African Americans between the ages of eighteen and sixty in Memphis and a one-mile radius of the city were taxed a dollar each to support the city's freedmen's hospital.[88] The community, in the face of such discrimination, attempted to provide what should have been public services for themselves.

The *Pennsylvania Freedmen's Bulletin* also debunked assertions of black dependence. "Much has been said about the expense entailed upon the government by furnishing rations to freedmen, but little is said as to the relative number of rations furnished to them and to whites in the same neighborhood. A gentleman just from Tennessee reports, that at Shelbyville, which has a colored population of one thousand, rations are issued to four hundred persons, not one of whom is colored."[89] In spite of such documentation, the misrepresentation of the freedpeople as depraved and idle persisted. It is to be remembered that white rebels were not forced to work for their keep as were African Americans.

George Clary, a white Union surgeon serving in Savannah, Georgia, also challenged, inadvertently, the opinion that only African Americans were receiving charity. "Provisions sent from Boston, New York, and Philadelphia are distributed every day to the multitudes of colored and poor white people who come with their baskets to receive them. How the upper (crust?) lives, I do not know, unless they send their darkeys to the same places to receive these charities for them."[90] He observed in another letter that New Bern, North Carolina was "overflowing with shiftless whites and newly fledged freemen of African descent . . . Gov't give free transportation to such of these refugees as wish to go North. I presume that not five in a hundred of them can read and write. They are a pitiable class, turned out of house and home by the stern necessity of seeking food as well as to escape from a grinding and tyrannical gov't. A good many Johnnies [rebels] have come down from Goldsboro and are being sent North in ships."[91] An earlier letter had made a class distinction with Clary saying, "Some of them whom I have talked with appear intelligent, but generally they are as ignorant as poor whites are supposed to be."[92]

Clary's observations point out the glaring difference in treatment of whites and African Americans. The white rebels, although "shiftless," destitute and uneducated are given free transportation to the North while African Americans are forced to work for the government or former plantation owners. The offer of free transportation was sometimes extended to African Americans but most often, the need for labor on the abandoned plantations and military operations overrode the possibility that African Americans would be allowed to leave voluntarily.

Nevertheless, in spite of the hardships they faced, African American women kept the faith and the hearth, literally and figuratively. Ann, a Paris, Missouri woman wrote movingly to her husband, Andrew Valentine, of the 2nd Missouri Colored Infantry: "My Dear Husband . . . You do not know how bad I am treated. They [her slave owners] are treating me worse every day. Our child cries for you. Send me some money as soon as you can for me and my child are almost naked . . . Do the best you can and do not fret too much for me for it won't be long before I will be free and then all we make will be ours. Your affectionate wife."[93]

Louisa Alexander of Naylor's Store, Missouri told a similar tale. She wrote to her husband who had escaped enslavement and was working as a spy for the Union army in Missouri that her master had not taken well to his offer to purchase her. "I received your letter yesterday, and lost no time in asking Mr. Jim if he would sell me, and what he would take for me. He flew at me, and said I would never get free only at the point of the bayonet . . . If I can get away I will, but the people here are all afraid to take me away." In spite of the odds, she and her daughter managed to escape, after her husband arranged for a German farmer to help them, two weeks after she wrote this letter.[94]

Perseverance and survival, therefore, signifies a type of heroic resistance because in the face of overwhelming odds, African American women simply did not give up. Their words and actions project a sense of optimism because they were looking to their own self-empowering resources to sustain and save themselves, their families and their community. Survival was the best revenge.

NOTES

1. Kent Anderson Leslie, *Woman of Color, Daughter of Privilege: Amanda America Dickson, 1849-1893* (Athens: University of Georgia Press, 1995), 53.

2. *New York Times*, 13 March 1865.

3. Marion B. Lucas, *A History of Blacks in Kentucky* (Frankfort: Kentucky Historical Society, 1992), 159.

4. Ibid.,158.

5. Eugene Genovese, *Roll, Jordan, Roll* (New York: Vintage Books, 1975), 97.

6. Victoria Bynum, *Unruly Women: the Politics of Social and Sexual Control in the Old South* (Chapel Hill: University of North Carolina Press, 1992), 114.

7. C. Vann Woodward, ed. *Mary Chesnut's Civil War* (New Haven, Connecticut: Yale University Press, 1981), 715.

8. Ibid., 833.

9. William W. Davis, *The Civil War and Reconstruction in Florida* (New York: Columbia University, 1913), p. 219.

10. Ervin L. Jordan, Jr., *Black Confederates and Afro-Yankees in Civil War Virginia* (Charlottesville: University Press of Virginia, 1995), 170.

11. Laura S. Haviland, *A Woman's Life-Work, Labors and Experiences* (Chicago: Publishing Association of Friends, 1889), pp. 273-275.

12. Jordan, 163.

13. Ibid., 75-76.

14. *Christian Recorder*, 28 May 1864. This incident is also told in Jordan's *Black Confederates and Afro-Yankees in Civil War Virginia*, page 163, which corrects the slaveowner's name, reported incorrectly as "Clayton" in the *Christian Recorder* and elsewhere. *Free At Last*, pages 115-116, edited by Ira Berlin, also relates this event.

15. Susie King Taylor, *Reminiscences of My Life in Camp*. (New York: Arno Press, 1968, 1902), pp. 67-68.

16. Luis Emilio, *A Brave Black Regiment: History of the Fifty-fourth Regiment of Massachusetts Volunteer Infantry 1863-1865* (New York: Bantam Books, 1992, 1894), 138.

17. George H. Hepworth, *The Whip, Hoe and Sword; or, the Gulf-Department in '63* (Boston: Walker, Wise and Company, 1864), 141.

18. James M. McPherson, *The Negro's Civil War*. (New York: Pantheon Book, 1965), p. 151.

19. James L. Smith, *Autobiography* (Norwich, Connecticut: Press of the Bulletin Company, 1881), 117.

20. This was probably the same prison camp mentioned in the previous case.

21. Willard W. Glazier, *The Capture, the Prison Pen, and the Escape* (Hartford, Connecticut: H.E. Goodwin, 1869), 219.

22. Ibid., 215.

23. George Clary Papers, Connecticut Historical Society, Hartford.

24. *Weekly Anglo-African*, 29 March 1862.

25. Ira Berlin, et al., eds., *Slaves No More* (New York: Cambridge University Press, 1992), 132.

26. Elizabeth H. Botume, *First Days Amongst the Contrabands* (New York: Arno Press, 1968, 1893), 56.

27. National Freedmen's Relief Association of the District of Columbia, *Fourth Annual Report* (Washington, DC: McGill & Witherow, 1866), 10-13.

28. Ibid.

29. Dorothy Sterling, ed., *We Are Your Sisters: Black Women in the Nineteenth Century* (New York: W.W. Norton, 1984), 241.

30. Ira Berlin, ed., *The Black Military Experience* (New York: Cambridge University Press, 1982), 714.

31. *Liberator*, 24 June 1864.

32. Berlin, *Slaves*, 160-161.

33. Lucas, 162.

34. Western Freedmen's Aid Commission, *Second Annual Report* (Cincinnati: Methodist Book Concern, 1865), 31.

35. Delaware, Maryland, Kentucky and Missouri did not secede from the Union; the western part of Virginia formed itself into a separate state, West Virginia, in 1863 to remain loyal to the Union. The fact that they did not secede did not mean they were anti-slavery. On the contrary, they were pro-slavery and anti-black but pro-Union.

36. Berlin, *Black*, 270-271.

37. Herbert G. Gutman, *The Black Family in Slavery and Freedom, 1750-1925* (New York: Vintage Books, 1976), 371.

38. Berlin, *Black*, 242-243.

39. *New York Times*, 13 March 1865.

40. Ira Berlin, et al., eds., *Free At Last: a Documentary History of Slavery, Freedom, and the Civil War* (New York: New Press, 1992), 222-223.

41. Ibid., 223.

42. Captain Horace James, the camp's military supervisor.

43. Berlin, *Free*, 224.

44. Berlin, *Black*, 729.

45. Berlin, *Free*, 208-209.

46. Ibid., 215.

47. Ibid., 181.

48. Gutman, 386.

49. Berlin, *Black*, 730.

50. Berlin, *Free*, 191.

51. Clary, June 22, 1865.

52. National Freedmen's Relief Association, New York, *By-Laws and Minutes* [Rare Books and Manuscripts Department, Boston Public Library]. Berlin, *Free*, 257.

53. Berlin, *Free*, 257.

54. *Christian Recorder*, 20 February 1864.

55. *Christian Recorder*, 25 June 1864.

56. Ibid., 244.

57. Berlin, *Free*, 464.

58. Ibid., 694-695.

59. Ibid.

60. Ibid., 687-688.

61. Ibid., 367.

62. Ibid., 696.

63. Ibid., 206-207.

64. William Wells Brown, *The Negro in the American Rebellion* (New York: Citadel Press, 1971, 1867), 177-181.

65. Ibid., 115, 184.

66. *New York Tribune*, 8 September 1865.

67. Ira Berlin and Leslie Rowland, eds., *Families and Freedom: a Documentary History of African-American Kinship in the Civil War Era* (New York: New Press, 1997), 88.

68. Emilio, 186.

69. Donald Yacovone, ed., *Voice of Thunder: the Civil War Letters of George E. Stephens* (Urbana: University of Illinois Press, 1997), 73.

70. Berlin, *Black*, 680.

71. Thomas Wentworth Higginson, *Army Life in a Black Regiment* (NY: Collier Books, 1962), 271.

72. Taylor, 51.

73. Ibid., 16.

74. Ibid., 21.

75. *Weekly Anglo-African*, 24 October 1863.

76. Berlin, *Black*, 682.

77. Ibid., 680.

78. Out of nineteen Union soldiers executed for mutiny during the Civil War, fourteen of them were African American. This number is far out of proportion to the number of African American servicemen. Of course, such a figure is evidence of probable discrimination.

79. Berlin, *Black*, 393.

80. Otto Friedrich, "We Will Not Do Duty Any Longer for Seven Dollars Per Month." *American Heritage* (February 1988), 64-73.

81. John W. Oliver, *History of the Civil War Military Pensions, 1861-1885* (Madison: University of Wisconsin, 1917), 89.

82. Berlin, *Free*, 169.

83. OR, Series III, Volume IV, 894.

84. Louis Gerteis, *From Contraband to Freedman: Federal Policy Toward Southern Blacks 1861-1865* (Westport, Connecticut: Greenwood Press, 1973), 19-20.

85. *Christian Recorder*, 10 June 1865.

86. Virginia Jeans Laas, ed., *Wartime Washington: the Civil War Letters of Elizabeth Blair Lee* (Urbana: University of Illinois Press, 1991), 301.

87. R.J.M. Blackett, ed., *Thomas Morris Chester, Black Civil War Correspondent: His Dispatches from the Virginia Front.* (Baton Rouge: Louisiana State University Press, 1989), 367-368.

88. Kathleen C. Berkeley, "'Colored Ladies Also Contributed': Black Women's Activities From Benevolence to Social Welfare, 1866-1896," *in The Web of Southern Social Relations: Women, Family, & Education* Eds. Walter Fraser, et al. (Athens: University of Georgia Press, 1985), 189-190.

89. *Pennsylvania Freedmen's Bulletin* , 1 August 1865.

90. Clary, February 2, 1865.

91. Ibid., April 4, 1865.

92. Ibid., March 28, 1865.

93. Berlin, *Black*, 686-687.

94. John Blassingame, ed., *Slave Testimony* (Baton Rouge: Louisiana State University Press, 1977), 119.

CHAPTER 10

Eloquent Appeals: The Pen and Voice As Weapons

The Civil War touched African American women in very personal ways, in every aspect of their lives. Because so many of their men were involved in some way or the other in the Civil War, the women felt the impact of the war in a very direct way. Lucy Stanton Day's stepbrothers enlisted in the Massachusetts 54th.[1] Sarah Swails' husband, Stephen, was a sergeant in the same regiment. Catherine Delany's husband, Martin, and her son, Toussaint L'Overture, were Union soldiers. Mary Ann Shadd Cary's brother, Abraham Shadd, served in the Massachusetts 55th. Susie King Taylor's first husband, Edward King, her father, Raymond Baker, and several uncles and cousins were Union soldiers. Margaret Sasportas' brother, Thaddeus, was a Union soldier. Caroline Wall Langston's husband, John Mercer, and her brother, O.S.B. Wall, both served in the Union army. Mary Smith Kelsey Peake's spouse was a Union spy.

Although Sojourner Truth had remarked sarcastically upon hearing that African American men were finally going to be recruited as soldiers: "Just as it was when I was a slave—the niggers always have to clean up after the white folks," she actively supported the recruitment of African American men.[2] She was quite proud that her grandson, James Caldwell, had volunteered for the Massachusetts 54th because, in his words, "Now is our time, Grandmother, to prove that we are men."[3] She asked the *National Anti-Slavery Standard* to publish his name in its pages so that "some one may go and see him,"[4] in order to aid and comfort him in her absence.

Because so many of their fathers, husbands, sons and brothers enlisted or were conscripted, African American women suffered enormous emotional, physical and mental strain due to the temporary and permanent loss of their men. They, therefore, understood quite clearly, that the fate of African Americans as a people was tied to the outcome of the conflict. The liberation of black men meant the liberation of African Americans. If the African American male could achieve "manhood" through his service as a soldier, then African American women would, by reflection, achieve "womanhood." As a result, black women were very vocal in their support of African American male participation in the Civil War. The reverse, a victorious South, was too horrible to imagine. In such a scenario, no African, free or enslaved, would have been safe.

The black press and public oratory were used to advantage. The women published letters to each other, recorded their speeches, wrote articles exhorting African American men to enlist, composed editorials in support of the recruitment of African American soldiers, placed advertisements seeking missing family members, solicited funds, announced their activities and gave advice in the pages of black newspapers. They wrote letters of appeal and demand to those in authority, seeking redress for injustices. They sang, lectured, composed songs and poems, gave dramatic readings to raise money and contend against oppression.

The deaths and maimings of their husbands, fathers, brothers, and sons caused emotional heartbreak as well as economic deprivation. Black women referred to such losses in their letters, diaries, speeches and memoirs, firmly establishing the Civil War as a defining event in African American history. Edmonia Highgate's brother was killed in the battle to take Petersburg, Virginia. Two of Sarah Smith Tompkins Garnet's brothers were killed in the War.[5] Sattira Douglas' husband, H. Ford, died shortly after the war ended as a result of contracting malaria during his stint as a soldier.

Charlotte Forten's father, Robert, served in the 43rd United States Colored Regiment during the Civil War, dying of typhoid fever in 1864. Nevertheless, she actively supported the participation of African American men in the army saying that "they . . . have shown that true manhood has no limitations of color."[6] In addition to her teaching duties, she helped in the Beaufort, South Carolina hospitals after the Fort Wagner attack, ministering to the wounded soldiers.

Elizabeth Keckley's son, James, a Wilberforce University student, was killed in action in 1861 at Wilson's Creek, Missouri after enlisting in the Union army. Using the name, George W.D. Kirkland, James, the result of Keckley's rape by her white owner, had enlisted as a white man before

African American men were officially allowed to join the Union army. Through her skill as a seamstress, Keckley had been able to purchase her own and her son's freedom in 1855. She received a pension for her son's service most likely because the official records listed him as white.[7] She, too, vigorously endorsed the enlistment of African American men.

Black women used the pen in personal quests to ameliorate individual suffering. Martha Wells wrote to the Adjutant General's Office from Berkeley Springs, West Virginia in 1866, seeking information about her soldier son's possible death. It is clear that she had devoted much time to investigating what might have happened to him. She had received word from that office that he had died, but she wanted them to continue searching because she thought they had made a mistake. "I hope you will make the search and gratify a poor distressed mother . . . if I am satisfied in my distressed mind that my son is dead I will go to Texas and bring him home."[8]

From Philadelphia, the wife of Samuel Brown wrote to Edwin Stanton, Secretary of War, concerning her missing husband. She included in her letter a plea from other Philadelphia women in the same situation. "I am in great trouble of mind about my husband. It is reported that he is dead. He has been gone over a year and I have not heard from him. His name is Samuel or Sandy Brown Co. C. 25th regiment U.S. Colored Troops Penn. He went with his brother and five cousins to enlist. None of them have been heard from only reports that they were dead which causes their wives great grief. You will be doing great charity by letting us know their whereabouts if alive so that we may write to them. Their names are . . . Daniel Brown, Asa Miller, Daniel Horsey, George Horsey, Samuel Horsey, George H. Washington . . . We have not received a cent from them since they left. We are all bad off . . . "[9]

The pages of African American newspapers and the podium were used to solicit support, financial and moral, for the Civil War effort. Sattira Douglas, wife of the famous abolitionist, H. Ford Douglas, regularly contributed articles to the *Weekly Anglo-African* and the *Christian Recorder*. She wrote to the *Christian Recorder* on behalf of the Colored Ladies' Freedmen's Aid Society of Chicago, the first organization to aid African American forces in the West of which she was a founder: "We . . . desire to announce, through your columns, what efforts we have made and are still making, toward promoting the object for which the Society was formed. We do this in order to give publicity to the fact, that the colored citizens of Chicago are not wholly indifferent to the demands of the needy freemen of the South."[10] Sattie, as she was called, later became an instructor of freedpeople in Leavenworth, Kansas.

Sarah Parker Remond, from the famous activist Salem, Massachusetts Remond family, sought diplomatic support for the Union in Great Britain through the International Congress of Charities, Correction, and Philanthropy. Because of its commercial ties with England through the cotton trade, the Confederacy counted on Great Britain to recognize it as legitimate by establishing diplomatic relations. However, through the efforts of the Union's statesmen and antislavery workers, such as Sarah Remond, Great Britain remained neutral, thereby dealing the Confederacy a serious blow.

Lancaster, England was a major center for the manufacture of raw cotton into finished cloth. "Nearly half of the cotton factory spindleage in the world was located in Lancaster and surrounding Lancashire."[11] Remond beseeched the British to "let no diplomacy of statesmen, no intimidation of slaveholders, no scarcity of cotton, no fear of slave insurrections, prevent the people of Great Britain from maintaining their position as the friend of the oppressed Negro, which they deservedly occupied previous to the disastrous civil war."[12]

As a member of the London Emancipation Society and the Freedmen's Aid Association, Remond lectured widely to influence British public opinion in favor of the Union. She wrote to William Lloyd Garrison from London in 1864: "We are now waiting with some anxiety and intense interest, the result of the Presidential election. Abolitionists generally desire the re-election of Mr. Lincoln, as any influence which defeats the 'Copperheads' must, to some extent, promote our cause. It is quite certain that the election of [George] McClellan would be received by the Confederates with enthusiasm, and also give fresh courage to their allies in Great Britain and France."[13] She returned only briefly to the United States in 1866 to help establish, along with her famous abolitionist brother, Charles Lenox Remond, the American Equal Rights Association which combined the battle for civil rights for African Americans with the female suffrage struggle.[14] She then expatriated to Florence, Italy where she studied and practiced medicine. Her sisters, Maritcha Remond and Caroline Remond Putnam, joined her there some years later.

Remond had been invited in 1858 to lecture in Great Britain by the Ladies and Young Men's Anti-Slavery Societies and remained in England to study at Bedford College for Ladies. For a while she stayed with the well-known fugitives, William and Ellen Craft, who had made a daring escape from enslavement in Georgia in 1848 with Ellen posing as a white planter while her husband pretended to be her servant. The Fugitive Slave Law of 1850 had forced them to relocate to Great Britain.

The eloquent orator and poet, Frances Ellen Watkins Harper, gave lectures to collect money for the war effort. She was a much sought-after speaker who received rave reviews for her oratory and appearance. "She has a noble head, the bronze muse; a strong face, with a shadowed glow upon it indicative of thought and of a nature most femininely sensitive, but not the least morbid. Her form is delicate, her hands daintily small . . . Her manner is marked by dignity and composure."[15]

An article in the Mobile, Alabama *Register* by a white observer of one of her post-bellum lectures said, "Her voice is remarkable—as sweet as any woman's voice we ever heard, and so clear and distinct as to pass every syllable to the most distant ear in the house. Without any effort at attentive listening we followed the speaker to the end, not discerning a single grammatical inaccuracy of speech, or the slightest violation of good taste in manner or matter. At times the current of thoughts flowed in eloquent and poetic expression, and often her quaint humor would expose the ivory in half a thousand mouths."[16]

She wrote a poem of celebration, vindication and lamentation, "The Massachusetts Fifty-Fourth," to honor the unit after more than half of the six hundred African American soldiers were killed at Fort Wagner, South Carolina:

Where storms of death were sweeping,
Wildly through the darkened sky,
Stood the bold but fated column,
Brave to do, to dare, and die . . .
Bearers of a high commission
To break each brother's chain;
With hearts aglow for freedom,
They bore the toil and pain . . .
Oh! not in vain those heroes fell,
Amid those hours of fearful strife;
Each dying heart poured out a balm
To heal the wounded nation's life.
And from the soil drenched with their blood,
The fairest flowers of peace shall bloom;
And history cull rich laurels there,
To deck each martyr hero's tomb . . . [17]

The Massachusetts 54th, the first African American regiment raised in the North, was used as proof of the worthiness of African American men as soldiers. The black community intensely monitored and empathized with the men in this unit, as they were eventually to do with all the battalions. Harper's poem reflects the high esteem they were held in, especially after the massacre at Fort Wagner. It also illustrates the responsibility for the race that the unit carried. Their success meant the African American community's elevation.

Another poem she wrote, entitled, "President Lincoln's Proclamation of Emancipation, January 1, 1863," celebrated the emancipation of enslaved Africans in states which had seceded from the Union:

It shall flash through coming ages,
It shall light the distant years;
And eyes now dim with sorrow
Shall be brighter through their tears . . .
It shall gild the gloomy prison
Darkened by the nation's crime,
Where the dumb and patient millions
Wait the better-coming time . . .
Soon the mists and murky shadows
Shall be fringed with crimson light,
And the glorious dawn of freedom
Break refulgent on the sight.[18]

The liberation, however limited, was a glorious thing because it erased some of the nation's shame. "Just a little while since the American flag to the flying bondman was an ensign of bondage; now it has become a symbol of protection and freedom."[19] Like the poem honoring the 54th, this verse, also, reflected the sentiments of the African American population.

Harper said of the Civil War: "We may look upon it as God's controversy with the nation, His rising to plead by fire and blood the cause of His poor and needy people."[20] In a November 15, 1864 speech which illustrated her powerful and forceful oratory, Harper attacked the idea that the war had failed to reunite the Union. For her, the liberation of enslaved Africans was much more to the point.

Tell me if the whole world of literature . . . can equal the music of these words:—'I grant you full, broad, and unconditional freedom.' . . . the Democrats tell us this war has been a failure to restore the Union. Why, that failure has been a grand success. The Union of the past, thank God, is gone. Darkened by the shadow of a million crimes, it has sunk beneath the weight of its own guilt, and now we stand upon the threshold of a new era—an era whose horizon is gilded with promise, and flushed with hope. The Union a failure? Go ask the hundred thousand freedmen in Maryland if the war be a failure, and let them point you to the homes which no soul-driver invades by law, where the crack of the whip, and the shrieks of tortured women, and groans of outraged men, no longer rise as swift witnesses to God against the terrible wrongs of slavery . . .

A new, more viable Union, with freedpeople as a part of it, would be put into place.

National defeats have been national gains . . . Slavery has brought us down to the dust of death, and it was poetic justice that we should have a general who would burrow in the mud, and muffle the thunders of his cannon before the wooden guns of Manassas.[21]

In keeping with the tradition of printing important speeches in newspapers, Harper's address was published in the African American press.

Later that month, on November 28, 1864, Harper participated as a featured speaker at a gala held at Cooper Institute in New York City which celebrated the emancipation of Africans in Maryland. One of the other participants was Rev. Henry Highland Garnet, the radical emigrationist who believed strongly in the right of enslaved Africans to engage in armed resistance. Another presenter, "Mrs. Sedgwick[22], of Philadelphia, . . . sang with precision and excellent effect the song—'*Viva l'America.* '"

The celebration had an especial significance for Harper because Maryland was the state of her birth. She was born to free parents in Baltimore and when she was orphaned at age three, her abolitionist uncle, William J. Watkins, raised her. However, while she was teaching in York, Pennsylvania, Maryland passed a law in 1852 which mandated enslavement or re-enslavement for any free African Americans entering the state. Harper, hence, considered herself an exile, noting at the gala that "she could now return to revisit . . . without fear of arrest."

Her speech on this occasion reiterated many of the same themes as her earlier work: the necessity of ensuring basic civil rights for African Americans, the significance of the war to the nation as a test of its commitment to espoused principles of freedom, and the valor and sacrifice of the African American soldier. Harper "declared that the lessons of the war . . . reads thus—Simple justice is the right of every race. Mrs. Harper claimed besides, that the war has introduced the colored man to the nation. Before, he was not known: if known, only as a menial and a slave." The

Massachusetts 54th received praise in her speech for teaching "the nation, by their own self-sacrifice, saying: 'We can afford to die, if it break our brother's chains.' That who could thus nobly die had evinced that the jewel which man prized above all others was the integrity of his soul."[23] Soldiers, not menial laborers, would be the salvation and elevation of the race.

Philadelphia's elite Social, Civil and Statistical Association gave a series of lectures to raise money to aid freedpeople. Harper was the fourth to speak in the series which included such speakers as William Wells Brown, Major General O.O. Howard, Major General Benjamin F. Butler, Rev. J. Sella Martin, John Mercer Langston, and Frederick Douglass. The broadside announcing her talk on January 31, 1867 at National Hall, entitled "National Salvation," proclaimed,

> It is needless to say that the abilities of Mrs. Harper as a speaker both natural and acquired are most wonderful, and that in presenting the claims of her race she never fails to interest by her beautiful language and eloquent appeals, even those ordinarily unfavorable to female lecturers.

Harper had been on a tour of the South to assess the condition of the freedpeople.

> She has for the last few weeks been delivering her New Lecture in Kentucky and Tennessee, much to the astonishment of the whites and the newly made free, which have had very marked effect, judging from newspaper notices from both Union and Rebel Journals.

Her oratory was so powerful and persuasive that the conveners were sure that even anti-black racists would benefit from her talk:

> But as she has spoken to the delight of large and intelligent audiences in this city on former occasions, we need only to add that we hope all friendly to Freedom and this Association, for the cause-sake, will exert themselves to hear this lecture, and to induce especially that class who are opposed to Equality before the Law to attend.[24]

The comment "ordinarily unfavorable to female lecturers" referred to the ongoing debate about the role of women in the African American community, and the larger society. It is to be remembered that men had jeered and pelted the fiery speaker and feminist, Maria Stewart, with rotten tomatoes in Boston in the early 1830's because they considered it presumptuous for a woman to engage in public speaking, especially public speaking which chastised men.[25]

Frances Ellen Watkins Harper inherited much the same animosity but Stewart had paved the way for her. Harper's fiery oratory made the way a little, very little, easier for Ida B. Wells who alienated some African American males, particularly ministers, with her outspokenness. And contemporary African American women who speak out about problems within and without the African American community owe a significant debt to these women.

Nevertheless, the conveners of this lecture series recognized Harper's unquestionable value as an audience drawer. The editors of the *Christian Recorder* commented in the February 25, 1865 issue: "the fame alone of this distinguished lecturess will bring out a better audience than any praise she could have from our pen . . . for elegance of expression this lady is unsurpassed."

In addition, Harper talked to freedpeople, especially the women, herself, going on tour in the South to assess their situation, "observing their social condition, and the working of the various Associations for their elevation."[26] She lectured for no set fee because of the destitute condition some of the refugees were in and she was often not paid at all. Still, she persevered, declaring triumphantly, "I am standing with my race on the threshold of a new era . . . with my limited and fragmentary knowledge, I may help the race forward a little."[27]

Harper spoke in Port Royal, South Carolina in September 1867. Laura M. Towne, a white teacher there, reported that Harper "gave the people some most excellent advice, which they liked very much. They were amazed at her power of expression."[28] After her southern tour, from which she decided that the formerly-seceded states were still "unreconstructed," she lectured in the north about her conclusions.

To collect money for refugees and African American soldiers, Sojourner Truth lectured, sang and composed inspirational songs, including one sung to the tune of "John Brown's Body" and later, the "Battle Hymn of the Republic":

> We are done with hoeing cotton, we are done with hoeing corn;
> We are colored Yankee soldiers, as sure as you are born.
> When Massa hears us shouting, he will think 'tis Gabriel's horn,
> As we go marching on.[29]

Unlike the "Battle Hymn," though, this song is about retribution against slaveholders.

Well-known locally, Louise De Mortie and Susa (Susie) Cluer of Boston gave dramatic readings as a way to raise funds. Described by William Wells Brown as "one of the most beautiful of her sex,"[30] De Mortie gave her first reading in concert with Cluer whose "reputation . . . [had] long been established" in March 1862. She received laudatory notices. "She possessed rare genius," according to the April 12, 1862 *Weekly Anglo-African* who also said, "Should Mrs. De Mortie make reading a profession, she will attain a high position."

Her performances were still being praised a year later. The February 6, 1863 *Liberator* stated that De Mortie, "with much ease and grace of manner . . . possesses a voice of great compass and strength, flexibility, sweetness, and power of expression." The writer went on to hope her public readings "may benefit her auditors by deepening in their minds the impression of the truths presented to them." The *Liberator* was saying in its December 9, 1864 edition, "The colored citizens of Cambridge held a public meeting at the City Hall, on Monday evening last, to celebrate the abolition of slavery in the State of Maryland . . . Addresses were delivered by Wm. Wells Brown, and Robert Morris, and two poems on Freedom were read by Madame Louise De Mortie, the talented colored lady whose public Readings are so acceptably heard through the New England States." She had apparently become famous for her skill by this time, appearing with someone as famed as William Wells Brown and being referred to as "Madame."

Along with Frances Ellen Watkins Harper, De Mortie became one of the most well known African American female speakers. As late as 1912, she was being praised for her expertise. "Madame Louise De Mortie of New Orleans, had this gift, and being magnetic and personally attractive, always appeared before large audiences."[31] At the peak of her popularity, however, De Mortie moved to New Orleans and in 1865 opened a home for African American children left orphaned by the Civil War. A notice in the June 24, 1865 *Christian Recorder* announced: "A home for colored orphans is being established in New Orleans, by Mrs. Louise De Mortie, with excellent success." Using her fame, she did extensive fundraising for this project, holding a two-week-long fair in May-June, 1865 which netted $1,083.75 for the orphanage.[32]

Caroline (Carrie) Le Count, of Philadelphia, also had a reputation as a performer. A graduate of the ICY, she "made many public appearances here and elsewhere in reading and recitation. She was popular after a fashion and was for many years in demand as an entertainer."[33] Le Count was active during the Civil War in relief, educational and civil rights activities.

The famous songstress, Elizabeth Taylor Greenfield, or the "Black Swan"[34] as she was called, "kindly volunteered to appear and furnish occasional airs at the opening and closing of each" of the Social, Civil and Statistical Association's lectures in Philadelphia which were given in the late 1860's "for the benefit of Freedmen, Sick and Wounded, &c."[35] She gave many concerts to aid refugees including a series at the Fifteenth Street Presbyterian Church in Washington, D.C. in 1864 to raise money for a recently established school for freedpeople in the city.[36]

One of Greenfield's protegees was Mary L. Brown, called "the American Nightingale," who was also active in relief efforts.[37] Brown organized a "soiree dansante" at Franklin Hall in Philadelphia in 1863 to raise money for a regimental flag for African American soldiers. She was also the niece of a well-known Philadelphia musician and bandleader, Frank Johnson. Brown and Greenfield sometimes appeared on programs together.

Black newspapers were used as vehicles for reuniting families and friends, or, at least, attempting to do so. Advertisements, which stayed in the papers for weeks, showed the disruption enslavement and the Civil War caused to African American families and the struggle women had in locating their families. These advertisements also belied white assertions that African Americans did not value marriage and close family ties. Rachel Shepherd of Portsmouth, Virginia sought information, through the *Christian Recorder*, on "the two brothers, Jordan Shepherd and Randall Shepherd, who left Norfolk, Va., some 18 or 20 years ago, or more. They are my brothers . . . " From West Chester, Pennsylvania, Catherine Jones asked for information about her cousin, John Burton "who enlisted in the 14th U.S.C.T."

Rev. Benjamin Tanner placed the following notice in the *Christian Recorder*: "Mrs. Letty Willis, of Frederick, Md . . . wishes to hear from her sister, Sophia Butler, wife of Mr. Lewis Butler. When last heard from, they were in Chambersburg, Penna., lately reduced to ashes by the rebels."[38] Harriet Mayo of Detroit, Michigan looked for information about Joseph, Richard, Aaron and Lucy Mayo who she thinks might be "some where within the lines of the Union army" since the last she had heard from them was when they were in Petersburg, Virginia.[39]

Hannah Cole of New Bedford, Massachusetts wanted to know: "Can anyone inform me of the whereabouts of John Person, the son of Hannah Person, of Alexandria, Va., who belonged to Alexander Sancter. I have not seen him for ten years. I was sold to Joseph Bruin, who took me to New Orleans. My name was then Hannah Person, it is now Hannah Cole. This is the only child I have and I desire to find him much."[40]

In many instances, African American women used the pen as a weapon as they vigorously sought redress for injustices, going so far as to write to the President, the Secretary of War, adjutant generals, anyone who might be thought of as having power to ameliorate their problems. They challenged the government to live up to its promises, implicit and explicit, to African Americans. In letter after letter and petition after petition, African American women showed that they were aware of the rights inherent in citizenship and that they had a right to demand that those liberties be respected.

The plaintive cries for justice are heartrending. African Americans expected the government, especially Abraham Lincoln, to address their needs. No matter how undeservedly, many black Americans saw Lincoln as the "Great Emancipator." Their letters to him show that they did not see the Emancipation Proclamation as a military maneuver designed to cripple the seceded South but rather as evidence of Lincoln's concern for them.

Mart Welcome's mother, Jane, wrote to Abraham Lincoln from Carlisle, Pennsylvania in 1864: "Mr. Abraham Lincoln. I want to know, sir, if you please, whether I can have my son released from the army. He is all the support I have now. His father is dead and his brother that was all the help that I had, he has been wounded twice . . . They say that you will sympathize with the poor . . . He belongs to the eighth regiment company of the U.S. Colored Troops . . . He is a sergeant."[41] In spite of the fact that she had already contributed one son to the service of the Union army, her request to have the other released was not granted.

Hannah Johnson, the mother of a Massachusetts 54th soldier who fought at, and fortunately survived, the infamous battle at Fort Wagner, South Carolina, wrote to President Lincoln demanding that he use his powers to protect African American troops from retaliatory treatment by Confederates when they were captured.

> My son is strong and as able to fight for his country and the colored people have as much to fight for as any . . . I have but poor education but I never went to school, but I know just as well as any what is right between man and man. Now I know it is right that a colored man should go and fight for his country, and so ought to a white man. I know that a colored man ought to run no greater risks than a white, his pay is no greater[;] his obligation to fight is the same. So why should not our enemies be compelled to treat him the same, made to do it.

She points out Lincoln's responsibility to the African American men who
risked their lives for the Union.

> My son fought at Fort Wagner but Thank God he was not taken
> prisoner, as many were. I thought of this thing before I let my boy go
> but then they said Mr. Lincoln will never let them sell our colored
> soldiers for slaves, if they do he will get them back quick. He will
> retaliate and stop it. Now Mr. Lincoln don't you think you ought to stop
> this thing and make them do the same by the colored men.

Johnson turned the stereotype of the indolent African on its head. In her
view, whites are lazy, shiftless exploiters. She also disputed the belief that
Africans in their native land were uncivilized. It was enslavement which
brought out the worse in people, white or black. Without the degrading
condition of enslavement, African men could achieve their rightful
manhood:

> They have lived in idleness all their lives on stolen labor and made
> savages of the colored people, but they now are so furious because they
> are proving themselves to be men . . . Ought one man to own another,
> lawful or not? Who made the law, surely the poor slave did not. So it is
> wicked, and a horrible outrage, there is no sense in it. Because a man
> has lived by robbing all his life and his father before him, should he
> complain because the stolen things found on him are taken. Robbing the
> colored people of their labor is but a small part of the robbery. Their
> souls are almost taken, they are made brutes of often.

She was aware of Lincoln's image as the "Great Emancipator" and she
wanted him to live up to the trust African Americans placed in him.

> It would seem cruel, but there is no other way, and a just man must do
> hard things sometimes, that show him to be a great man. They tell me,
> some do, you will take back the [Emancipation] Proclamation, don't do
> it. When you are dead and in Heaven, in a thousand years that action
> of yours will make the angels sing your praises.

For Hannah Johnson, Lincoln could only be a great man if he insured
equitable treatment for African American soldiers.

> You must put the rebels to work in State prisons to making shoes and
> things, if they sell our colored soldiers, till they let them all go. And
> give their wounded the same treatment . . . Will you see that the colored

men fighting now, are fairly treated. You ought to do this, and do it at once, not let the thing run along. Meet it quickly and manfully, and stop this mean cowardly cruelty. We poor oppressed ones, appeal to you, and ask fair play.[42]

A wife wrote to Edwin M. Stanton, Secretary of War, beginning her letter with the righteously indignant: "I have taken the liberty to write you a few lines which I am compelled to do. I am colored it is true but I have feelings as well as [a] white person and why is it the colored soldiers letters can't pass backward and forwards as well as the white ones?" Lucy Bailey of Detroit then asked for information about her missing husband, John Bailey, a drum major for the 100th USCI.[43]

Those African American women who had such skills used their pens and their voices as mighty weapons in the battle for black liberation. They spoke and wrote in common cause with all African Americans to challenge injustice and to exhort their people to continued resistance. The particular circumstances of the Civil War perhaps tested those attributes more than most times in African American history but black women rose to the occasion to make their eloquent appeals to the hearts and consciences of America.

NOTES

1. Ellen Lawson, *The Three Sarahs: Documents of Antebellum Black College Women* (New York: Edwin Mellen Press, 1984), 198.
2. Carleton Mabee, *Sojourner Truth: Slave, Prophet, Legend.* (New York: New York University Press, 1995), 116-117.
3. Ibid.
4. Frances W. Titus, *Narrative of Sojourner Truth.* (New York: Arno Press, 1968, 1878), 145.
5. Jessie Carney Smith, ed., *Notable Black American Women* (Detroit, Michigan: Gale Research, 1992), 389.
6. Lewis C. Lockwood, *Two Black Teachers During the Civil War* (New York: Arno Press, 1969, 1864), 86.
7. Ervin L. Jordan, Jr., *Black Confederates and Afro-Yankees in Civil War Virginia* (Charlottesville: University Press of Virginia, 1995), 119.
8. Ira Berlin, ed., *The Black Military Experience* (New York: Cambridge University Press, 1982), 675-676.
9. Ibid., 665.
10. *Christian Recorder*, 12 March 1864.
11. C. Peter Ripley, ed., *Black Abolitionist Papers, Volume V: the United States, 1859-1865* (Chapel Hill: University of North Carolina Press, 1992), 25.

12. Sarah Parker Remond, "The Negroes in the United States of America," *Journal of Negro History* 26 (April 1942): 218.

13. *Liberator*, 11 November 1864.

14. Ruth Bogin, "Sarah Parker Remond: Black Abolitionist From Salem," *Essex Institute Historical Collections* 110 (April 1974): 147.

15. Hallie Q. Brown, *Homespun Heroines and Other Women of Distinction* (New York: Oxford University Press, 1988, 1926), 102.

16. William Still, *The Underground Railroad* (New York: Arno Press, 1968, 1872), 775.

17. *Anglo African*, 10 October 1863.

18. L. Maria Child, *Freedmen's Book* (New York: Arno Press, 1968, 1865), 250-251.

19. William Still, *The Underground Railroad* (New York: Arno Press, 1968, 1872), 766.

20. Melba Joyce Boyd, *Discarded Legacy: Politics and Poetics in the Life of Frances E.W. Harper 1825-1911* (Detroit, Michigan: Wayne State University, 1994), 51.

21. *Christian Recorder*, 31 December 1864. There were two battles at Manassas, Virginia (or Bull Run), the first in 1861 and the second in 1862. The Union lost both.

22. This is probably Sarah Sedgwick Brown who Scruggs (pp. 340-341) says was called the "Colored Nightingale." She was well known in Philadelphia. Sedgwick was the daughter of the well-to-do John Bowers, Sr. and the sister of Thomas J. and John, Jr. who were a musician and tailor, respectively. Her sister was Henrietta Bowers Duterte, an activist who became the first woman undertaker in Philadelphia.

23. *Liberator*, 9 December 1864.

24. Broadside, Historical Society of Pennsylvania.

25. Rodger Streitmatter, "Maria W. Stewart: the First Female African-American Journalist," *Historical Journal of Massachusetts*, 21 (Summer 1993): 56.

26. *Pennsylvania Freedmen's Bulletin* (October 1867).

27. William Still, *The Underground Railroad* (New York: Arno Press, 1968, 1872), 772.

28. Ibid.

29. Benjamin Quarles, *The Negro in the Civil War* (New York: Da Capo, 1989, 1953), 228-229.

30. Jessie Carney Smith, ed., *Notable Black American Women, Book II* (Detroit, Michigan: Gale Research, Inc., 1996), 174.

31. *Philadelphia Tribune*, 18 May 1912.

32. Ibid., 174-175.

33. *Philadelphia Tribune*, 18 May 1912.

34. A reference to Jenny Lind, called the "Swedish Nightingale"

35. Broadsides, Historical Society of Pennsylvania.

36. Melvin R. Williams, "A Blueprint for Change: the Black Community in Washington, D.C., 1860-1870," *Records of the Columbia Historical Society*, 48 (1972): 367.

37. Smith (1992), 415-416.

38. *Christian Recorder*, 4 February 1865.

39. *Christian Recorder*, 18 February 1865.

40. *Christian Recorder*, 24 June 1865.

41. Berlin, *Black*, 664.

42. Ira Berlin, et al., eds. *Free At Last: a Documentary History of Slavery, Freedom, and the Civil War*. (New York: New Press, 1992), 450-451.

43. Berlin, *Black*, 665-666.

CHAPTER 11

The Honor of the Whole African Race on Her Shoulders: Conclusion

Fanny Jackson Coppin voiced the belief that race was more of an impediment than gender when she wrote: "I never rose to recite in my classes at Oberlin but I felt that I had the honor of the whole African race upon my shoulders. I felt that, should I fail, it would be ascribed to the fact that I was colored."[1] Coppin expressed these feelings as an African American, not as a woman because the burden of racism was experienced by all African Americans, regardless of gender.

Although African American women were more concerned with the effects of the Civil War on their community as a whole, gender issues, nonetheless, received some attention, no matter how muted by the vicissitudes of war. However, discussions of gender took place outside the view of the larger white society and the debate was always nuanced by the role race played in determining the life chances of all African Americans. Gender problems were, therefore, secondary to the larger issue of black liberation. For example, when white women sought the right to vote, often at the expense of black men, African American women came down solidly in favor of race. Black women, while desiring suffrage for themselves, most often voluntarily made their struggle for the franchise secondary to black male suffrage.

Despite such strong commitment to racial solidarity on the part of black women, there was an attempt by some African American men, especially religious leaders, to define the role of black women based on the traditional role assumed to be possessed by white women. That traditional "white" gender role, however, involved the concept of woman as property. For African Americans to adopt such tradition meant that black women, who had set aside gender distinctions in order to survive the

Civil War, were no longer to be the property of whites, but now were to be considered the property of African American men. In a generalized way, black men were looking to be the equals of white men, rather than partners of African American women.

According to Paula Giddings, the assertiveness that black women exhibited during the Civil War—because of exigencies which had necessitated survival—was to be challenged by African American men in the conflict's aftermath. "Following the Civil War, men attempted to vindicate their manhood largely through asserting their authority over women. For their part, women sometimes welcomed that assertion, sometimes were forced to acquiesce to it, and sometimes resisted it. Influencing the masculine determination was the history of the White man's proprietary 'rights' over Black women, and the consequent struggle of Black men to reclaim them."[2]

The white abolitionist, Laura M. Towne, noted this tendency in her diary in 1867 when she recorded how quickly the newly-freed African American men on St. Helena Island accepted the "superior male" attitude. At a meeting held to form a Republican Party on the island so that African American men could exercise their recently-received right to vote, it was decided to exclude women from the proceedings. "Two or three white men . . . got up and said women and children ought to stay at home on such occasions . . . To-day in church Mr. [John A.]Hunn announced another meeting next Saturday. 'The females must stay at home?' asked Demas [minister] from the pulpit. 'The *females* can come or not as they choose,' said Mr. Hunn, 'but the meeting is for men voters.' Demas immediately announced that 'the womens will stay at home and cut grass,' that is, hoe the corn and cotton fields—clear them of grass! It is too funny to see how much more jealous the men are of one kind of liberty they have achieved than of the other! . . . [D]omestic freedom—the right, just found, to have their own way in their families and rule their wives—that is an inestimable privilege! . . . Several speakers have been here who have advised the people to get the women in their proper place . . . [T]he notion of being bigger than women generally, is just now inflating the conceit of the males to an amazing degree."[3] These were the same women who very ably carried on the work of the farms and plantations while the men were away fighting in the war.

A more direct indication of attempts to place black women in a traditionally subservient role as property can be seen in the "Declarations of Wrongs and Rights" issued by the men at the National Convention of Colored Citizens of the United States, which met in October 1864 in

Syracuse, New York. Among one of the "wrongs" visited on African American men was the following: "As a people, we have been denied the ownership of our bodies, our wives, homes, children, and the products of our own labor . . . we have been forced to silence and inaction in full presence of the infernal spectacle of . . . our daughters ravished, our wives violated . . . "

This National Negro Convention was convened in the midst of the Civil War by the leading African American men of the day to discuss the issues facing the African American community. A very short roll-call of the delegates shows how important the convention was: Thomas J. Bowers; William Wells Brown, historian; Joseph C. Bustill; Francis L. Cardozo; Octavius Catto; abolitionist William Howard Day; Frederick Douglass; Rev. Henry Highland Garnet; John Mercer Langston; Rev. Jermain Loguen; Rev. J. Sella Martin; Rev. J.W.C. Pennington; lawyer John S. Rock; George L. Ruffin; John Sampson, the editor of the *Cincinnati Colored Citizen* and brother to Joseph E. Sampson, an officer of the Colored Ladies Auxiliary of the Soldier's Aid Society in Northern Ohio; George Vashon; the editor of the *Christian Recorder*, Rev. Elisha Weaver; and many, many more. Many of the delegates were married to, related to or associated with prominent female activists and many were staunch supporters of equal rights for women.

Even though this assembly, unlike most of the other National Negro Conventions, departed from tradition by allowing Frances Ellen Watkins Harper and Edmonia Highgate to address the gathering, women were not treated as full members. After 1848, women could attend the meetings but were not allowed to share in making policy. Women, of course, protested their exclusion from the process of making decisions about racial matters which affected them. Not wishing to allow men to speak for them, they logically equated the sexist behavior of the black men at the conventions with white racist behavior. The women at the Ohio State Convention in 1849, led by Jane P. Merritt, demanded the right to be heard at the conferences. Mary Ann Shadd Cary was seated at the 1855 Philadelphia Negro Convention but only after a very heated debate in which she defended her right to be a part of the convention. By 1859, however, the men at the New England Convention of Colored Citizens had elected Ruth Remond and Mrs. Lawton to their business committee and Ellen Sherman and Anne E. Gray to the finance committee.[4] Ruth Remond was Sarah Parker and Charles Lenox Remond's sister-in-law. Charles Remond had been a longtime feminist and had argued for equal rights for women for years.

Undoubtedly the large number of Christian ministers who attended the National Negro Conventions accounted for the exclusion of women. The Pauline doctrine of male authority over females was apparently in operation: "The husband is the head of his wife . . . woman is the reflection of man . . . Indeed, man was not made from woman, but woman from man. Neither was man created for the sake of woman, but woman for the sake of man . . . Women should be silent in the churches. For they are not permitted to speak, but should be subordinate, as the law also says. If there is anything they desire to know, let them ask their husbands at home."[5] Nevertheless, the vicissitudes of the times had demanded a re-ordering of the old, conventional gender mores and women were contributing to the re-ordering through their activism. Many African American male leaders like William C. Nell, Rev. Jermain Loguen, William J. Watkins (Frances Ellen Watkins Harper's uncle and benefactor), Robert Purvis, Robert B. and William D. Forten and Frederick Douglass, also rejected those sexist norms.

Martin Delany, a steadfast feminist, had written in 1852: "Let our young women have an education; let their minds be well informed; well stored with useful information and practical proficiency, rather than the light superficial acquirements, popularly and fashionably called accomplishments. We desire accomplishments, but they must be *useful*."[6] In keeping with the prevailing thought of his day, he had placed the responsibility for the race squarely on African American women's shoulders: "Our females must be qualified, because they are to be the mothers of our children. As mothers are the first nurses and instructors of children; from them children consequently, get their first impressions, which being always the most lasting, should be the most correct. Raise the mothers above the level of degradation, and the offspring is elevated with them . . . No people are ever elevated above the condition of their *females*; hence, the condition of the *mother* determines the condition of the child. To know the position of a people, it is only necessary to know the *condition* of their *females* . . . "[7]

Some measure of Delany's commitment to furthering the position of African American women can be seen in his choice of Mary Ann Shadd Cary as a Civil War recruiter at a time when it was not fashionable for women to operate in what were seen as male spheres of activity. He did not exclude women from conferences and collaboration, calling on them as well as African American men, to engage in discussions concerning his emigration schemes. At the 1854 National Emigration Conference in

Cleveland, Ohio, there were twenty-nine "fully accredited" female delegates, including Delany's wife, Catherine (Kate) A. Richards Delany.[8]

Kate, who bore eleven children[9] and endured Delany's extended absences from home as a result of his activism, including service during the Civil War, must have been the epitome of Delany's ideal woman. Frances Rollin, a teacher of freedpeople and Martin Delany's biographer, said Kate, "a fine-looking, intelligent, and appreciative lady, possessed of fine womanly sympathies, and always entering fully into [Martin's] pursuits, has contributed no little aid to his success."[10] Her son, Toussaint L'Overture, enlisting at the young age of eighteen, served in the Massachusetts 54th.

Ultimately, however, as Delany's comments show, the responsibility for the moral structure of the black community devolved on the shoulders of African American women. They, like black men, were expected to be credits to their race. Black women were to do this by projecting an image of untarnished, virtuous womanhood, assertive when it came to survival but docile in their relations with men. So, not only did African American women carry the responsibility of combating the negative images of them which abounded in the white community, they also had to bear the weight of African American male expectations of them. It was a burden they were willing to bear for the sake of racial unity, however.

Sallie Daffin, teacher of freedpeople, raised the specter of gender during the conflict in an article in the June 25, 1864 *Christian Recorder*, entitled simply "Woman." Although she did not speak of female submission to men, she was not advocating equality. Instead, she placed women in traditional roles as uncomplaining helpmates and nurturers. She wrote, "In whatever sphere of life it has been the lot of woman to be cast, she has so fulfilled her destiny, as to become an ornament to the world, and a blessing to her fellow-creatures . . . "

According to Daffin, men rely on their physical prowess and assume an intellectual preeminence over women, but, in fact, women have similar attributes: "Man boasts of his strength, courage, and great mental superiority over woman. To her, he attributes a quickness of perception; but less discretion, firmness, and maturity of judgment. But history presents us numerous examples of female heroism, decision of character, and profound mental worth . . . "

Daffin used Joan of Arc and Empress Josephine as models of women who had shown unparalleled courage. Although conditions may have been different from the periods which spawned Joan of Arc and Empress Josephine's greatness, the women of Daffin's day were still able to offer something: " . . . in a thousand ways does she contribute to the welfare and happiness of her nation, by the continued practice of those acts of patience and self-denial, which man, how much soever strength he may glory in, is incapable of performing . . . " The woman's contribution, notwithstanding all her positive attributes, is to be made in the traditional sphere. "In the domestic and social circle, who is there that has not felt, even if he fails to acknowledge it, that the mission of woman is a noble and meritorious one? comprehending a range so extensive, as to be immeasurable."

Readers were reminded by Daffin of the sacrifices that women made in linking their lives and fortunes to the men they "chose" to marry, assuming that women could exercise a basic agency:

> Viewing women in the position of wife . . . with what a self-sacrificing spirit, she tears herself from the fond embrace of loving parents, and dear friends; from whom, perhaps, she has never experienced an unpleasant look or word, to launch out upon the ocean of life, with nothing but the hand of a stranger to guide and support her . . . she goes forth reposing her all upon him, whom she has chosen as her life companion.

Although she did not attribute this behavior directly to African American men, she alludes to one of the major gender relations issues which was to plague the African American community after the war as women sought to secure a place for themselves—the mistreatment of African American women by African American men. Frances Ellen Watkins Harper, Sojourner Truth, among other women, condemned this behavior in their speeches and writings because they had expected that African American men would not assume the mien of white men in their treatment of black women. After all, had they not all just battled on a genderless front for black liberation?

> And how often has her confidence been misplaced—how often her devotion, which she has so lavishly bestowed upon him, been compensated with unkind words, and ill treatment. Say not, then, the mission of woman is a trifling one; for all are, to a great extent, indebted to her, for her many acts of kindness, self-denial, and love.

Harper, however, refused to allow the possibility of black male sexism to be used by white women to keep African American men from the vote, even if women did not get the franchise. The problem of abuse among African Americans was the black community's alone to deal with.

Perhaps in response to Daffin's article, in July 1864 Rev. William Reid suggested that God had ordained a subservient role for women. According to Reid, "the 'ruling power' is unquestionably lodged in the husband; and where reason and persuasion fail of securing sympathy, or of making his choice the wife's, then it is the duty of submission that belongs to the wife, 'except in affairs of religion and the conscience . . . What wife, having . . . Divine instruction in her possession, and at the same time, refusing to submit to her husband's authority, can dare to hope for the smiles of that God whose commands she is constantly and knowingly disregarding?"[11]

Amanda Turpin continued the topic in the August 20, 1864 *Christian Recorder* with a challenge to the African American community to put aside gender issues and focus on uplifting the race as a whole. "There is a great field of labor opening, and the influential female is called to perform a great portion of the work; therefore, let us rally to a post of duty, and help to burst open the dark prison-doors of ignorance, that the light of intelligence, mental and moral improvement, may break forth and shine into the minds of our once down-trodden and oppressed, but now freed race." Turpin outlined what she saw as the female's role in society—that of "influencing" men—but she felt that "surely, the female must have been created for some greater and more eminent position than she has yet attained." She stopped short, nonetheless, of advocating equal rights for women, saying "we are *almost* persuaded to speak in behalf of women's rights." It is significant that many African American female activists did exactly that—they turned their attention to the women's rights movement after the war and formed clubs and other organizations to work for the interests of African American women as well as the rights of all African Americans.

One area which received their full attention was the relentless white attacks against the moral character of black women. The disparagement of African American women affected the whole African American community because such verbal and written assaults allowed physical depredations as well as those insidious, subliminal manifestations of racism. African American men knew that by extension, their honor was also being attacked. Through their activism, African American women like Josephine St. Pierre Ruffin, Frances Ellen Watkins Harper, Anna Julia Cooper, Ida B. Wells, Mary Church Terrell, Fannie Barrier Williams, and a host of others deliberately challenged the negative images of black women, promoted by the white community, which had been around as long as the existence of the enslavement of Africans. They attempted to refigure the "disfigured images" that Patricia Morton writes about and to consciously repudiate the myth of the degraded and degenerate black woman to which Angela Davis refers. They were about the business of constructing a gender identity for African American women which was to be defined by themselves and in the process they intended to elevate the community as a whole.

Josephine St. Pierre Ruffin remarked on this crusade at the 1895 Inaugural National Conference of Colored Women , noting that "an army of organized women standing for purity and mental worth . . . deny the charge . . . " of being "ignorant and immoral" leveled against African American women. "Too long have we been silent under unjust and unholy charges; we cannot expect to have them removed until we disprove unjust charges through individual efforts . . . " The women had come together to show "that we are truly American women, with all the adaptability, readiness to seize and possess our opportunities, willingness to do our part for good as other American women." They were determined "for the sake of our own dignity, the dignity of our race, and the future good name of our children . . . to stand forth and declare ourselves and principles, to teach an ignorant and suspicious world that our aims and interests are identical with those of all good inspiring women." However, African American women had special racial needs which compelled them to organize: "the training of our children, openings for our boys and girls, how they can be prepared for occupations and occupations may be found or opened for them, what we can do in the moral education and physical development, the home training it is necessary to give our children in order to prepare them to meet the peculiar conditions in which they shall find themselves, how to make the most of our own, to some extent, limited opportunities."[12] They understood that racism, not sexism, was the most limiting, life-denying force facing the African American community.

Much earlier, Frances Ellen Watkins Harper had gone directly to the women most affected during one of her post-bellum southern tours. She lectured to freedwomen about the particular and special problems facing black women. "Part of my lectures are given privately to women, and for them I never make any charge, or take up any collection . . . I . . . talk with them about their daughters, and about things connected with the welfare of the race. Now is the time for our women to begin to try to lift up their heads and plant the roots of progress under the hearthstone."[13]

The predominant white belief maintained that African American women, particularly enslaved African American women, were sexually depraved and promiscuous, that they somehow invited, in fact, pursued sexual liaisons with white men. "The lack of chaste sentiment among the female slaves is exhibited by their yielding without objection, except in isolated cases, to the passion of their master. Indeed, the idea of the superiority of the white race was so universally admitted that the negress felt only pride at bearing offspring that had an admixture of the blood of the ruling class . . . So loose was the tie of marriage among the slaves, that the negro husband felt little or no displeasure when the fancy of the master chanced to light upon his wife."[14] This negative vision of enslaved women was transferred to free African American women who were also considered to be sexually loose.

This opinion held despite all evidence to the contrary. In fact, white sources often pointed out the existence of mixed race people as an example of the degrading influence of enslavement on whites as well as blacks. Colonel James Montgomery, white commander of the 2nd South Carolina Volunteers, alluded to miscegenation in an insulting speech to the Massachusetts 54th but he placed the blame, and the solution, for the "problem" on African American men. "Your yellow faces are evidences of rascality. You should get rid of this bad blood. My advice to you is the lightest of you must marry the blackest woman."[15]

White northern soldiers, visiting the South for the first time, were amazed to see nearly white enslaved Africans. "I saw to day a white slave, a girl about 18 with blue eyes, yellow hair nearly straight and a complexion lighter than a majority of Northern women. I should never have suspected her African blood if I had not seen her with other slaves."[16]

African Americans disputed the idea that black women invited the sexual attention of white men. The African American perspective on miscegenation emerged in the following article from the September 1862 *Douglass' Monthly*:

> An officer of the seventeenth Massachusetts Regiment, writing from Newbern, North Carolina, alludes to a phase of slavery that recently came under his notice . . . Such instances as he mentions are not rare in the slave states. Speaking of a contraband, a pretty yellow girl about 15 years old, who passed over the ferry in company with others fleeing from servitude, he says:
> She was the daughter of her master . . . She was brought up on the plantation of her father until about 14 years old, when the old planter, her father, began to think her old enough for use. She now carries the scars on her back where she was whipped before she would submit to her own father's lustful embraces.—Day after day she went through the flogging, but at last her spirit, as well as the flesh, was broken. She could withstand the monster no longer. The master and father triumphed

over his helpless victim, and after due course of time, she had a baby by her own father.—This baby, a few days ago, was forcibly taken from his mother, (when they heard the Yankees were coming,) and sent into the country towards Goldsboro, thinking of course the mother would sooner sacrifice liberty than her child; but the woman[17] had made up her mind that when the Yankees did come she would go with them, no matter the consequence.

Well, the mother is here, the child is—she don't know where.

The author placed the onus squarely on white men and a white system which held little regard for African womanhood (and childhood.) Black people saw such unions for what they were - another type of white male depredation, this time sexual, against the African American community.

W.E.B. Du Bois attacked the sexual hypocrisy of white southerners: "Southerners who had suckled food from black breasts vied with each other in fornication with black women, and even in beastly incest. They took the name of their fathers in vain to seduce their own sisters."[18] J.B. Roudanez, a free mechanic who was employed on plantations in New Orleans and was publisher of the *New Orleans Tribune*, confirmed Du Bois' assertion in 1864 when he presented his views on miscegenation on the plantations in a personal, eye-witness report to the War Department: "The young masters were criminally intimate with the negro girls; it was their custom; the girls copulate at fourteen years, and under; have known girls to be mothers at that age; some of the French planters had children by slave women; the planters' sons preferred these half-sisters for concubines . . . "[19]

Miscegenation was, therefore, an abiding concern because the large number of people of mixed racial heritage were very visible reminders that enslaved black women did not have the right to their own bodies and that black men could not protect black women from white male outrage. Jourdon Anderson, formerly enslaved by P.H. Anderson of Big Spring, Tennessee, wrote in 1865 from Ohio to his former master who was asking him to return to work for him, this time for wages. In his letter which clearly showed he had no intention of returning (he asked for eleven thousand six hundred and eighty dollars for back wages for him and his wife while they were enslaved), he asked to be reassured that his daughters would not suffer the fate of so many comely African American women. ". . . Please state if there would be any safety for my Milly and Jane, who are now grown up, and both good-looking girls. You know how it was with poor Matilda and Catherine. I would rather stay here and starve—and die, if it come to that—than have my girls brought to shame by the violence and wickedness of their young masters."[20]

Anderson's letter shows that these unions were not often consensual. Force, which he rightly called "violence and wickedness," is inherent in any sexual encounter between the enslaver and the enslaved. This point can be seen in the narratives of enslaved women, women like Harriet Jacobs and Elizabeth Keckley, who condemned the white men who raped or tried to rape them. Both of these women went on to become leaders in African American relief activities, in spite of the attacks.

Jacobs was very open and angry about the unwanted sexual attention her master showed her, an almost unheard of admission in those days but her tale gave voice to the thousands of enslaved women who could not tell their stories. When he died, she rejoiced, "There are wrongs which even the grave does not bury. The man was odious to me while he lived, and his memory is odious now."[21] When there was a possibility that her daughter might be recaptured after they had escaped enslavement, she became incensed: "I thought of what I had suffered in slavery at her age, and my heart was like a tiger's when a hunter tries to seize her young."[22] Her anger spilled over after a white friend bought her freedom so she would not be forced to live as a fugitive. "A human being *sold* in the free city of New York! The bill of sale is on record, and future generations will learn from it that women were articles of traffic in New York, late in the nineteenth century of the Christian religion."[23]

Keckley loved her son, James, although he was the product of her rape by her white owner. Unlike Jacobs, she wrote of the violation in oblique tones, "He persecuted me for four years, and I—I—became a mother. The child of which he was the father was the only child I ever brought into the world. If my poor boy ever suffered any humiliating pangs on account of birth, he could not blame his mother, for God knows that she did not wish to give him life; he must blame the edicts of that society which deemed it no crime to undermine the virtue of girls in my then position [enslavement.]"[24] Keckley's son enlisted as a white man in the Union army and was killed in battle.

Another example of the sexual depredations committed by white men is an incident in December 1863 which caused six white officers of 4th Corps d'Afrique, stationed at Fort Jackson, Louisiana to be dismissed from the United States Army for the attempted rape of African American laundresses attached to their command.[25] Brigadier General William Dwight, in reporting his decision to arrest one of the officers, divulged, "In this Regiment thus commanded was practiced every species of disgusting vice; what should have been the performance of duty was made a means of low and vile licentiousness among the officers, of outrage toward the women of their race which could not fail to be known to these soldiers, and the demoralization thus caused was repressed by violent punishment miscalled discipline."[26]

A correspondent to the *New York Evening Post* noted that "It has been found necessary, for the good order of the men and the good behavior of officers, to send all Black women out of this camp, except a few who are lawfully married to privates in the regiment, and are retained as laundresses for the regiment."[27] This was in keeping with the idea that African women were lewd, lascivious temptresses of white men.

Bell Wiley, a white southern apologist historian, in referring to this attack, continued the stereotype after the Civil War when he placed the blame on the women in an attempt to excuse this offense. "Negro women were sometimes employed as laundresses and as hospital nurses. An extensive use of colored females around the camps was discouraged by the authorities because of the demoralizing influences resulting therefrom. 'Prostitution, 'observed one officer 'is worse than slavery.'"[28]

It is significant, however, that the same regiment of African American soldiers had mutinied just a month before, in December 1863, as a result of brutal, inhumane treatment from the unit's white officers, including those dismissed for the attack on the women. The attempted rapes simply reflected the racist attitudes that the white officers felt toward *all* Africans. The soldiers, most of them formerly enslaved, had been subjected to the most vicious treatment imaginable by their white commanders—whippings, being hung by the thumbs or tied to stakes, beatings—treatment too reminiscent of their recent enslavement. And like enslavement, the African American women attached to this unit were thought to be available for the sexual gratification of the white men. It did not matter that the women were, more than likely, related in some way to some of the soldiers. It is also significant that the white men got off very lightly for their infractions—they were not beaten, shot or tied up by the thumbs. Being treated like gentlemen, they were simply dismissed from the service.

In another incident, a white soldier excused his sexual misconduct with a young African American woman as "natural" saying, "I have only obeyed nature's first law . . . intercourse with the opposite sex is absolutely necessary to the preservation of good health."[29] He, of course, meant sex with black women, because, presumably, white women were not "natural" enough to engage in illicit sex and, apparently, he did not have a traditional sexual right to white women.

A white Union physician wrote home about another sensational case of assumed white sexual prerogative in which three white men from Augusta, Georgia killed a white officer of the 33rd USCI, Captain Hausley. Hausley, "a gentlemanly appearing officer, (white), was spending the evening (late) with a very bright and pretty mulatto. Three young men of the upper families of the city came to the windows and began to make a noise whereupon the Capt. went out and was met by them and shot and stabbed. One of the young men had visited the girl frequently. Jealousy of Yankee usurpation of exclusively southern privileges is supposed to be the cause of the foul murder."[30] The assailants were arrested. The fact that the perpetrators and the victim were white made this case "a fruitful topic" for white observers. Had any of them been black, there would have, no doubt, been a different outcry and result.

General Rufus Saxton, white military governor of the Sea Islands, also remarked on the presumption of white male sexual prerogative in his official December 1864 report to Secretary of War Edwin Stanton. "The [black] women were held as the legitimate prey of lust, and as they had been taught it was a crime to resist a white man they had not learned to defend their chastity. Licentiousness was widespread; the morals of the old plantation life seemed revived in the army of occupation."[31]

African American soldiers did not subscribe to white notions of the lewd and lascivious black woman, however. Of course, black women were their wives, mothers, sisters, daughters, cousins; to denigrate them was to impugn the morals of the whole race. A soldier from the 3rd USCI stationed in Jacksonville, Florida wrote to the August 6, 1864 *Christian Recorder* not only about how savagely African American soldiers were treated by their white officers but also about the sexual abuse of the African American women connected to the division. This regiment also mutinied due to sadistic and barbarous treatment. Six African American soldiers were executed as a result, one received a sentence of fifteen years imprisonment at hard labor, two received ten years, and another got a year. All were dishonorably discharged and had their pay and pensions forfeited so that their families were not compensated for their service.[32] Like the Fort Jackson incident, the treatment of the African American soldiers was inextricably linked to the odious mistreatment of their women.

This despicable behavior was noted by a Mrs. Harlan, a white agent for the NFRA, who used the reality of sexual depredations against black women in an attempt to get the association to do more for refugee women than give mere material aid. She made the following report to them in March 1862: "The negro women have . . . been abused most shamefully [by the Union army.] From these outrages there can, of course, be no redress except through the interposition of the superior officers. But even they cannot now restore that which has been so thoroughly destroyed, and retrieve these poor creatures from the grave to which loathsome and retributive disease will rapidly hurry hundreds of them unless charity bring the necessary aid speedily."[33] In true Victorian fashion, her anger centers on the sexual violation of the women because not only does she see them as irredeemably tarnished morally but they are physically damaged because of sexually transmitted diseases such as syphilis and gonorrhea. Hers is one of the few references made to this aspect of the sexual abuse of African American women.

White sexual illusions about black women were manifested in very concrete ways, especially in public policy. White Union commanders used this threadbare fable to excuse their disruptive abuse of African American families. Colonel F.W. Lister, who had driven the wives and children of black soldiers away from a camp in Bridgeport, Alabama, wrote to Brigadier General William D. Whipple in 1865: "The marital relationship is but little understood by the colored race, and if possible still less respected . . . In fact the larger portion of the enlisted men change their so called wives as often as the regiment changes stations." He alleged, "Large herds of colored prostitutes flocked to Bridgeport from both ends of the line."[34]

The myth, and its impact, continued after the war. In many of the apologist Civil War histories written at the turn of the century, African American unions and familial feelings were denigrated, providing a handy rationale for the continued denial of basic human rights to African Americans. William W. Davis wrote in 1913: "They shed husbands, children, wives, and other dependents with an ease and rapidity which makes even a modern divorce court in comparison seem a conservative institution."[35] Of course, Davis, in his racist diatribe, did not acknowledge that because they were enslaved, African Americans had no "rights," including marriage or child rearing. Marriages between enslaved Africans were usually not legally sanctioned or recognized during enslavement.

One way that the black community challenged the myth was by placing a premium on marriage and family. The institution was seen, by African Americans, as evidence that they were properly civilized and morally elevated from the degrading condition of enslavement. First of all, marriage was seen as a basic civil right. Secondly, it served as proof that

African Americans were ready for citizenship. Consequently, many freedpeople sought to establish the "traditional" family structure of the man as head of the household so long denied to them.

The Adjutant General's Office used marriage as a means of gaining black recruits, issuing General Order No. 33 in March 1865 which,

> for the purpose of encouraging enlistments . . . , it is hereby enacted that the wife and children, if any he have, of any person that has been, or may be, mustered into the military or naval service of the United States, shall, from and after the passage of this act, be forever free, any law, usage, custom whatsoever to the contrary notwithstanding.

In addition to freeing the wives and children of self-liberated men, this act recognized the special circumstances facing Africans concerning marriage due to enslavement. It delineated the criteria officials were to use in deciding a marriage's legitimacy.

> In determining who is or who as the wife and who are the children of the enlisted person herein mentioned, evidence that he and the woman claimed to be his wife have cohabited together, or associated as husband and wife, and so continued to cohabit or associate at the time of enlistment, or evidence that a form or ceremony of marriage, whether such marriage was or was not authorized or recognized by law, has been entered into or celebrated by them, and that the parties thereto thereafter lived together, or associated or cohabited as husband and wife, and so continued to live, cohabit, or associate at the time of enlistment, shall be deemed sufficient proof of marriage for the purposes of this act; and the children born of any such marriage shall be deemed and taken to be the children embraced within the provisions of this act, whether such marriage shall or shall not have been dissolved at the time of enlistment.[36]

African American men rushed to enlist so their families could be free and many women entered into marriages so that they and their children could be free. The significance of these legal unions can be seen in later petitions for pensions made by widows of Civil War soldiers as African American women had to "prove" their marriages were authentic. Military officials and bureaucrats at the United States Pension Bureau looked with little favor on these petitions, often deciding they were not legitimate.

General Order No. 33 countermanded an earlier directive by a white commander of the 60th USCI in Helena, Arkansas, John G. Hudson, who, no doubt, was influenced by the negative stereotypes of African American women. "Information has been received at these Head Quarters, that the enlisted men of this command, are much in the habit of marrying Common place women of the town, this must be stopped at once . . . All Marriage Certificates given by the Rev. J.I. Herrick, Minister of the Gospel and Post Chaplain, are annulled from this date."[37]

Harper's Weekly discounted the biased view that the "tie of marriage" was loose among enslaved Africans. The August 16, 1862 issue carried the story of an army cook, "Aunt Charlotte," whose "domestic relations . . . are well-ordered . . . She has children, grand-children, and great grand-children. Her old husband—'Uncle Sam' . . . at the age of seventy-five, is General [Ambrose E.] Burnside's gardener. It is touching to witness the habitual care which 'Old Aunty' takes of this venerable partner of her life and her bondage." Although the tone of the article is patronizing, with the use of "Aunty" and "Uncle" to refer to elderly Africans, the message is benign. The use of these terms by whites indicated distance—African Americans were seen as one step removed from white humanity and one step closer to the ape. Nevertheless, the story challenged the white view that blacks did not value marriage.

Advertisements in newspapers, narratives, letters, reminiscences and actions of African Americans represent a truer picture of marital commitment. From Wilmington, Delaware, Raady Hooper placed an ad in the *Christian Recorder* asking for information about her husband, Elias Hooper "who joined the Fifth Massachusetts Dis. Cavalry in January last."[38] Fannie Perry wrote lovingly to her husband, Norflet, who was at the front in Texas: "I haven't forgot you nor I never will forget you as long as the world stands, even if you forget me. My love is as great as it was the first night I married you, and I hope it will be so with you. My heart and love is pinned to your breast, and I hope yours is to mine. If I never see you again, I hope to meet you in Heaven . . . If you love me like I love you no knife can cut our love in two."[39] It is clear from African American sources that a high value was placed on familial ties.

So, despite gender inequality and other problems within the African American community, after the Civil War black women did what they had always done—fought the enemy without and forged alliances within. They faced many of the same problems they had endured before and during the conflict but at least they knew what they were up against and they rolled up their sleeves and set about making a place for themselves. Becoming active in women's rights activities, they spoke out endlessly against oppression and the denigration of African women and they established aid societies to help their less fortunate sisters. They formed organizations specifically to deal with the problems they faced as African women. To completely demolish the myths about them, they enrolled in educational pursuits so they could have precise proof of their elevation. As the records show, these noble ladies were nothing like the stereotype. They willingly and competently carried the honor of the whole African race on their shoulders.

NOTES

1. Fanny Jackson Coppin, *Reminiscences of School Life and Hints on Teaching* (Philadelphia, PA: A.M.E. Book Concern, 1913), 15.

2. Paula Giddings, *When and Where I Enter: the Impact of Black Women on Race and Sex in America* (New York: Bantam Books, 1984), 61.

3. Laura M. Towne, *Letters and Diary* (New York: Negro Universities Press, 1969, 1912), 183-184.

In an interesting aside, note that Towne, white, gives the title, "Mr." when referring to white men, but refers to African American men by their first names. She may be aware of the gender issue but she misses the racism in her own action.

4. Sharon Harley and Rosalyn Terborg-Penn, eds., *The Afro- American Woman: Struggles and Images* (Port Washington, New York: Kennikat Press, 1978), 29.

5. I Corinthians 11:7-9; 14:34-35.

6. Martin Delany, *Condition, Elevation, Emigration, and Destiny of the Colored People of the United States* (New York: Arno Press, 1968, 1852), 196.

7. Ibid., 196, 199.

8. Harley, 34.

9. Kate and Martin Delany named their children after famous Africans: Toussaint L'Overture, Charles Lenox Remond, Alexandre Dumas, Ramses Placido, Saint Cyprian, Faustin Soulouque, and Ethiopia Haile Amelia.

10. Frank [Frances] A. Rollin, *Life and Public Services of Martin R. Delany* (New York: Arno Press, 1969, 1883), 28.

11. *Christian Recorder*, 9 July 1864.

12. Elizabeth Davis, *Lifting As They Climb: the National Association of Colored Women* (Boston: National League of Afro- American Women, 1895), 17-18.

13. William Still, *The Underground Railroad* (New York: Arno Press, 1968, 1872), 772.

14. James Ford Rhodes, *History of the United States From the Compromise of 1850 to the Final Restoration of Home Rule at the South in 1877*, volume 1 (New York: Macmillan Company, 1910), 335.

15. *Weekly Anglo-African*, 24 October 1863.

16. Stephen W. Sears, *For Country, Cause & Leader: the Civil War Journal of Charles B. Haydon* (New York: Ticknor & Fields, 1993), 291.

17. The raconteur's own bias is apparent: the 15-year-old "girl" becomes a "woman" after she is raped and bears a child.

18. W.E.B. Du Bois, *Black Reconstruction in America 1860-1880* (Cleveland: World Publishing Company, 1962), 125.

19. Ira Berlin and Leslie Rowland, eds., *Families and Freedom: a Documentary History of African-American Kinship in the Civil War Era* (New York: New Press, 1997), 12-13.

20. L. Maria Child, *The Freedmen's Book* (New York: Arno Press, 1968, 1865), 267.

21. Harriet Jacobs, *Incidents in the Life of a Slave Girl* (New York: Oxford University Press, 1988, 1861), 294.

22. Ibid., 299.

23. Ibid., 300.

24. Elizabeth Keckley, *Behind the Scenes: Thirty Years a Slave and Four in the White House* (New York: Arno Press, 1968, 1868), 39.

25. *New Orleans Times*, 23 March 1864.

26. Fred H. Harrington, "The Fort Jackson Mutiny," *Journal of Negro History* 27 (October, 1942): 429-430.

27. *New Orleans Times*, 23 March 1864.

28. Bell I. Wiley, *Southern Negroes 1861-1865* (New Haven, Connecticut: Yale University Press, 1938), 341-342.

29. Joseph T. Glatthaar, *Forged in Battle: the Civil War Alliance of Black Soldiers and White Officers* (New York: Free Press, 1990), 92.

30. George Clary Papers, September 4, 1865, Connecticut Historical Society, Hartford.

31. OR, Series III, volume 4, 1029.

32. B. Kevin Bennett, "The Jacksonville Mutiny," *Civil War History* 38 (1992): 48.

33. National Freedmen's Relief Association, New York, *By-Laws and Minutes* [Rare Books and Manuscripts Department, Boston Public Library]

34. Ibid., 714.

35. William W. Davis, *The Civil War and Reconstruction in Florida*. (New York: Columbia University, 1913), 341-342.

36. OR, Series III, volume 4, 1228.

37. Ira Berlin, ed., *The Black Military Experience* (New York: Cambridge University Press, 1982), 709.

38. *Christian Recorder*, 27 August 1864.

39. Ruthe Winegarten, *Black Texas Women: 150 Years of Trial and Triumph* (Austin: University of Texas Press, 1995), 35.

Bibliography

American Freedman [New York]

American Missionary [New York]

Aptheker, Herbert, ed. (1979, 1951) *A Documentary History of the Negro People in the United States: From the Colonial Times Through the Civil War*. New York: Citadel Press.

Atlantic Monthly

Beeching, Barbara. (1995) *Primus Papers: an Introduction to Hartford's 19th Century Black Community*. Unpublished M.A. Thesis, Trinity College, Hartford, Connecticut.

Bell, Howard H. (1969) *Minutes of the Proceedings of the National Negro Conventions 1830-1864*. New York: Arno Press.

Bennett, B. Kevin. (1992) "The Jacksonville Mutiny," *Civil War History*, 35:39-50.

Berlin, Ira, et al., eds. (1992) *Free at Last: a Documentary History of Slavery, Freedom, and the Civil War*. New York: New Press.

Berlin, Ira, ed. (1982) *The Black Military Experience*. New York: Cambridge University Press.

Berlin, Ira, et al., eds. (1992) *Slaves No More*. New York: Cambridge University Press.

Berlin, Ira and Leslie Rowland, eds. (1997) *Families and Freedom: a Documentary History of African-American Kinship in the Civil War Era*. New York: New Press.

Blackett, R.J.M., ed. (1989) *Thomas Morris Chester, Black Civil War Correspondent: His Dispatches from the Virginia Front*. Baton Rouge: Louisiana State University Press.

Blackett, R.J.M. (1989) *Beating Against the Barriers: the Lives of Six Nineteenth-Century Afro-Americans*. Ithaca, New York: Cornell University Press.

Blassingame, John W., ed. (1977) *Slave Testimony*. Baton Rouge: Louisiana State University Press.

Blockson, Charles L. (1994) *African Americans in Pennsylvania: a History and Guide*. Baltimore, Maryland: Black Classic Press.

Bogin, Ruth. (April 1974) "Sarah Parker Remond: Black Abolitionist From Salem," *Essex Institute Historical Collections*, 110: 120-150.

Botume, Elizabeth H. (1968, 1893) *First Days Amongst the Contrabands*. New York: Arno Press.

Boyd, Melba Joyce. (1994) *Discarded Legacy: Politics and Poetics in the Life of Frances E.W. Harper*. Detroit: Wayne State University Press.

Bradford, Sarah. (1994, 1886) *Harriet Tubman: Moses of Her People*. New York: Citadel Press.

Brown, Hallie Q. (1988, 1926) *Homespun Heroines and Other Women of Distinction*. New York: Oxford University Press.

Brown, William Wells. (1971, 1867) *The Negro in the American Rebellion*. New York: Citadel Press.

Busby, Margaret, ed. (1992) *Daughters of Africa*. New York: Ballentine Books.

Butchart, Ronald E. (1980) *Northern Schools, Southern Blacks, and Reconstruction: Freedmen's Education, 1862-1875*. Westport, Connecticut: Greenwood Press.

Butchart, Ronald E. (1994) "'We Best Can Instruct Our Own People': New York African Americans in the Freedmen's Schools, 1861-1875," *in African Americans and Education in the South, 1865-1900* Ed. Donald G. Nieman. New York: Garland Publishing.

Bynum, Victoria. (1992) *Unruly Women: the Politics of Social and Sexual Control in the Old South*. Chapel Hill: University of North Carolina Press.

Charles Blockson Collection, Temple University, Philadelphia, Pennsylvania.

Cheek, William and Aimee L. Cheek (1989) *John Mercer Langston and the Fight for Black Freedom 1829-65*. Urbana: University of Illinois Press.

Child, L. Maria. (1968, 1865) *The Freedmen's Book*. New York: Arno Press.

The Christian Recorder [Philadelphia, Pennsylvania]

Clark, Peter H. (1864) *The Black Brigade of Cincinnati*. Cincinnati: Joseph B. Boyd.

Clary [George] Papers, Connecticut Historical Society, Hartford.

Collier-Thomas, Bettye. (1984) *Black Women Organized for Social Change 1800-1920*. DC: Bethune Museum-Archives.

Committee of Merchants for the Relief of Colored People, Suffering from the Late Riots in the City of New York. (1963) *Report*. New York: George A. Whitehorne.

Coppin, Fanny Jackson. (1913) *Reminiscences of School Life, and Hints on Teaching*. Philadelphia: A.M.E. Book Concern.

Cowan, Tom and Jack Maguire (1994) *Timelines of African American History: 500 Years of Black Achievement*. New York: Perigee Books.

Creel, Margaret Washington. (1988) *"A Peculiar People": Slave Religion and Community-Culture Among the Gullahs*. New York: New York University.

Dabney, Wendell Phillips. (1927) *Maggie L. Walker and the Independent Order of St. Luke: the Woman and Her Work*. Cincinnati: The Dabney Publishing Co.

Daniel, Sadie Iola. (1970) *Women Builders*. Washington, DC: Associated Publishers.

Dannett, Sylvia G. (1964) *Profiles of Negro Womanhood, 1619-1900*. New York: M.W. Lads.

Davis, Angela. (December 1971) "Reflections on the Black Woman's Role in the Community of Slaves," *Black Scholar* 3: 2-15.

Davis, Elizabeth. (1895) *Lifting As They Climb: the National Association of Colored Women*. Boston: National League of Afro-American Women.

Davis, Marianna W., ed. (1981) *Contributions of Black Women to America*. Columbia, South Carolina: Kenday Press.

Davis, William W. (1913) *The Civil War and Reconstruction in Florida*. New York: Columbia University.

DeBoer, Clara M. (1995) *His Truth is Marching on: African Americans Who Taught the Freedmen for the American Missionary Association 1861-1877*. New York: Garland Publishing.

Delany, Martin (1968, 1852) *Condition, Elevation, Emigration, and Destiny of the Colored People of the United States*. New York: Arno Press.

Diggs, Ellen I. (1983) *Black Chronology: From 4000 B.C. to the Abolition of the Slave Trade*. Boston: G.K. Hall.

Dorsey Collection, Center for African American History and Culture, Temple University, Philadelphia, Pennsylvania.

Douglass' Monthly [Rochester, New York]

Du Bois, W.E.B. (1962) *Black Reconstruction in America 1860-1880*. Cleveland: World Publishing Company.

Du Bois, W.E.B. (1994, 1899) *The Philadelphia Negro*. Millwood, New York: Kraus-Thomson Organization Limited.

Eggleston, G.K. (July 1929) "The Work of Relief Societies During the Civil War," *Journal of Negro History*, 14: 272-299.

Emilio, Luis F. (1992, 1894) *A Brave Black Regiment*. New York: Bantam Books.

Fee, John Gregg. (1891) *Autobiography of John G. Fee*. Chicago: National Christian Association.

Fincher, Jack. (October 1990) "The Hard Fight Was Getting Into the Fight At All," *Smithsonian*, 21: 46-60.

Fleming, John E. (August/September 1975) "Slavery, Civil War and Reconstruction: a Study of Black Women in Microcosm," *Negro History Bulletin*, 38: 430-433.

Foner, Philip, ed. (1992) *Frederick Douglass on Women's Rights*. New York: Da Capo Press.

Foner, Philip and Ronald Lewis, eds. (1989) *Black Workers: a Documentary History From Colonial Times to the Present*. Philadelphia: Temple University Press.

Foster, Frances Smith, ed. (1990) *A Brighter Coming Day: a Frances Ellen Watkins Harper Reader*. New York: Feminist Press at the City University of New York.

Fraser, Walter J., et al., eds. (1985) *The Web of Southern Social Relations: Women, Family & Education*. Athens: University of Georgia Press.

Freedman's Friend [Philadelphia]

"Freedmen at Port Royal" (July, 1865) *North American Review*, 101: 1-28.

Freedmen's Record [Boston, Massachusetts]

Friedrich, Otto. (February, 1988) "We Will Not Do Duty Any Longer for Seven Dollars Per Month," *American Heritage*, 39: 64-73.

Friends' Association of Philadelphia, and Its Vicinity, for the Relief of Colored Freedmen. (1864) *Statistics of the Operations of the Executive Board*. Philadelphia: Inquirer Printing Office.

Genovese, Eugene D. (1975) *Roll, Jordan, Roll: the World the Slaves Made*. New York: Vintage Books.

Gerteis, Louis S. (1973) *From Contraband to Freedman: Federal Policy Toward Southern Blacks 1861-1865*. Westport, Connecticut: Greenwood Press.

Giddings, Paula. (1984) *When and Where I Enter: the Impact of Black Women on Race and Sex in America*. New York: Bantam Books.

Glatthaar, Joseph T. (1990) *Forged in Battle: the Civil War Alliance of Black Soldiers and White Officers*. (New York: Free Press.

Glazier, Willard W. (1869) *The Capture, the Prison Pen, and the Escape*. Hartford, Connecticut: H.E. Goodwin.

Gooding, James Henry. (1991) *On the Altar of Freedom: a Black Soldier's Civil War Letters From the Front*. New York: Warner Books.

Grand United Order of Tents. (1909) *In Memoriam of Annetta M. Lane, Founder of the Grand United Order of Tents of the J.R. Giddings and Jollifee Union*. Richmond, Virginia: St. Luke Herald Press. [Virginia Historical Society, Richmond]

Grimke, Charlotte Forten. (1988) *Journals of Charlotte L. Forten Grimke*. New York: Oxford University.

Gutman, Herbert G. (1976) *The Black Family in Slavery and Freedom, 1750-1925*. New York: Vintage Books.

Harley, Sharon. (1995) *Timetables of African-American History*. New York: Simon & Schuster.

Harley, Sharon and Rosalyn Terborg-Penn, eds. (1978) *The Afro-American Woman: Struggles and Images*. Port Washington, New York: Kennikat Press.

Harper's Weekly [New York]

Harrington, Fred Harvey (October 1942) "The Fort Jackson Mutiny," *Journal of Negro History*, 27: 420-431.

Haviland, Laura S. (1889) *A Woman's Life-Work, Labors and Experiences*. Chicago: Publishing Association of Friends.

Hepworth, George H. (1864) *The Whip, Hoe, and Sword; or, the Gulf-Department in '63*. Boston: Walker, Wise and Company.

Higginson, Thomas W. (1962) *Army Life in a Black Regiment*. New York: Collier Books.

Hine, Darlene Clark, et al., eds. (1993) *Black Women in America: an Historical Encyclopedia*. Bloomington: Indiana University Press.

Hine, Darlene Clark, et al., eds. (1995) *We Specialize in the Wholly Impossible*. Brooklyn, New York: Carlson Publishing.

Home for Aged and Infirm Colored Persons. (1866) *Constitution, By-Laws and Rules and Proceedings of the Second Annual Meeting.* Philadelphia: Merrihew Son.

Home for Destitute Colored Children. (1879) *24th Annual Report.* Philadelphia: Press of Lewis and Greene.

Hull, Gloria, et al. (1982) *All the Women Are White, All the Blacks Are Men, But Some of Us Are Brave: Black Women's Studies.* Old Westbury, New York: Feminist Press.

Jackson, Luther Porter (1945) *Negro Office-Holders in Virginia, 1865-1895.* Norfolk, Virginia: Guide Quality Press.

Jacobs, Harriet. (1988, 1860) *Incidents in the Life of a Slave Girl.* New York: Oxford University Press.

Johnson, Clifton H. (April/May 1971) "Mary Ann Shadd: Crusader for the Freedom of Man," *Crisis,* 78: 89-90.

Jones, Jacqueline. (1985) *Labor of Love, Labor of Sorrow: Black Women, Work and the Family from Slavery to the Present.* New York: Vintage Books.

Jones, Robert. (1894) *Fifty Years in the Lombard Street Central Presbyterian Church, Philadelphia.* Philadelphia: Edward Stern & Co., Inc.

Jordan, Ervin L., Jr. (1995) *Black Confederates and Afro-Yankees in Civil War Virginia.* Charlottesville: University Press of Virginia.

Katz, William Loren. (1990) *Breaking the Chains: African-American Slave Resistance.* New York: Atheneum.

Katz, William Loren, ed. (1969, 1871) *History of Schools for the Colored Population.* New York: Arno Press.

Keckley, Elizabeth. (1968, 1868) *Behind the Scenes: Thirty Years a Slave and Four in the White House.* New York: Arno Press.

Keto, C. Tsehloane. (1991) *The African Centered Perspective of History.* Blackwood, New Jersey: K.A. Publications.

Knox, Thomas P. (1864) *Startling Revelations from the Department of South Carolina, and Expose of the So Called National Freedmen's Relief Association.* Boston: William M. Kendall.

Laas, Virginia Jeans, ed. (1991) *Wartime Washington: the Civil War Letters of Elizabeth Blair Lee.* Urbana: University of Illinois Press.

Ladies' Union Association, Philadelphia. (1867) *Report of the Ladies' Union Association, formed July 20th 1863 for the Purpose of Administering to the Wants of the Sick and Wounded Colored Soldiers.* Philadelphia: G.T. Stockdale. [New York Public Library - Schomburg Center for Research in Black Culture]

Lanning, Michael Lee. (1997) *The African American Soldier: From Crispus Attucks to Colin Powell*. Secaucus, New Jersey: Birch Lane Press.

Lawson, Ellen N. (1984) *The Three Sarahs: Documents of Antebellum Black College Women*. New York: Edwin Mellen Press.

Lerner, Gerda, ed. (1972) *Black Women in White America: a Documentary History*. New York: Vintage Books.

Leslie, Kent Anderson. (1995) *Woman of Color, Daughter of Privilege: Amanda America Dickson 1849-1893*. Athens: University of Georgia.

The Liberator [Boston, Massachusetts]

Lockwood, Lewis. (1969, 1863) *Mary S. Peake: the Colored Teacher at Fortress Monroe in Two Black Teachers During the Civil War*. New York: Arno Press.

Loewenberg, Bert J. and Ruth Bogin, eds. (1976) *Black Women in Nineteenth- Century American Life: Their Words, Their Thoughts, Their Feelings*. University Park: Pennsylvania State University.

Logan, Rayford W. and Michael R. Winston, eds. (1982) *Dictionary of American Negro Biography*. New York: W.W. Norton.

Logan, Shirley W., ed. (1995) *With Pen and Voice: a Critical Anthology of 19th-Century African American Women*. Carbondale: Southern Illinois University Press.

Long, Richard A., ed. (1988) *Black Writers and the American Civil War*. Secaucus, New Jersey: Blue and Grey Press.

Lucas, Marion B. (1992) *A History of Blacks in Kentucky*. Frankfort: Kentucky Historical Society.

Mabee, Carleton. (1995) *Sojourner Truth: Slave, Prophet, Legend*. New York: New York University Press.

Main, Ed M. (1970, 1908) *The Story of the Marches, Battles and Incidents of the Third United States Colored Cavalry*. New York: Negro Universities Press.

Majors, M.A. (1893) *Noted Negro Women: Their Triumphs and Activities*. Chicago: Donohue & Henneberry.

Massey, Mary Elizabeth. (1966) *Bonnet Brigades*. New York: Alfred A. Knopf.

McCain, Diana Ross. (1984) *Black Women of Connecticut: Achievement Against the Odds*. Hartford: Connecticut Historical Society.

McLain, Guy, et al., eds. (1990) *Springfield Fights the Civil War*. Springfield, Massachusetts: Connecticut Valley Historical Museum.

McPherson, James. (1991) *Marching Toward Freedom: Blacks in the Civil War 1861-1865*. New York: Facts on File.

McPherson, James. (1965) *The Negro's Civil War*. New York: Pantheon Books.

Messenger Family Papers, Connecticut Historical Society, Hartford.

Moebs, Thomas T. (1994) *Black Soldiers, Black Sailors, Black Ink: Research Guide on African-Americans in U.S. Military History, 1526-1900*. Chesapeake Bay, Maryland: Moebs Publishing Company.

Morris, Robert C. (1981) *Reading, 'Riting, and Reconstruction: the Education of Freedmen in the South, 1861-1870*. Chicago: University of Chicago Press.

Morton, Patricia. (1991) *Disfigured Images: the Historical Assault on Afro-American Women*. New York: Praeger Publishers.

Nalty, Bernard C. and Morris J. MacGregor. (1981) *Blacks in the Military: Essential Documents*. Wilmington, Delaware: Scholarly Resources, Inc.

National Association for the Relief of Destitute Colored Women and Children. (1867, 1868, 1877) *Annual Reports*. [Philadelphia: Historical Society of Pennsylvania]

National Freedman [New York]

National Freedmen's Relief Association, NY. (1862-1868) *By-Laws and Minutes*. [Rare Books and Manuscripts Department, Boston Public Library, ms.f. Am 2328]

National Freedmen's Relief Association, Washington, D.C. (1866) *Fourth Annual Report*. DC: McGill & Witherow. [Historical Society of Pennsylvania, Philadelphia].

Oliver, John W. (1917) *History of the Civil War Military Pensions, 1861-1885*. Madison: University of Wisconsin.

Painter, Nell I. (1996) *Sojourner Truth: a Life, a Symbol*. New York: W.W. Norton.

Pearson, Elizabeth W., ed. (1969, 1906) *Letters from Port Royal, 1862-1868*. New York: Arno Press.

Pennsylvania Freedmen's Bulletin [Philadelphia]

Perkins, Linda. (1984) "The Black Female American Missionary Association Teacher in the South, 1861-1870," *in Black Americans in North Carolina and the South*. Eds. Jeffrey Crow and Flora Hatley. Chapel Hill: University of North Carolina Press.

Peterson, Carla L. (1995) *Doers of the Word: African American Women Speakers and Writers in the North (1830-1880)*. New York: Oxford University.

Petry, Ann. (1955) *Harriet Tubman: Conductor on the Underground Railroad*. New York: Crowell.

Philadelphia Tribune, Charles Bolivar's "Pencil Pusher" Column [Charles Blockson Collection, Temple University, Philadelphia.

Piccin, Nancy. (May 25, 1987) "Family's Civil War Artifacts Trace History," *Springfield, Massachusetts Morning Union*, 1+

Primus Family Papers, Connecticut Historical Society, Hartford.

Quarles, Benjamin. (1989, 1953) *The Negro in the Civil War*. New York: Da Capo Press, Inc.

Redkey, Edwin S., ed. (1992) *A Grand Army of Black Men: Letters from African American Soldiers in the Union Army, 1861-1865*. New York: Cambridge University Press.

Remond, Sarah Parker. (April 1942) "The Negroes in the United States of America," *Journal of Negro History*, 27: 216-18.

Rhodes, James Ford. (1910) *History of the United States From the Compromise of 1850 to the Final Restoration of Home Rule at the South in 1877*. New York: Macmillan Company.

Richardson, Joe M. (1986) *Christian Reconstruction: the American Missionary Association and Southern Blacks, 1861-1890*. Athens: University of Georgia Press.

Richardson, Marilyn, ed. (1987) *Maria W. Stewart: America's First Black Woman Political Writer: Essays and Speeches*. Bloomington: Indiana University Press.

Ripley, C. Peter, ed. (1992) *Black Abolitionist Papers, Volume V: the United States, 1859-1865*. Chapel Hill: University of North Carolina Press.

Rollin, Frank [Frances] A. (1969, 1883) *Life and Public Services of Martin R. Delany*. New York: Arno Press.

Rose, Willie Lee. (1964) *Rehearsal for Reconstruction: the Port Royal Experiment*. New York: Bobbs-Merrill Company.

Salvatore, Nick. (1996) *We All Got History: the Memory Books of Amos Webber*. New York: Times Books.

Salem, Dorothy C. (1993) *African American Women: a Biographical Dictionary*. New York: Garland Publishing, 1993.

Saunders, John A. (1964) *100 Years After Emancipation: the History of the Philadelphia Negro 1787-1963*. Philadelphia: Free African Society.

Scruggs, L.A. (1893) *Women of Distinction: Remarkable in Works and Invincible in Character*. Raleigh, North Carolina: L.A. Scruggs.

Sears, Stephen W. (1993) *For Country, Cause & Leader: the Civil War Journal of Charles B. Haydon*. New York: Ticknor & Fields.

Sillen, Samuel. (1955) *Women Against Slavery*. New York: Masses and Mainstream Press.

Silber, Nina and Mary Beth Sievens. (1996) *Yankee Correspondence: Civil War Letters Between New England Soldiers and the Home Front*. Charlottesville: University Press of Virginia.

Simmons, William J. (1968, 1887) *Men of Mark: Eminent, Progressive and Rising*. New York: Arno Press.

Sketch of the Life of Rev. Charles B. Ray (1887) New York: Press of J.J. Little. [New York Public Library - Schomburg Center for Research in Black Culture]

Smith, James L. (1881) *Autobiography*. Norwich, Connecticut: Press of the Company.

Smith, Jessie Carney, ed. (1992) *Notable Black American Women*. Detroit, Michigan: Gale Research, Inc.

Smith, Jessie Carney, ed. (1996) *Notable Black American Women*, Book II. Detroit, Michigan: Gale Research, Inc.

State Equal Rights Convention of the Colored People of Pennsylvania. (1865) *Proceedings, February 8th, 9th, and 10th, 1865*. Philadelphia: The Convention.

Steady, Filomina Chioma, ed. (1981) *The Black Woman Cross- culturally*. Cambridge, Massachusetts: Schenkman Publishing Company.

Sterling, Dorothy, ed. (1984) *We Are Your Sisters: Black Women in the Nineteenth Century*. New York: W.W. Norton.

Stewart, Maria. (1832) *Meditations from the Pen of Mrs. Maria W. Stewart, Negro*. Boston: Garrison and Knapp.

Still, William. (1968, 1872) *The Underground Railroad*. New York: Arno Press.

Streitmatter, Rodger. (Summer 1993) "Maria W. Stewart: the First Female African-American Journalist," *Historical Journal of Massachusetts*, 21: 44-59.

Taylor, Frank H. (1913) *Philadelphia in the Civil War, 1861 - 1865*. Philadelphia: The City.

Taylor, Susie King. (1968, 1902) *Reminiscences of My Life in Camp with the 33rd United States Colored Troops*. New York: Arno Press.

Tidings [Philadelphia]

Titus, Frances W., ed. (1969, 1878) *Narrative of Sojourner Truth*. New York: Arno Press.

Towne, Laura M. (1969, 1912) *Letters and Diary*. New York: Negro Universities Press.

Truth, Sojourner. (1993) *Narrative of Sojourner Truth*. New York: Vintage Books.

U.S. War Department. (1880-1901) *The War of the Rebellion: a Compilation of the Official Records of the Union and Confederate Armies*. Washington, DC: Government Printing Office.

Vaz, Kim M., ed. (1995) *Black Women in America*. Thousand Oaks, California: Sage Publications.

Walker, Robbie Jean, ed. (1992) *The Rhetoric of Struggle: Public Addresses by African American Women*. New York: Garland Publishing Company.

Warner, Robert Austin. (1940) *New Haven Negroes: a Social History*. New Haven, Connecticut: Yale University.

Weekly Anglo-African [New York]

Wesley, Charles and Patricia Romero. (1967) *Negro Americans in the Civil War*. New York: Publishers Company, Inc.

Western Freedmen's Aid Commission. (1865) *Second Annual Report*. Cincinnati: Methodist Book Concern.

Westwood, Howard C. (1985) "The Cause and Consequence of a Union Black Soldier's Mutiny and Execution," *Civil War History*, 31: 222-236.

White, Deborah Gray. (1985) *Ar'n't I a Woman?: Female Slaves in the Plantation South*. New York: W.W. Norton.

Wiley, Bell I. (1938) *Southern Negroes 1861-1865*. New Haven, Connecticut: Yale University Press.

Williams, George Washington. (1969, 1888) *A History of the Negro Troops in the War of the Rebellion 1861-1865*. New York: Negro Universities Press.

Williams, George Washington. (1874) *History of the Twelfth Baptist Church, Boston, Massachusetts*. Boston: James H. Earle. [Rare Books and Manuscripts Department, Boston Public Library, #8N7549A.82]

Williams, Melvin R. (1972) "A Blueprint for Change: the Black Community in Washington, D.C., 1860-1870," *Records of the Columbia Historical Society*, 48: 359-93.

Wilson, Joseph T. (1968, 1890) *The Black Phalanx*. New York: Arno Press.

Winegarten, Ruthe. (1995) *Black Texas Women: 150 Years of Trial and Triumph*. Austin: University of Texas Press.

Woodward, C. Vann, ed. (1981) *Mary Chesnut's Civil War*. New Haven, Connecticut: Yale University Press.

Yacovone, Donald, ed. (1997) *A Voice of Thunder: the Civil War Letters of George E. Stephens*. Urbana: University of Illinois Press.
Yee, Shirley J. (1992) *Black Women Abolitionists: a Study in Activism, 1828-1860*. Knoxville: University of Tennessee Press.

Index

241